THE OCCULT SCIENCES.

THE·

OCCULT SCIENCES

A COMPENDIUM OF TRANSCENDENTAL DOCTRINE
AND EXPERIMENT

EMBRACING

AN ACCOUNT OF MAGICAL PRACTICES; OF SECRET SCIENCES
IN CONNECTION WITH MAGIC; OF THE PROFESSORS OF
MAGICAL ARTS; AND OF MODERN SPIRITUALISM,
MESMERISM AND THEOSOPHY

BY

ARTHUR EDWARD WAITE

LONDON
KEGAN PAUL, TRENCH, TRÜBNER & CO., Ltd.
[SUCCESSORS TO GEORGE REDWAY]·
1891

19. N. 117

PREFACE.

THE subject of occultism, by which we mean those sciences, called transcendental and magical, a knowledge of which has been transmitted and accumulated in secret, or is contained in books that have an inner or secret meaning, has been very fully dealt with during recent years by various students of eminence. But the works of these well-equipped investigators are, in most instances, unsuited to an elementary reader, and they are all somewhat expensive. It has remained for the results of their studies to be condensed into a portable volume, which shall conduct the inquirer into the vestibule of each branch of "the occult sciences," and place within his reach the proper means of prosecuting his researches further in any desired direction. It is such an unpretending but useful task which we have set ourselves to perform in the present volume, which embraces, as we would claim, in a compressed and digested form, the whole scope of occult knowledge, expressed in the language of a learner.

We have sought as far as possible to distinguish between theory and practice, between facts which it is possible to ascertain and explanations over which views may diverge. We have checked our individual judgments and modified our individual opinions not only by the best authorities in the literature of the several subjects treated, but by the collaboration of many living writers who are specialists in distinct branches of esoteric science. In this respect the book may be accepted as the result of a collective endeavour rather than of an unaided effort, and it will be received with an increased confidence on this ground.

CONTENTS.

PART III.

PROFESSORS OF MAGICAL ART.

PART IV.

MODERN PHENOMENA.

INTRODUCTION.

THE claims of Hermetic philosophy to the consideration of serious thinkers in the nineteenth century
are not to be confounded with those merely of an
exalted intellectual system, or of a sublime and legitimate
aspiration. These may, indeed, be urged in behalf of it
with the force of unadulterated truthfulness, but not as
the principal point. What the philosophy which is indiscriminately called transcendental, Hermetic, Rosicrucian,
mystical, and esoteric or occult, submits in its revived
form to the scrutator of life and her problems as a suffic-
ing and rational cause for its resuscitation, and as an adequate ground for its recognition, is tersely this :—That it
comprises an actual, positive, and realisable knowledge
concerning the worlds which we denominate invisible,
because they transcend the imperfect and rudimentary
faculties of a partially developed humanity, and concerning the latent potentialities which constitute, by the
fact of their latency, what is termed the interior man.
In more strictly philosophical language, the Hermetic
science is a method of transcending the phenomenal
world, and attaining to the reality which is behind
phenomena. At a time when many leaders of thought
have substantially abandoned all belief in the existence
of intelligence outside of the visible universe, it is almost
superfluous to say that the mere claim of the mystics
has an irresistible magnetic attraction for those who are
conscious that deep down in the heart of every man
there exists the hunger after the supernatural.

The mode of transcending the phenomenal world, as
taught by the mystics, consists, and to some extent
exclusively, of a form of intellectual ascension or development, which is equivalent to a conscious application of
selective evolutionary laws by man himself to man.

Those latent faculties which are identified as Psychic Force pass, under this training, into objective life; they become the instruments of communication with the unseen world, and the modes of subsistence which are therein. In other words, the conscious evolution of the individual has germinated a new sense by which he is enabled to appreciate what is inappreciable by the grosser senses.

The powers of the interior man, and the possibility of communication with the unseen, are the subject of historical magic, which is filled with thaumaturgic accounts of experiments with these forces, and of the results of this communication. Whether these alleged occurrences are to be accepted as substantiated facts is not the question on which the enlightened mystic desires to insist. The evidence which supports them may be, and is, important; it may be, and is, overwhelming; but it is not upon the wonders of the Past only that the Hermetic claim is sought to be established, or demands recognition, in the Present. Whatever be the evidential value for the success of the psychic experiments conducted by the investigators of old, they may at least be said to constitute a sufficient ground for a new series of scientific inquiries on the part of those persons who are devoting their intelligence and their energy to the solution of the grand mysteries of existence. Otherwise, the transcendental philosophy would be simply the revival of an archaic faith, and would be wholly unadapted to the necessities of to-day. It should be remembered, however, when speaking of scientific inquiry, that the reference is not confined to the professed scientists of the period, but to all who are capable of exact observation, and can appreciate the momentous character of the issues involved.

The standpoint indeed is this: the successful experiments of the past are capable of repetition in the present, and it is open to those who doubt it to be convinced by individual experience. In one of his most mystical utterances, Christ is recorded to have said that there are those who are eunuchs from their mother's womb, and that there are those who become eunuchs in the interests of the Kingdom of God : so also there are natural magicians and magicians who are the product of art, yet, generally speaking, the magician, unlike the poet, is not born but made, for the same potentialities abide in the whole of humanity, and they can be ultimately developed in all. What is wanted, therefore, is not merely persons possessed of the gifts of clairvoyance, or even of lucidity, of prophetic foresight, or of the qualities called mediumistic, but those who by the nature of their aspirations, and by the help of a favourable environment, are able to apply the arcane laws of evolution to their own interior selves. But there is another and an indispensable condition, namely, the power to distinguish between Hermetic truth and the shameless frauds which have encompassed it from time immemorial. At present, the intellectual world is substantially divided into those who reject esoteric doctrine and practice as unmixedly fraudulent, and those whose credulity identifies its worst impostures and most puerile perversions with its highest forms of truth. Transcendentalism is concerned with the development and application of certain powerful forces resident in the interior man, and as these forces have been developed and applied in various directions, from many motives, and with a multiplicity of ends in view, historical mysticism is very diverse in its character, is often puerile, superstitious, dangerous, malevolent, and obscene, and from its very nature has been always peculiarly liable to the counterfeits of charlatans.

Certain sections of modern mystics have expressed somewhat too freely their indignation against the Christian churches for the abuses and corruptions which they have generated during the undermining process of the ages. Now, the history of no doctrine and of no religion can compare in its abuses and corruptions with that of Magic ; for every species of abomination, of "unnatural love and more unnatural hate" have been fostered under the tenebrous wings of the goetic part of mysticism. There, as in other matters, the height of aspiration finds its exact counterpoise in the abysses of spiritual degradation. It is the custom with many to shield occultism from the responsibility of these dishonourable histories

by means of transliteral interpretations, just as it is the
custom among the more credulous section of spiritualists
to cloak every phase of fraud among "mediums" by
accrediting the "spirit world" with the impostures of
many of those who pose as the avenues of communication
between the seen and the unseen.   In the current
periodical literature of our newest and most elaborated
mysticism may be found attempts to erect Cagliostro,
the Sicilian mesmerist, into an adept of divine magic, on
the plea that a person accepting the notorious facts of his
life and character as historical truth, would be adopting
a shallow and puerile view.   Even the most obvious and
direct contradictions which are to be found in the French
mystics have been qualified and excused by a separation
of the conflicting statements into different planes of
thought.   In the same manner, at a number of private
séances where the non-professional avenues of communication refused all remuneration, and where, as a consequence, the essential element of fraud might be safely
deemed wanting, the most incessant and clumsy imposture has been explained by the hypothesis that the
unbuyable "avenues" were completely entranced and
unconscious, that they were utilised in this manner by
the "holy spirit world" in order to economise psychic
force, and "form-manifestations" were being witnessed.

But nevertheless the transcendental philosophy is the
one hope of an age which is sick unto death of its own
unprofitable speculations.   It asks no faith; it offers a
positive knowledge.   But it is well that we should
recognise the existence and proximity of its darker side.
It is well also for all who approach the subject, and
desire to preserve the even balance of an unbiassed and
well-regulated mind, to discount much of the gorgeous
claim put forward by modern mystics concerning the
antique masters.   Hierophants who are supposed by
their admirers to have achieved all heights, ought surely
to have enjoyed an immunity from the "cosmogonical"
ignorance of their age, whereas their writings reveal them
as by no means advanced students of physical science.
Those who are believed to have stood on the threshold
of Deity might have enunciated theological views of a

broader character; nevertheless, we find that in most questions of religion they appear to have adhered to the doctrines which were current at their particular epochs. These facts suggest limitations which will, we fear, be conclusive proof to a large number of thinkers that the achievements of adepts in the past are of a somewhat imaginary nature. However, a comparison of their claims with the known facts of modern psychology will establish the general truth of their statements; and the higher and unexplored possibilities which to-day are indicated by psychic science, and which are known to advanced experimentalists, will be found, on comparison, to be precisely in the direction of the more exalted claims of the mystics. But in spite of the attainments of some brilliant exceptions, there is little reason to suppose that the *turba philosophorum*, as a whole, did much more than extend our actual psychic experiments—mesmeric, hypnotic, and spiritual—for a marked but a measurable distance beyond ourselves, and that the grand altitudes of occultism, of which we write and dream, were the Promised Land of their own aspirations, and not attained in their lives.*

This being the case, it is better for the present to confine our attention in the main to the repeatable experiments of the mystics. To serious students it is possibly permissible, with excessive discrimination and caution, to extend the circle of investigation to some of the branches of Black Magic (such as the control of evil spirits), knowledge and not gain being the only end in view. The alleged dangers in connection with magical practices are insignificant in comparison with the ends which are to be achieved, and the existing secret brother-

---

* There is, however, an alternative view which it is only just to cite. It is advanced that the hierophants of the past were forced of necessity to speak the cosmological language of their day. When transcendental doctrine was rendered in the language of the current philosophy, the mystic could not seem *much* above the errors of the day. Otherwise, his over-science would have been additionally incomprehensible. On the transcendental plane, he probably knew all, but in physical science he may have been limited by the knowledge of the period. In either case, the translation of the secret wisdom for the public use could only be accomplished by writing down theologically as well as philosophically to the public level.

hoods, more especially Masonry, which is founded on esoteric doctrine, could be utilised by the mystics in subservience to these ends.

The common presumptions established by modern science against the spiritual nature of man and the existence of spiritual intelligences outside the visible universe, are based on a sharp distinction between the substances respectively denominated *material* and *spiritual*, which offers a singular instance of the verbal tyrannies to which we subject our minds. No more abundant source of intellectual misconception and blunder can well be adduced than is comprised in the two words SPIRIT and MATTER. Believers and sceptics alike have exhausted the methods of philosophy in their attempt to establish the two conceptions at antipodean poles of thought. It is now universally admitted that we are exclusively limited to an acquaintance with the appearances of this world which we term material ; of matter in its ultimate nature we know nothing whatever. No scientific analysis can throw light upon its eternally inscrutable problem. It is also admitted that, in the intellectual order, man realises that he is a conscious being by a reflex and not a direct act, and the ultimate nature of the ego is a book permanently sealed. Once more, we are familiar alone with certain modes of manifestation ; ever the reality escapes us. It is therefore impossible rationally to establish fundamental distinctions between substances about which we are fundamentally ignorant, and as, for all practical purposes, mind is identical with the vague concept which we denominate spirit, we may enunciate the following axiom with complete truth :—*The distinction between matter and spirit is philosophically futile and frivolous.* A direct consequence follows ; those who affirm the existence of matter and deny spirit may be unconsciously contradicting themselves. Though identified in the common darkness which involves them, it is philosophically impossible, of course, to affirm their substantial identity ; therefore reservation of judgment is the only prudent course. This reservation must be, moreover, extended in another and important direction. Seeing that the phenomena called thaumaturgic, magical and spiritual may be simply uninvestigated modes of manifestation in one force infinitely differentiated in the universe, it is unreasonable to deny their possibility on à priori grounds, for the possible modes of manifestation in an ultimately unknown substance cannot be theoretically limited. As a fact, we are unconsciously landed in pure Spinozism, for it is one of the tenets of this grand and singular thinker that matter and mind are but two finite manifestations of one infinite substance, which may be capable of an infinite number of other finite manifestations of which we can and do know nothing. It is outside the present order of inquiry, but these considerations lead us to touch briefly on a still more important subject. The existence of a creative mind exterior to the visible universe, and standing in relation thereto as its almighty author and architect, has been debated for long ages without the possibility having occurred to dialecticians on either side that the efficient cause of matter and mind may be something so totally transcending them both, and equally in nature and substance, that it cannot be identified with either. If the pantheistic identification of deity with the titanic forces of the Cosmos be a narrow and inadequate solution of the mystery of God, the anthropomorphic identification with mind is liable to the same objection.

If there be any philosophic accuracy in this method of reasoning, it follows that by virtue of our absolute and irretrievable ignorance concerning the fundamentals of matter and mind, mere speculations on the problems of life, on the possibility of intellectual subsistence devoid of a physical organism—in other words, on the existence of disembodied humanities, and of hierarchies of spiritual beings above or below humanity—can never ultimate in any solid knowledge; they will ever be speculations only, devoid of conviction and satisfaction. It follows, also, that there is no possible refuge from permanent agnosticism except by a formal act of faith in some system of alleged revelation, or by experimental researches, if possible, into the nature and powers of the mind. But faith is no longer what it was in the days of St Paul, "the substance of things hoped for, the evidence of things not seen;" it is not a source of scientific conviction; it is aspiration formulated as creed; and by its nature it is unable to provide a true intellectual certainty.

It is at this point that the transcendental philosophy appears, and in the name of a thousand histories, and of ten thousand times ten thousand traditions and legends, declares it is possible to know by experimental research that disembodied humanities can and do subsist, that there are hierarchies of intelligence above and below humanity, that in this life, and with this environment, the potentialities of the interior man may be so developed as to put him in communication with forms of intellectual subsistence which transcend his normal mode; that the positive knowledge which is the result of such research can be attained now as it was attained in the past, and that a scientific solution of the problems of life is actually within the limits of every earnest man.

Such are the claims of the Hermetic philosophy, and such is the scientific basis of mysticism. On these claims the spiritual future of the world may be reasonably considered to depend. On this basis, if on any, must the religion of the future be built, if by religion we are to understand the establishment of a vital and vivifying correspondence between that which is highest in man and that which is supreme in the universe. The choice lies between agnosticism and the science of the mystics. If mysticism be a true science, grand and illimitable is the prospect which awaits the psychic man. If it be grounded in superstition and imposture, even from agnosticism itself we may devise a chilly consolation, for so insoluble is the mystery of the universe that no aspiration can be extinguished as wholly impossible of fulfilment; even in the insoluble mystery there is room for a forlorn hope.

PART I.

———0———

DEFINITIONS.

EVERY branch of the occult or secret sciences may be included under the word MAGIC, with the sole exception of astrology, which, important and interesting as it is, can hardly be termed a branch of arcane wisdom, as it depends solely on abstruse astronomical calculations, and on the appreciation of the value of those influences which are supposed to be diffused by the planets and the starry heavens over the lives of nations and individuals. But the doctrines concerning the nature and power of angels, ghosts, and spirits; the methods of evoking and controlling the shades of the dead, elementary spirits, and demons; the composition of talismans; the manufacture of gold by alchemy; all forms of divination, including clairvoyance in the crystal, and all the mysterious calculations which make up kabbalistic science, are all parts of magic. It is necessary to make this statement at the outset to prevent misconception, because in an elementary hand-book it would be clearly a source of confusion to include subjects so apparently distinct under a single generic title; and we have therefore determined to make a few introductory remarks upon magic viewed as a whole, and then to treat each of its branches under special titles which will be readily intelligible to those who are seeking for the first time an acquaintance with the mysteries of the esoteric sciences.

The popular significance attached to the term magic diverges widely from the interpretations which are offered by its students. By the term magic, according

to the common opinion, there is generally implied one
of two things—either that it is the art of producing
effects by the operation of causes which are apparently
inadequate to their production, and are therefore in
apparent defiance of the known order of nature; or that
it is the art of evoking spirits,* and of forcing them to
perform the bidding of the operator. The second alternative may be practically resolved into the first, for the
invocation of invisible intelligences is inseparably connected in the minds of the vulgar with a certain hocus-
pocus of preposterous rites and formulæ, including the
utterance of barbarous and, to them, meaningless words,
which certainly appear to be inadequate to produce
so stupendous an effect as a direct manifestation from a
hidden side of Nature. Now, to establish communication with worlds which are normally beyond our reach
is undoubtedly included in the great claims of the
magus; and the art of evoking spirits, taken in its true
and its highest sense, is the head and crown of Magic;
but it is not in fact a violation of immutable natural
laws, and the causes which are set in operation by its
qualified initiates are really adequate to the effects which
are produced, wonderful and incredible as they may
appear. The popular conception of Magic, even when it
is not identified with the trickeries of imposture and the
pranks of the mountebank, is entirely absurd and gross.

"Magic, or, more accurately, Magism," says Christian

* Four classes of the intelligences called "spirits" are recognised by the science of the magi. There are the Angels who are
the offspring of primeval creation, made and not begotten; there
are the Devils, or Demons, the angelical hierarchies who fell
from their first estate. There are the Elementary Spirits, who
inhabit the four elements of ancient physical science, and are
divided into Sylphs, Undines, Gnomes, and Salamanders—intelligences who reproduce their species after the manner of mankind. Finally, there are the Souls of departed men and women
whose actual locality in the unseen world is variously described.
Angels are invoked in the higher branches of white magic, and
Demons in the operations of the black art; Elementary Spirits are
the classes most easily commanded, and they are the "familiars"
of the middle ages. The Souls of the Dead were conjured
commonly for the revelation of mundane secrets, occasionally
for the disclosure of future events, but most frequently in the
interests of bereaved affection.

in his *Histoire de la Magie*, "if anyone would condescend to return to its antique origin, could be no longer confounded with the superstitions which calumniate its memory. Its name is derived to us from the Greek words MAGOS, a Magician, and MAGEIA, Magic, which are merely permutations of the terms MOG, MEGH, MAGH, which in Pehlvi and in Zend, both languages of the eldest East, signify 'priest,' 'wise,' and 'excellent.' It was thence also that, in a period anterior to historic Greece, there originated the Chaldæan name Maghdim, which is equivalent to 'supreme wisdom,' or sacred philosophy. Thus, mere etymology indicates that Magic was the synthesis of those sciences once possessed by the Magi or philosophers of India, of Persia, of Chaldæa, and of Egypt, who were the priests of nature, the patriarchs of knowledge, and the founders of those vast civilisations whose ruins still maintain, without tottering, the burden of sixty centuries."

Ennemoser, in his " History of Magic " (as translated by Howitt), says : " Among the Parsees, the Medes, and the Egyptians, a higher knowledge of nature was understood by the term Magic, with which religion, and particularly astronomy, were associated. The initiated and their disciples were called Magicians—that is, the Wise—which was also the case among the Greeks. . . . Plato understood by Wisdom nothing less than a worship of the Divinity, and Apuleius says that Magus means, in the Persian language, a priest. . . . India, Persia, Chaldea, and Egypt, were the cradles of the oldest Magic. Zoroaster, Ostanes, the Brahmins, the Chaldean sages, and the Egyptian priests, were the primitive possessors of its secrets. The priestly and sacrificial functions, the healing of the sick, and the preservation of the Secret Wisdom, were the objects of their life. They were either princes themselves, or surrounded princes as their counsellors. Justice, truth, and the power of self-sacrifice, were the great qualities with which each one of these must be endowed; and the neglect of any one of these virtues was punished in the most cruel manner."

A theosophical writer who is said to belong to the most

advanced school, Dr Franz Hartmann, who is said to be a
practical as well as theoretical student, who also lays claim
to the successful performance of recondite alchemical experiments by the application of spiritual forces to material
things, and who, therefore, should at any rate be com-
petent to provide us with a tolerable definition of his art,
has the following assertion at the beginning of one of his
books :—" Whatever misinterpretation ancient or modern
ignorance may have given to the word *Magic*, its only
true significance is *The Highest Science, or Wisdom, based
upon knowledge and practical experience.*" This definition
reads an absolute value into a term which it does not
historically possess, for though Magic be undoubtedly
derived from a word which signifies Wisdom, it is
Wisdom as conceived by the Magi to which it is alone
equivalent, and so far as philosophy is concerned, magian
Wisdom either may or may not be identical with the
absolute and eternal Wisdom.

Magic, says Eliphas Lévi, is "the traditional science
of the secrets of Nature which has come down to us
from the Magi," a definition devoid of nonsense, and
narrowly escaping perfection, the limitation of the source
of esoteric knowledge to the Persian hierarchs being, we
think, its sole defect.

By these definitions it is plain that Magic is not merely
the art of invoking spirits, and that it is not merely concerned with establishing a communication with other forms
of intelligent subsistence in the innumerable spheres of
the transcendental. If such invocation be possible, if such
communication can be truly established, it is evidently by
the intervention of certain occult forces resident in the
communicating individual, man. Now, it is reasonable to
suppose that the same forces can be applied in other
directions, and the synthesis of the methods and processes
by which these forces are utilized in the several fields of
experiment, combined with a further synthesis of methods
and processes by which the latent potentialities of a
variety of physical substances are developed into manifest activity, constitutes Magic in the full, perfect, and
comprehensive sense of that much abused term.

The maltreatment and odium of centuries has eliminated from the word Magic its original and sublime significance. Once, in the dead language of starry Chaldea, the solemn sanctuary, the cradle, if not the birthplace, of the sciences called transcendental, it was the equivalent of supreme wisdom; once its professors were the priests, the wise, the excellent: but the science is confounded with the impostures which have encompassed its history, and the initiates are identified with the rabble of rogues and charlatans. So it would almost seem as if the term Magic had become a word whose accepted meaning is a libel on the science which it signifies, and a slur on the memory of its grand masters. Fortunately, however, it is not the only term by which that science is described; esoteric wisdom, occult knowledge, the transcendental philosophy and practice are inter-convertible terms which all signify Magic, and are used indiscriminately throughout this volume, less to avoid tautology than to minimise the depreciatory effect of a now debased word by connecting it with the equivalents of its first and true significance.

We have already explained in the Introduction to this work what we conceive to be the objects of the present revival of mysticism, and the exact nature of its claims on the consideration of the nineteenth century. The origin and destiny of Man are the absorbing and vital problems which, in the present age, demand more urgently than ever a complete and satisfactory solution. Such a solution is offered, it is claimed, by Magic. Latent energies, undeveloped faculties, generally unknown possibilities, are affirmed by that science to be actually resident in man. By their effectual evolution it is said that the horizon of his energies and his perceptions can be so enlarged as to extend over a new range of existence. It is demonstrated that his physical envelope is not his real self, that he can transcend it without destroying, while he can establish a direct connection with numberless forms of intelligence who are dissevered from their perishable bodies, and with others of every rank who have never been joined with flesh. The desire of the long ages is promised a complete fulfilment in this sublime programme of an abandoned knowledge.

The psychological experiments of the past masters of mysticism are alleged to have brought them into communication with various classes of intelligences, such as angels, elementary spirits, demons, and the disembodied souls of men. The fundamental principle of this communication was in the exercise of a certain occult force resident in the Magus and strenuously exerted for the establishment of such a correspondence between two planes of Nature as would effect his desired end. This exertion was termed the evocation, conjuration, or calling of the spirit, but that which in reality was raised was the energy of the inner man; tremendously developed and exalted by combined will and aspiration, this energy germinated by sheer force a new intellectual faculty of sensible psychological perception, and enabled the prepared mystic to see into a new world, and communicate with its several populations. To assist and to stimulate this energy into the most powerful possible operation, artificial means were almost invariably used. The ordinary faculties and senses were worked upon, and frequently the narrow line which intervenes between exaltation and frenzy was overstepped in the temerity of the process. The appeal to the senses by a gorgeous and overwhelming ritual, which has been attended with grand success in the hierarchic religions of Christianity, was made also by the hierarchic magic of the past. The synthesis of these methods and processes was called Ceremonial Magic, which in effect was a tremendous forcing-house of the latent faculties of man's spiritual nature. Undoubtedly the end was occasionally accomplished by violent and unnatural means, for intellectual exaltation can be achieved by laudanum and haschisch as much as by divine grace applied to the soul; but the ethical value of the end cannot be impeached by the use of discreditable methods, though the operator may be personally discredited and permanently maimed thereby.

The gospel according to the mystics has, it will be seen, its darker side. As the known forces of modern material science can be used to preserve or destroy, so can the arcane potencies developed by magic be directed to a good or an evil end. In the suggestive language of the alchemists, coals may be turned into gold, but also it is possible to convert the precious metal into coal. We can rise into communion with the exalted understanding of the angels; we can sink into correspondence with the psychic deformities of the devils; we can compose the Universal Medicine and the arcane poison of the second death.

There is white and there is black magic. The lawful application of the arcane forces which are known to esoteric science constitutes White Magic; the lawless and vicious application of the same forces is the Black or infernal Art.

The seat of the law abides in the intention and will of the operator. That which is well meant must eventually work well. Actions must be appraised by their intention and not their effect alone, as the significance of words is extended, contracted, or changed by a reference to their philological origin. Black Magic has two preponderating elements—the diabolical, and the superstitious or absurd. The use of the term diabolical is not to be interpreted in an absolutely theological sense.

The contrast obtained by the epithets white and black may be considered to countenance their use, but such emblematical language has frequently been misapplied. Then we have red magic, which is characterized as the cream of the secret sciences and other fanciful designations.

As this book is by no means intended for an advanced student, but is exclusively addressed to the postulant in the pronaos of the mystical temple, as its information is therefore elementary, although practical, the supreme altitudes of magical science (where the adept passes into the saint, where communication with spiritual intelligences is transcended, and a union is said to be established with the fontal source of souls, with the divine, universal life) are not described herein, and the way of attainment in this transcendental branch is not delineated.

Here it is sufficient to observe that the mystics continually refer to the existence of an absolute and universal science which is not beyond possession by

finite man. This divine knowledge is intimately associated with a divine power which may be either developed
in man, or with which he may be energised from without.
As it is impossible to conclusively determine that such
heights have ever been truly scaled, the modern mystic
will be unwise to insist on their existence, though he
may feel personally assured of the fact.

For merely historical references to Magic among the
Arabs, the Romans, the Chinese, the Early Christians,
the Egyptians, the Greeks, the Israelites, the Germans,
the Laplanders, and the Orientals, the reader is referred
to Ennemoser's work, translated by Howitt and published under the title of "The History of Magic."
There is also a learned work, translated in 1877 from
the French of Lenormant, and called "Chaldean Magic,"
in which are translated some curious incantations in the
cuneiform character. Del Rio's *Disquisitionum Magicarum*,
a voulme of 1100 pages, published in 1657, is an early
authority, and contains a chapter on Fascination. An
antiquarian work called "Narratives of Sorcery and
Magic from the most Authentic Sources," was published
by Thomas Wright, F.S.A., in 1851. Francis Barrett's
"The Magus," an expensively illustrated work printed
in 1801, is the work of one who styled himself a " professor " of occult science. In France the writings of
Eliphas Lévi—especially his *Histoire de la Magie*, and
his *Dogme et Rituel de la Haute Magie* — are justly
esteemed.

Pererius in 1598, Tiedemann in 1787, Freytag in
1710, Christophorus in 1711, have all written tracts on
the subject of Magic, which are sometimes met with.

WHITE MAGIC.

THE EVOCATION OF ANGELS.

THE highest orders of intelligence known to the Christian mystics, and derived, like their general conceptions of the Cosmos of matter and mind, from their Jewish initiators, were the messengers of Scriptural tradition, who are called in the Greek *angelos*, and in the Hebrew *malak*. The ambassadorial office has long been eliminated from our conception of these beings, who, in a condition of ecstatic adoration and in undiversified permanence of beatitude, seem to have survived their *raison d'être*. According to the Rabbinical commentary on Genesis, written by Rabbi Jacob, the angels have no free will, "for they, being of a pure understanding, and having an inclination to good only, cannot be otherwise than good;" and this is an actual doctrine of the Latin church. Practically, however, the angels of Catholic history and legend, in spite of their consummate perfection, would appear to rejoice in the plenary possession of that freedom which an abstract theology denies them. They respond to invocations, they perform miracles, they garner the prayers of the faithful, they overwatch human beings, and they engage everlastingly in a spiritual warfare with the emissaries of perdition and darkness.

This practical aspect of orthodox angelology corresponds to that of western magic, both being undoubtedly derived from the ancient faith of Israel, which in turn was indebted for the elements of its pneumatic hypotheses to Egypt, Babylon, and Chaldea, whence the doctrine of the Incommunicable Name, with the powers and virtues thereof, was derived by Rabbinical theosophists. The latter evolved out of its diverse combina-

B

tions a complex hierarchy of intelligence, analogous to the Alexandrian system of successive emanations, differentiated by a downward egression out of the one and eternal substance.

The Incommunicable Name came to be considered a fountain of arcane power, and, by an easy and natural transition, it was at length regarded as the source of life. The letters which composed it were deemed especially prolific in the creations of intelligence, illumination, and harmony. A measure of their power was extended to the entire Hebrew alphabet, which was endowed with an abstruse mystical significance. It is necessary to explain this point in order to understand the angelical doctrines of the Jewish Magi. Each of the alphabetical symbols represented a vital and creative principle resident in the intelligible world. Just as out of the letters of an ordinary alphabet is evolved the vocabulary of a great language, so from the arcane potencies which were signified by the Hebrew signs, the variations of an infinite existence were divinely elaborated. Now, the supposition of an exact correspondence between the arcane potencies in question and the signs by which they were represented, as well as between the inexhaustible vitalities of the Cosmos and the language developed from the signs, constituted the magical character of the Jewish tongue.

In an interesting and valuable manuscript, entitled, "The Cabalistic Science, or the Art to Know the Good Genies," there is the following explanation of the mysteries which are contained in the Hebrew alphabet.

By the sequence of symbols extending from Aleph to Jod was symbolised the Angelical World, or the hierarchy of sovereign intelligences directly derived from the first Eternal Light, and attributed to Jod in first and superior correspondence. By the sequence from Caf to Tsad were represented the several orders of angels who inhabit the visible, or astronomical and astrological worlds, mystically attributed to Jah, each individual sphere being under the special safeguard of a particular presiding intelligence. The sequence from Tsad to Thau is in arcane correspondence with the elementary world, which is attributed by philosophers to Jaho in the paramount

order. The destinies of humanity are dispensed in the
elementary sphere, and its angelic intelligences preside
over animated Nature.

Orthodox Christian theosophy enumerates nine choirs
of angelical beings which differ from each other in order
and in degree of glory, but are all of the same nature.
In the mystical writings attributed to the apostolic
Areopagite, an account of these hierarchies is given in
an extended form, and it is undoubtedly to this transcendentalist that theology is indebted for the angelical
doctrines subsequently developed by S. Thomas. Now
the advanced mystic who borrowed the name of
Dionysius was indebted in turn to the Kabbalists for
his pneumatic hypotheses, as will be seen in the following tabulation of the attributes of the Divine Names,
and of the intelligences in correspondence with each of
the Hebrew letters.

I. The first letter of the Hebrew alphabet is called
Aleph ; it is in correspondence with EHEIEH, the fontal
name of God, which is interpreted as Divine Essence.
Its seat is in the world called Ensoph, which signifies
Infinity, and its attribute is Keter, the Crown. It rules
over the Angels called by the Hebrews Haioth-ha-
Kodesch, or The Living Creatures of Holiness, who are
otherwise named Seraphim, and constitute the first and
supreme choir.

II. The second letter is Beth, and the Divine name
which corresponds to it is BACHOUR, or *electus juvenis.*
It is the sign of the Ophanim, who are the Angels of the
second order, and the Cherubim of exoteric theology.
By their ministry, Jehovah unfolded and cleared the
primordial chaos. The attribute of BACHOUR is Hocmah,
or Divine Wisdom.

III. The third letter is Ghimel. It corresponds to
the name GADOL, which signifies Grand or Great, and is
assigned to the Angels of the third order whom the
Hebrews called Aralym, the mighty and strong. These
are the Thrones of the Kabbalists, and the third choir.
By their ministry Tetragrammaton Elohim establishes
and maintains the form of the Fluidic Matter. Its
attribute is Binah, or Intelligence.

IV. The fourth letter is Daleth. It represents the name DAGOUL, which is equivalent to Insignis, and it corresponds to the Angels of the Hasmalim, or Angels of the fourth order, who are the Dominions of current theology. By their ministry were elaborated the diverse forms of matter, and especially the human body. Hesed is the attribute of El, and it signifies Mercy and Goodness.

V. The fifth letter is He, which typifies the name NADOUR, significant of the majesty of God, and corresponding to the fifth angelical hierarchy, which is the choir of might and power, and its Intelligences are called Powers. By their ministry the elements were evolved by Elohim-Gibor, whose numeration is Pachad, which signifies Fear and Judgment, and whose attribute is Geburah, which signifies Strength and Power.

VI. The sixth letter is Vau, whence is developed the name VEZIO, *cum splendore;* it stands for the Angels of the sixth order, the Malakim, or Virtues, by whose ministry Eloah-Vaudahat produces the metals and other substances which belong to the mineral kingdom. His attribute is Tiphereth, which signifies Beauty and Splendour.

VII. The seventh letter is Zain, which originates the name ZAKAI, equivalent to *purus mundus.* It corresponds to the Angels of the seventh order, the Kabbalistic Children of Elohim, who are the Principalities of orthodox faith. By their ministry the vegetable kingdom was produced by Tetragrammaton-Sabaoth, whose attribute is Nezah, which, interpreted, is Triumph and Justice.

VIII. The eighth letter is called Cheth. It designates the name CHASID, which is equivalent to *misericors.* It corresponds to the Angels of the eighth choir, the Bene-Elohim, or Sons of God, who are identical with the archangelical host. By their ministry the animal creation was developed by Elohim-Sabaoth, whose attribute is Hod, which is Praise.

IX. The ninth letter is Teth. It corresponds to TAHOR, or the *Mundus purus,* and to the Cherubim or ninth choir of Angels, who preside at the birth of man and inspire him with the light which is needed to direct him to eternal life. By their ministry are Guardian Angels devoted to the whole of humanity by Shaday and Elhaï, whose attribute is the Foundation, or Jesod.

X. The tenth letter is Jod, which gives power to the name JAH, which is equivalent to *Deus*. It designates the tenth numeration of the Hebrews—Adonay-Melech, or the God-King, whose attributes are the Kingdom, the Temple, and the Empire. Its influences extend to the Issim—strong, happy, and blessed Men, located in the sphere of the spirit. By their ministry, intelligence, industry, and the knowledge of divine things descend as an influx to embodied humanity.

The Angelical World is completed with the tenth letter, but the rest of the Hebrew alphabet corresponds to individual princes of intelligence, governors of innumerable hosts, and severally enacting an important part in the economy of the mystical universe. Mettatron is in correspondence with Caf, the eleventh letter; by his ministry, the sensible world receives deific virtues. He belongs to the first Heaven of the Astronomic World. There is also the final Caf, which corresponds to the Intelligences of the second order, who govern the Heaven of the fixed stars, and especially the zodiacal signs. Their supreme chief is Raziel. Lamed, the twelfth letter, corresponds to the Intelligences of the third Heaven, who preside in the sphere of Saturn. Their lord is Schebtaïel, whose attribute is the Hidden God. Mem, which is the thirteenth letter, corresponds to the fourth Heaven, or sphere of Jupiter. The sovereign Intelligence who governs this planet is called Tsadkiel. There is also the final Mem, which is analogous to the fifth Heaven, or sphere of Mars, with Camaël for its supreme Intelligence. He is the strength and fire of God, and presides over many princes. Nun is the fourteenth letter, and corresponds to the sixth Heaven, which is that of the Sun. Now, the first sovereign Intelligence which governs the grand luminary is the splendid and mighty Raphaël, the House of God. Nun in its aspect as a final corresponds to the sphere of Venus, which is also the seventh Heaven, and has

Haniel for its sovereign lord, who is the love, justice, and grace of God. Samech, the fifteenth letter, corresponds to the eighth Heaven, which is that of the star Mercury, and is governed by Michael. The sixteenth letter is Oin, which is analogous to the ninth Heaven, the sphere of the Moon, governed by the messenger-intelligence Gabriel. The Astrologic and Astronomic worlds finish with this letter, and the succeeding sequence of arcane correspondences is concerned with the Elementary Plane.

Thus Phé, the seventeenth letter of the Hebrew alphabet, has reference to the first of the mystical elements, which is held to be Fire, and its sovereign Intelligence is Seraphim. Phé final corresponds to the Air, which is the abode of the Sylphs, whose lord is Cherubim. Tsadé, the eighteenth letter, has reference to Water, which is the abode of the Nymphs. Now the Queen of the Nymphs is Tharsis. Koph is the nineteenth letter; it is in correspondence with Earth, which is the sphere of the Gnomes, having Ariel for its presiding Intelligence. Resh, which is the twentieth letter, applies to the Animal Kingdom, including Man; Schin corresponds to all vegetable substances, and Tau, the last symbol of the Hebrew alphabet, refers to the world of minerals.*

Besides the celestial hosts, which are enumerated in the above tabulation, the mystical calculus of the Hebrews establishes the existence of other angelical sequences, as, for example, the angels who encompass the Great White Throne, and whose names are entirely extracted from three mysterious verses in the fourteenth chapter of Exodus. Such elaborations of a multitude of titles, by means of Kabbalistic computations, and their endowment with corresponding powers and formal periods of influence, were prized by rabbinical writers as containing the keys of the government of the universe.

It is hardly on their own merits that we have included these speculations in a practical handbook of occultism, although they are almost venerated by a certain section

---

* In this list, by some mischance, the rulers of the Air and of the Earth have become confused; for Cherubim is usually referred to the latter element, and Ariel to the former.

of modern mystics. But they are vitally important as establishing the exact nature of Kabbalistic conceptions concerning those worlds of invisible intelligences, whose outer fringes are contiguous to our own horizon, of which they had glimpses as we have, but of which they had little real knowledge, and could formulate no adequate hypothesis. The inadequacy of their speculation is embarrassing to believers in the infallibility of the Hebrew mystics, but it offers no obstacle to those who are investigating the actual scope of ancient knowledge concerning the facts of psychology, and can distinguish the landmarks of true experimental progress amidst a wilderness of distraught speculations.

The rites to be used in the conjuration of the more exalted intelligences are found in the "Key of Solomon," an excellent edition of which has been issued by Mr. Mathers. Intelligences of this nature are generically denominated angels, but they often partake of the character of superior elementary spirits, and this is undoubtedly the case with most of those who are supposed to be controlled by the imprecations and threats of the Magus.

An anonymous German work published at Frankfort in 1686, and entitled *Theosophia Pneumatica*, appears to comprise in a comparatively small space the most satisfactory formulæ for the invocation of the supreme angels. A translation in manuscript, made by Dr J. M. Rieder, having recently come into our hands, we have made it the foundation of the citations which follow. Students will perceive that it is somewhat similar to the treatise by Arbatel on "Magic." The classifications and names of the angels, as they exist in this curious work, are not in correspondence with those which have been already given, but as it is acknowledged by the mystics that the true names — which is equivalent to saying, the real and ultimate natures—of all unseen beings are inaccessible to human research, importance should not be ascribed to any of the variations. Titular distinctions in matters of magical practice have little but literary utility. Once in the presence of an angel, it is said, the soul has no need of speech, much less of the ordinary methods of social address.

The magical treatise in question has the common disability of all works of its age and class; its aspirations its intentions, and its practical value as a ritual must be sedulously separated from its crude philosophical setting. Whatever the spiritual knowledge attained by the Magus of old, it was seemingly insufficient to raise him above the intellectual limitations of his time, and it must ever be remembered that the modern scheme of mystical criticism which seeks to account for such obvious philosophical inadequacies as exist in the ancient mystics by assuming that, in spite of superior attainments, they condescended for concealed reasons to countenance current opinions, scientific or religious, is without any actual warrant in known fact.

In "Pneumatic Magic," the names of the angels are classified under the title of Olympian, or Celestial spirits, who abide in the firmament and the supreme constellations: "it is their function to acknowledge the Fata and to administer the inferior destinies. Each Olympic spirit accomplishes and teaches whatsoever is portended by the star in which he is insphered. Yet can he do nothing of his own power, nor without a special command from God.

"There are Seven Stewards of Heaven by whom God is pleased to administrate the world. To wit:—ARA-THRON, BETHOR, PHALEG, OCH, HAGITH, OPHIEL, PHUL. They are thus called in the Olympian language, and each of them has a numerous army and grand chivalry of the firmament.

ARATHRON commands over 49 visible regions.
BETHOR	,,	,,	42	,,	,,
PHALEG	,,	,,	35	,,	,,
OCH	,,	,,	28	,,	,,
HAGITH	,,	,,	21	,,	,,
OPHIEL	,,	,,	14	,,	,,
PHUL	,,	,,	7	,,	,,

"The Olympic Regions are in all one hundred and ninety-six, over which the Seven Stewards extend their policy. The mysteries of these regions and of the firmaments are explained in the sublime science of transcen-

dental astrology, and the means of establishing communication with the powers and principalities therein.

"Arathron appears on a Saturday at the first hour, and
gives a true answer for his regions and their inhabitants.
So also with all the others, each at his own day and
hour, and each presiding over a space of four hundred
and ninety years. The functions of Bethor began in
the fiftieth year before the birth of Christ, and were
extended till the year of Christ 430. Phagle reigned
till A.D. 920; Och till the year 1410; Hagith will
govern till A.D. 1900. The others shall follow in succession. These intelligences are the stewards of all the
elements, energising the firmament, and, with their
armies, depending from each other in a regular hierarchy.

"The names of the minor Olympian spirits are interpreted in divers ways, but those alone are powerful
which they themselves give, which are adapted to the
end for which they have been summoned. Generically,
they are called ASTRA, and their power is seldom prolonged beyond one hundred and forty years.

"The heavens and their inhabitants come voluntarily
to man and often serve against even the will of man,
but how much more if we implore their ministry. That
evil and troublesome spirits also approach men is accomplished by the cunning of the devil, at times by conjuration or attraction, and frequently as a penalty for
sins; therefore, shall he who would abide in familiarity
with celestial intelligences take pains to avoid every
serious sin; he shall diligently pray for the protection
of God to vanquish the impediments and schemes of
Diabolus, and God will ordain that the devil himself
shall work to the direct profit of the Theosophist.

"Subject to Divine Providence, some spirits have
power over pestilence and famine, some are destroyers
of cities, like those of Sodom and Gomorrah, some are
rulers over kingdoms, some guardians of provinces, some
of a single person. The spirits are the ministers of the
word of God, of the Church and its members, or they
serve creatures in material things, sometimes to the
salvation of soul and body, or, again, to the ruin of

both. But nothing, good or bad, is done without knowledge, order, and administration."

Arathron is the celestial spirit of Saturn; he can
operate natural things prepared by astrological influences;
he may change everything into stone, whether animals
or plants; but they will preserve their exterior appearance. He changes treasures into coals and coals into
treasures. He gives familiar spirits with definite power.
He teaches alchemy, magic, and natural philosophy.
He joins men to gnomes and earth spirits. He renders
people invisible. He governs fertility and conception;
he teaches the discovery of lead, its manipulation, and
its change into gold. He teaches the art of curing the
smaller animals of their diseases, such as goats, poultry,
&c. He gives intelligence of prisoners and of sick
people, despatches ministering spirits, who serve after
his own manner, enlarges the understanding, gives excellent advice on all elevating subjects, and is most
exact in his calculations.

He must be invoked on a Saturday, at the first hour
of sunset in the increasing moon.

Bethor administers the influence of Jupiter; he who
can obtain his assistance may rise to the highest dignities;
he dispenses treasures, subjects the spirits of the air to
the Magus, and gives a true answer. These intelligences
carry all things, even precious stones, with marvellous
medicines, from one place to another. The spirit of
Jupiter gives other ministering spirits of the firmament:
he can extend life to seven hundred years, God willing.
He has subject to him forty-two kings, thirty-five
princes, twenty-eight dukes, one-and-twenty counsellors,
fourteen servants, seven messengers, and two thousand
nine hundred legions of spirits; he instructs judges in
the administration of equal justice to the poor as well as
to the rich; he inspires his Magus with the love of
justice, gives him true vision-haunted dreams, and assists
in the attainment of venerable functions and dignities.
He gives understanding to the old, even to fools and
idiots, strengthens the weak memory, beautifies men under
his influence, endows them with eloquence before princes
and the great of this world, and makes them gentle,

courteous, and noble; he gives a number of serving spirits for various purposes; and he appoints ministering spirits to teach the manufacture of gold from tin. This princely angel is Good Fortune *ipsâ personâ;* he dispenses a profusion of gifts, especially of a spiritual kind; his ministers can bring the object of your desires even from India and other lands of the Orient; they teach distillation from various herbs and roots, and the preparation all kinds of physics and spices. This spirit must be adjured on Monday in Pentecost at the first hour of sunrise.

Phaleg is the master of matters which are ascribed to Mars, but he is also a prince of peace; whosoever receives his signum is exalted to supreme dignities. He teaches military science and medicine; how to judge and govern well, to find, extract, and manipulate iron, and how to manufacture gold.

He must be called on a Tuesday at the first hour of sunrise, between seven and eight in the morning, and between two and three in the afternoon, during the increasing moon.

Och is a sovereign over things belonging to the sun; he can extend life to six hundred years, insuring constant health and wisdom; he sends the most excellent angels, teaches a perfect medical science, can change anything into the purest gold, gives a purse in which gold grows, prepares the precious metal in the mountains during a long period, by alchemy in a briefer space, and by magic in a single moment. Whosoever receives his sign the kings of the earth must venerate as a divine being. He commands thirty-six thousand five hundred and thirty-six legions of spirits; he alone administers all things; all intelligences serve him. He and his subjects seldom exalt anyone till they have attained middle age, neither can they impart the highest rank, but their advice is excellent in several matters, especially in medicine, including the cure of wounds caused by the bite of a snake, scorpion, or spider.

The spirit of Sol must be invoked on a Sunday morning at sunrise.

Hagith administrates in Venereal concerns. He makes

beautiful the being to whom he gives his sign, and endows him with physical grace. He changes copper into
gold instantaneously, gives spirits full of faithful service,
has four thousand legions of angels, with kings occasionally established over them—one over every thousand.
He teaches the knowledge of herbs, plants, roots, and
spices; he instructs in the arcana of health, skill, and
beauty; he is the most rapid of all spirits; he gives good
counsellors, embroiderers, sempstresses in silk — the
latter all neat and skilful."

He must be invoked in the increasing moon, on a
Friday, at the first hour of sunrise or sunset.

Ophiel administers mercurial things. His legions
exceed one hundred thousand. He grants ministering
angels willingly, teaches all arts, and to whomsoever
he gives his sign he imparts the power of instantaneously extracting the philosophical stone out of
mercury. From him you may learn astrology, the
learned professions, mining, alchemy, statuary, painting,
the removal of mountains into the sea, the erection of
bridges, the preparation of magic mirrors and other
instruments, excellence in letter writing, editing, and
penmanship; also, elocution, jurisprudence, and interpretation of Holy Writ. He gives good counsel, right
judgment, and skill in all subtle arts.

He must be adjured on a Wednesday, at the first hour
of sunrise, and during the increasing moon.

Phul administers all things belonging to the moon.
He can change all metals into silver, heal dropsy, give
Undines serving man in visible, corporeal shapes, and can
lengthen life to three hundred years. You may obtain
from him an angel, who is a physician, a philosopher, an
artist, and a naturalist or transcendentalist. He gives
physic for the eyes, and remedies against vertigo, epilepsy
and strabism, or presbitism. He grants also a good sight
and reliable information on many subjects, including
things future which are of a personal character.

He is called on a Monday, at the first hour of sunrise,
in the increasing moon.

The ritual informs us that each of the Seven Celestial
Stewards can operate after a number of methods, either

according to the common course of nature, or by the more arcane exercise of will-power, and that each can accomplish in a very brief period what, without his interference, would require much time and preparation. Each of these intelligences must be invoked between seven and eight in the forenoon, or between two and three in the afternoon, on any day of the week, but solely in the hours which he governs, the moon being on the increase.

An acquaintance with the names and offices of these spirits is by no means sufficient to enter into a state of correspondence with their exalted intelligence, and many preparations for the successful evocation of angels are described by the authority I have cited, of which some are methodically enumerated after the following fashion :—

I.

The Talmid (otherwise the Magus, in his earlier grade of initiation) shall ponder day and night on the method of attaining a true knowledge of God, not only by the Word which has been manifested from the beginning of the world, but also from the laws of the Cosmos, and the admirable practical secrets which may be learned from the study of the visible and invisible creatures of God.

II.

The Magus shall learn to know himself, to distinguish between his mortal and immortal parts, and the spheres to which they severally belong.

III.

By his immortal nature he shall study to love God, to adore and to fear him in spirit and in truth. But he must also in his mortal body endeavour to be useful to his neighbours, and glorify his maker. These are the highest commandments of Magic, by which you shall obtain the veritable Pneumatology through Divine Truth and Wisdom, and you shall be served by angelical creatures not only in secret, but publicly, and face to face.

IV.

As every one is destined from his mother's womb to a certain commerce of life, the disciple should pause to consider whether he is born to Magic, and to what branch. By noting the measure of success in the different sections of operation, he may soon ascertain the second point.

V.

An intending Magus shall be discreet and faithful; he shall never reveal what he has been told by a spirit. Daniel was commanded to set a seal on several matters; Paul was forbidden to reveal what he beheld in his ecstasy. The importance of this ordination cannot be exaggerated.

VI.

Say very frequently with David :—Take not thy Holy Spirit of strength away from me. Lead me not into temptation.

VII.

Accustom yourself to the evocation of spirits. You cannot gather grapes from thorns, nor figs from thistles. Prove all things and hold fast that which is good. Avoid all that is contrary to the will of God.

VIII.

Avoid all superstition, which consists in the attribution of divine power to things which are without divinity, and in the acceptation of divine service without a command from God. The illusions of diabolical magic, which arrogates to the prince of darkness the adoration due to God, are included under this name.

IX.

Avoid the deceitful imitations of the devil, who, by the perversion of the theurgic powers concealed in the Word of God, becomes a fraudulent imitator of things which belong to God.

When these conditions have been fulfilled, and the operator proceeds to the practice, he should devote a special prefatory period to profound contemplation on the serious and sacred business which he has voluntarily taken in hand, and must labour to present himself before his Supreme Teacher with a pure heart, an undefiled mouth, and innocent hands : "he must bathe his body and purge it from all uncleanness, wear newly washed garments, confess his sins, and abstain from wine, as well as all unchastity" for the space of three days. He should also give alms to the poor, and when the eve of operation has at length arrived, he must dine moderately at noon, and sup on bread and water. Then on the following day, he must seek a retired and uncontaminated spot, where, free from observation, he can recite the prescribed invocations, *e.g.* :

Prayer.

Holy, Holy Father! Increase my faith and confirm me that I may believe stedfastly in Thy willingness to vouchsafe me that which I am now asking through Jesus Christ Thy Son. Amen.

And further :—

ALMIGHTY, EVERLASTING, MERCIFUL GOD, who didst create all things to thine own honour and praise, and to the benefit of mankind, I pray Thee to send me the spirit OCH—of the race of the suns—in a visible form to teach me that which I would ask him, namely to give me a plain and brief instruction in the preparation of the angelic water, for the cure of all external and internal diseases in seven days.* That he may direct one of his spirits to visit me all the days of my life, giving true answers, and instructing me in all questions

* *Obiter nota :* the angelic water in all seven metals in ☉ philos : regenerated elixir and *metalla potabilia* mixed together. *Ut si plumbum regeneratum est elixir plusquam in massa respicemus Saturnam et Arathron et Signa ejus et liquefactum est aqua fixa reliqua.* And all metals solved, also discover their nature, so that also ☿ and all other metals can be changed into gold in an instant —and gold which is good, right, and resisting all proofs.

and in all matters on which I require information. Give
me a docile heart to understand and remember, also to
apply my knowledge to Thy glory and the benefit of
man. O Lord, take not Thy Holy Spirit from me, confirm me in divine joy. Lead us not into temptation, but
deliver us from evil.

Holy, Holy Father, I pray Thee, do not abandon me
to the spirit of untruth, as Thou didst give him power
over Achab, but preserve me in thine own truth. In
all things Thy will be done. Through Jesus Christ.
Amen.

When the spiritual exaltation of the Magus has been
accomplished by these and other prayers (varied of
course to suit the purpose intended), and by various
ceremonial practices, the spirit is, in magical language,
compelled to appear. That is to say, the operator has
passed into a condition when it would be as impossible
for a spirit to remain invisible to him as for an ordinary
mortal to conceal himself from our common sight,
without an intervening shelter, in the blaze of a noon-
day sun.

When the angel has arrived, continues the Ritual,
briefly make known what you wish, write down his
answer ; do not ask more than three questions ; preserve
what you learn in your memory, and consider it as
sacred. As soon as your answer has been obtained,
say to the angel :—" Since thou didst come peacefully,
thanks be to God the Lord, in whose name thou art
commissioned, return now in peace unto thy rank and
sphere, and come again when I invoke thee according
to the order and functions which the Almighty has
vouchsafed thee. Amen."

———

Thus we see that the magician of old who had any
desire unfulfilled, by his knowledge of the different
spiritual potencies and their respective functions, was
able, by evoking that one whose powers corresponded to
his own desire, to obtain whatever he sought. Whether
such evocations are now practised, and if so to what

extent, it is impossible here to say, for probably the modern magician who attained such knowledge would have attained it only after such a novitiate as would render him unable or unwilling to disclose the facts. Indeed, it is the general opinion of modern occultists that the initiated mystic never disclosed anything except to his brother adepts, and that what has transpired in these matters has been through persons who failed in the process, but had advanced as far as a certain point.

The theological literature of angelology is exceedingly extensive, and one of its most important developments is that of St Thomas of Aquinas, who is called the angelical doctor. In general literature, perhaps the most curious work is Heywood's "Hierarchy of the Blessed Angels," which is a storehouse of curious research. Other works are "*De apparitionibus omnis generis Spirituum*," by the Jesuit, Peter Thyræus, date 1600; "Pneumatalogia; or, a Discourse of Angels, their Nature and Office or Ministry," anonymous, 1701; but a methodical history of angelology has not yet been written.

WHITE MAGIC.

THE EVOCATION OF THE SPIRITS OF THE ELEMENTS.

TO the old magical doctrine of the Spirits of the Elements we owe some of the most graceful and enchanting fictions in literature. It supplied Pope with the supernatural machinery for his inimitable "Rape of the Lock," while an old Latin treatise of Paracelsus suggested the groundwork of "Undine," one of the most dainty and delicate of all German fairy tales. Oriental romance is also replete with the operative wonders of these and kindred beings, for the Peris, Jinn, and Afreets of Arabian imaginative writers are substantially identical with Western conceptions concerning Elementary Spirits.

The possible existence of such intelligences has been seriously debated even by the scientific writers of this epoch. In the "Unseen Universe" a chapter is filled with speculations as to the association of delicate cosmical processes in this visible universe with the operations of unseen intelligences residing within it.

The belief in the connection of personal agents with the more startling natural phenomena is admitted to have been extensively prevalent during the middle ages, when imagination peopled the "four elements" with intelligences, normally unseen, "some of them friendly to man, some of them his deadly enemies. They are powerful and conscious of their power, but at the same time profoundly and mournfully aware that they are without a soul. Their life depends upon the continuance of some natural object, and hence for them there is no immortality. Sometimes, however, an elementary spirit procures a soul by means of a loving union with one of the human race. At other times, the reverse happens, and the soul of the mortal is lost, who, leaving the haunts of men, associates with those soulless, but often amiable and affectionate beings."

On the other hand, there are writers who, also at this day, believe, or profess to believe, that "the planets of our system may be directed in their 'continual speaking changes' by their several crowds of governing spirits"— that "spirits are everywhere the directors of matter"— that "there exist upon the earth reasonable creatures other than man, having like him a body and soul, being born and dying like him"—that these are "the forces of the wind, the fire, and the flood,"—that, in fact, whatever superstition generated in the past, whatever imagination has endowed with a habitation and a name, has an invisible but certain existence. The doctrine of planetary intelligences has been countenanced as hypothetically admissible even by Mr W. S. Lilly, who is one of the most cultured and thoughtful of later philosophical writers.

The idea of living forces existing in the elements is not merely of mediæval, or even of Gnostic, origination, for this belief was cherished in the earliest ages of the world's history. As a proof of this we may instance two very ancient Accadian or early Assyrian Incantations, addressed to the Elements of Fire and of Water. The originals were translated by Mr Ernest Budge, the Egyptologist, and published in "The Records of the Past."

The 108th chapter of the Ancient Egyptian "Ritual of the Dead," the "Per-M-Hru," is called "the Chapter of Knowing the Spirits of the West." Several of the chapters which immediately follow are devoted to the knowledge of the Spirits of various denominations, the Spirits of the East, the Spirits of Tu, the Spirits of An, &c.

Thus we see that the most ancient nations believed in the existence of certain living forces of Nature, whose chiefs they named and invoked; and we shall find the same ideas prevalent in both the Scandinavian and the Indian mythology.

The discriminating disciple of mysticism, however, while admitting the complete possibility of the existence of intelligences both inferior and superior to humanity, will do well to remember that some of the elaborate hypotheses concerning them are devoid of scientific value, being structures equally clumsy and inadequate which have been based upon partial-experiment.

The most popular presentation of the doctrine of Elementary Spirits is found in a little book entitled the "Comte de Gabalis," a work of the Abbé de Villars, published at the close of the last century. It possesses the merit—which is rare in a popular handbook—of being quite representative and accurate so far as it goes, and albeit so doubtful in its character as to have frequently passed for a satire, it is an excellent tract for citation within its individual lines.

It is sufficient for our purpose to state—what is very generally known—that the four official elements have from time immemorial been supposed to swarm with a variety of, on the whole, sub-human intelligences, who are formally grouped into four broad species. The air is inhabited by the amiable race of Sylphs, the sea by the delightful and beautiful Undines, the earth by the industrious race of swarthy Gnomes, and the fire by the exalted and glorious nation of Salamanders, who are supreme in the elementary hierarchy. There is a close analogy in the natures of all these intelligences with the more lofty constitution of certain angelical choirs, for in the "Compendious Apology for the Society called Rosicrucian," written by Robert Fludd, it is stated that the Seraphim, Virtues, and Powers are of a fiery character, the Cherubim are terrestrial, the Thrones and Archangels are aquatic, while the Dominations and Principalities are aerial.

"When you shall be lifted among the children of the philosophers," says the 'Comte de Gabalis,' "when your eyes shall have been fortified with the use of the most sacred medicine, you will immediately discover that the elements are inhabited by singularly perfect beings, of whose knowledge the sin of Adam hath deprived his most wretched posterity. Yon immense space which intervenes between earth and heaven hath far more noble inhabitants than birds or gnats; those vast seas have in-

numerable other guests than the whales and the dolphins;
the profundities of the earth are not for the moles alone,
and the more noble element of fire was not created to
remain void and useless. The air is full of an innumerable
multitude of people of human form, somewhat fierce in
their aspect, but in reality tractable, great lovers of
science, excessively subtle, officious to the sages, and
only hostile to the foolish and ignorant. Their wives
and daughters are beauties of a masculine character,
much after the manner of the Amazons. The seas and
rivers are inhabited as well as the air, and the beings
who fill them were denominated Nymphs or Undines by
the antique doctors of wisdom. They beget but few
males, but the women are abundant, they are exceedingly beautiful, and the daughters of men cannot
compare with them. The earth is populated to a short
distance of its centre with gnomes, people of a low
stature, the guardians of buried treasure, of mines, and
of precious stones. They are ingenious, amicable to
humanity, and commanded with facility. They supply
the Children of the Sages with the money which they
need, and desire no other wages for their labours but
the glory of the service. The Gnomides, their wives,
are diminutive but exceptionally pretty, and very quaint
in attire. As to the Salamanders, the igneous inhabitants of the fiery region, they serve the philosophers, but
are not anxious to court their company, and their wives
and daughters are rarely visible. The wives of the
Salamanders are more beautiful than any of the rest, for
their element is purer, and you will be more charmed with
the beauty of their minds than even with their physical
perfections. Yet you cannot but pity these hapless
creatures when I tell you that their souls are mortal,
and that they have no hopes of enjoying that Eternal
Being whom they know and religiously adore. Composed
of the purest parts of the elements which they inhabit,
and having no contrary qualities, they subsist, it is true,
for many ages, yet what is time in comparison with everlasting? They must eventually return to the abyss of
nothing. So much does this thought afflict them that it
is frequently hard to console them. But God, whose

mercy is infinite, revealed to our fathers, the philosophers, a remedy for this evil. They learned that in
the same manner that man by the alliance which he hath
contracted with God has been made partaker of divinity,
so may the Sylphs, Gnomes, Undines, and Salamanders,
by an alliance with man be made partakers of immortality, and of the bliss to which we aspire, when one of them
is so happy as to be married to a sage, while Elementaries
of the masculine kind can attain the same glorious end
by effecting a union with the daughters of the human
race.

"The Salamanders are composed of the most subtle
parts of the sphere of fire, conglobated and organised by
the universal fire, so called because it is the principle of
all the motions of Nature. In the same manner, the
Sylphs are composed of the purest atoms of air, Nymphs
of the most ethereal particles of water, and Gnomes
of the most refined earth. The primeval Adam was in
correspondence with these perfect creatures, because
being composed of the finest matters of the four elements, he contained in himself the physical perfection
of each of these four races, and was therefore their
natural king. But when sin had precipitated him
among the excrements of the four elements, this harmony was shattered, he became gross and impure, and
no longer bore any proportion with these so pure and
subtile substances."

Though not definitely stated in the "Comte de Gabalis,"
it is obvious that the end of a magical communication
with Elementary Spirits is to restore our Edenic correspondence between man and the harmonial world of
spirits, which in effect would be a restoration of the
celestial condition of primordial humanity. Now the
traditions of aboriginal perfection and aureoline splendour may be possibly untrue for the past but they are
certainly prophetic for the future ; they are the ultimate
stage of evolution forecast at remote periods, and while
taking form as reminiscences of a vanished glory, they
are also a dim foreshadowing of a glory which is still to
come.

A recipe for the transfiguration of the Magus in the

direction of Salamandrine perfection is vouchsafed in
the "Comte de Gabalis;" it is completely unintelligible
in its literal sense, while the unserious nature of the
entire work will not reasonably warrant the supposition
that it contains an arcane meaning, though it may be
admitted that its wording is suggestive from the mystical standpoint.   The recipe is as follows :—If you would
recover the empire over the Salamanders, purify and
exalt the NATURAL FIRE that is within you.   Nothing is
required for this purpose but the concentration of the
FIRE OF THE WORLD by means of *concave mirrors* in a
globe of glass.   In that globe is formed a SOLARY POWDER,
which being of itself purified from the mixture of other
elements, and being prepared according to 𝔄ℜ𝔗, becomes in a very short time a sovereign process for the
exaltation of the *Fire that is within you,* and will transmute you into an igneous nature.

It is clear that a great part of the secret and mystery
is in the nature of the mirrors and in the nature of the
vessel of glass, and those who devote themselves to the
unravelling of this Gordian Knot should direct their
especial attention to these points, which, if allegory may
be credibly assumed, should not be very far to seek.

We are assured by the Abbé de Villars that by the
use of this recipe the inhabitants of the Sphere of Fire
will become our inferiors, and ravished to behold our
mutual harmony restored, they will have the same love
and friendship for us that they entertain for their own
kind.

Amidst the rich imagination of these fantastic reveries,
the student will do well to remember that the experiments of the old magicians brought them into communication with many classes of extra-mundane intelligence,
and that they elaborated many hypotheses to account
for them.

But it must be further recollected that among Elemental Spirits themselves there exist many classes and
natures in each category.   For instance ; in the case of
the Fire-Spirits there are those which are friendly, hostile,
and neutral as regards men ; there are those which are
compounded of a purer essence, partaking of the nature

of the lower angels without being exactly of their genus; there are those which are violent and cruel, approximating to a demoniac nature, and whose tendency is to stir up wrath, hatred, and envy. Then there are those again which are pure living Spirits of Flame, operating in all things of a fiery nature, and directing the currents of that element. Besides all these there are those which more resemble the Spirits of fairy-lore, and which may, perhaps, be best described as a species of *igneous* mankind having a more physical organisation than certain of the other classes. Yet, again, there are certain whose natures form a link between the Spiritual World and the Vegetable Kingdom; others again control the fiery nature in the Mineral World; and others are Volcanic in nature and operation, whence they were called by certain of the mediæval writers " Ætneans." But even these classes are but few in comparison with the enormous number of subdivisions in each Element alone. And, besides this, it must be remembered that there are all the millions upon millions of Elemental Spirits of the Planets, of the Zodiac, and of the Fixed Stars; so that the mind is bewildered in the endeavour to trace out fully all the classes even under one Element. Then in each Element there are Spirits partaking of all forms, mixed and simple, of the Animal Kingdom, every form of bird, beast, fish, reptile, and insect, sometimes in the simple form, but more often compounded with each other and with Man:—*e.g.*, a frequent form of certain Fire-Spirits is a compound of a Man, a Lion, and a Serpent. Some of the most repulsive of the Elemental forms, however, are the various compounds of huge insect or crustacean forms with either human or animal heads. Such are veritable nightmares, and Darwin's " missing link" seems to be easily discoverable on the Elemental plane. The snakes, dogs, and insects, seen by some sufferers from " *delirium tremens*," are—according to a modern occultist —simply forms taken by some of the lowest Elementals who have been attracted to the drink-sodden atmosphere of the habitual drunkard, following the same law by which vultures and jackals are drawn to rotting and putrefying carrion. Yet, nevertheless, it would be just as incorrect to call even the lowest and worst of the Elementals "devils," as to say that a Scorpion or an Adder was really a fiend.

Another and more difficult matter to grasp, regarding the Elemental Spirits, is that they partake only of the nature of one Element respectively, and that in that Element they can live, breathe, and move; but that another Element, and especially one opposite in nature, is to them a bar and obstacle.

Though the evocation of Elementary Spirits was an important part of theurgic practice during the middle ages, we are unacquainted with any ritual which expounds the method of communicating with these intelligences in any complete way. A considerable section of so-called angelical magic was in reality devoted to the control of the Spirits of the Air, who are the Sylphs of Paracelsian mythology, and it is frequently hard to distinguish between the angels and the ' elementaries ' of old writers on account of this uniform confusion. Much of the Black Magic of the past was also undoubtedly concerned with the lower hierarchies of Nature Spirits, and just as the " Comte de Gabalis " identifies the gracious creations of the classic Pantheon—its Astartes, Dianas, and Egerias with the beautiful tribe of Nymphs—so did the devils of the Sabbath, by a variety of characters and qualities, approach the lowest of the elementals, and had actually but little that was in common with the thunderstruck angels of orthodox Christian theology.

A method for the interrogation and government of elementary intelligences is given in the initiations of Eliphas Lévi; but the source of its extraction is unnamed, and it is of a very fragmentary nature. It is, however, the most available of its kind, and, with a few supplementary recipes, may be sufficient for practical purposes.

To dominate the Elementary Spirits, and become thus the king of the occult elements, it is necessary, says the last of the French initiates, to experience the four trials of antique initiation; and, as these initiations exist no longer, they must be supplied by analogous processes;

as, for instance, by exposing oneself with courage in a burning house, by crossing a precipice on a plank or the trunk of a tree; by ascending a perpendicular mountain in a storm; and by vigorously plunging through a cascade or dangerous whirlpool. He who is afraid of the water will never reign over the Undines; he who shrinks from the flames will never command Salamanders; let him who is subject to vertigo leave the Sylphs in peace, and forbear from irritating the Gnomes, for inferior spirits will obey no power which has not asserted its supremacy in their own individual element.

When courage and indomitable energy have acquired this incontestable power, the Logos of will-force must be imposed on the elements by particular consecrations of air, fire, earth, and water, this being the indispensable beginning of all magical operations.

The air is exorcised by the sufflation of the four cardinal points, the recitation of the Prayer of the Sylphs and the following formula:—The Spirit of God moved upon the water, and breathed into the nostrils of man the breath of life. Be Michael my leader and be Sabtabiel my servant, in the name and by the virtue of light. Be the power of the word in my breath, and I will govern the spirits of this creature of Air, and by the will of my soul, I will restrain the steeds of the sun, and by the thought of my mind, and by the apple of my right eye. I exorcise thee, O creature of Air, by the Pentagrammaton, and in the name Tetragrammaton, wherein are steadfast will and well directed faith. Amen. Sela. So be it.

Water is exorcised by the laying on of hands, by breathing, and by speech, mixing consecrated salt with a little of the ash which is left in the incense pan. The aspergillus is made of branches of vervain, periwinkle, sage, mint, ash, and basil, tied by a thread taken from a virgin's distaff, with a handle of hazelwood which has never borne fruit, and on which the characters of the seven spirits must be graved with the magic awl. The salt and ashes of the incense must be separately consecrated. The Prayer of the Undines should follow.

Fire is exorcised by casting salt, incense, white resin,

camphor, and sulphur therein, and by thrice pronounc-ing the three names of the Genii of fire—MICHAEL, king of the sun and of the lightning; SAMAEL, king of volcanoes; and ANAEL, king of the Astral Light; then by reciting the prayer of the Salamanders.

The earth is exorcised by the sprinkling of water, by breathing, and by fire, with the perfumes proper to each day, and the prayer of the Gnomes.

It must be borne in mind that the special kingdom of the Gnomes is at the north, that of the Salamanders at the south, that of the Sylphs at the east, and that of the Undines at the west. They influence the four tempera-ments of man, that is to say, the Gnomes influence the melancholic, Salamanders the sanguine, Undines the phlegmatic, and Sylphs the bilious. Their signs are—the hieroglyphs of the Bull for the Gnomes, who are commanded with the magic sword; of the Lion for the Salamanders, who are commanded with the forked rod, or magic trident; of the Eagle for the Sylphs, who are ruled by the holy pentacles; and, finally, of Aquarius for the Undines, who are evoked by the cup of libations. Their respective sovereigns are Gob for the Gnomes, Djin for the Salamanders, Paralda for the Sylphs, and Necksa for the Undines.

Like so much of occult nomenclature, these names are of a generic and arbitrary kind, and appear to be devoid of real importance; in the present instance, they are borrowed from folk-lore.

It must be remembered that the words "Elemental" and "Elementary" are not exactly convertible terms; as the latter is frequently used by "theosophists" to denote the astral remains, or "shell," of a deceased person who has led a gross and evil life on earth, and whose vanishing personality remains for some time in the earth atmosphere, seeking to annoy the living.

When an elementary spirit torments, or, at any rate, troubles, the inhabitants of this world, continues Eliphas Lévi, it must be adjured by air, water, fire, and earth, by breathing, sprinkling, the burning of perfumes, and by tracing on the ground the Star of Solomon and the sacred Pentagram. These figures should be absolutely correct, and drawn either with the ash of consecrated fire, or with a reed soaked in various colours, mixed with pulverised loadstone. Then, holding the pentacle of Solomon in the hand, and taking up by turns the sword, rod, and cup, the Conjuration of the Four should be repeated.

This Conjuration should be preceded and terminated with the sign of the cross, made after the Kabbalistic manner. Raising the hand to the forehead, the Magus should say : " Thine is," then, bringing it to the breast, "the kingdom;" transferring it to the left shoulder, "justice;" finally, to the right shoulder, " and mercy ;" then, joining both hands, " through the generating ages."

To conquer and subjugate the elementary spirits, we must never be guilty of the faults which are their characteristics. Never will a capricious and changeable mind be able to rule the Sylphs. Never will a soft, cold, and fickle disposition be qualified to govern the Undines ; anger irritates the Salamanders, and gross covetousness makes those whom it enslaves the sport and plaything of the Gnomes. But we must be prompt and active, like the Sylphs; pliant and observant as the Undines; energetic and strong like the Salamanders ; laborious and patient, like the Gnomes : in a word, we must overcome them in their strength without ever being overcome by their weakness.

Mediæval magic abounds with the histories of familiar spirits attached to the persons of magicians, and frequently performing their commands without any apparent reward, and without exacting from their mortal master any of the spiritual sacrifices which are usually supposed to be required from dealers with the infernal world. The evidential value of these histories has been weakened with time, but they are absolutely paralleled in the wonders of modern Spiritualism, and there is a mass of contemporary testimony in affirmation of a domestic ministry of unseen intelligences, who in their characters and performances are substantially identical with the familiar spirits of the past. The ritual for the evocation of familiars is therefore not to be identified with infernal magic; current psychology would regard it as a communion with the souls of the dead, an opinion which is wholly in conflict with the consensus of mystical authority, and from the standpoint of historic magic, it seems safe on the whole to include it as a part of elemental practice. The following antique ceremonial for the control of familiars may be therefore recorded here.

Fix, in the first place, upon a spot proper for thy purpose, which must be either a subterranean vault, hung round with black, and lighted by a magical torch; or else in the centre of some thick wood or desert, or upon some extensive, unfrequented plain; or amidst the ruins of ancient castles, abbeys, monasteries, &c., or amongst the rocks on the sea-shore; in some private detached churchyard, or any other solemn, melancholy place, between the hours of twelve and one in the night, either when the moon shines very bright, or else when the elements are disturbed with storms of thunder, lightning, wind, and rain; for in these places, times, and seasons, it is contended that spirits can with less difficulty manifest themselves to mortal eyes, and continue visible with the least pain in this elemental world.

When the proper time and place are fixed on, a magic circle is to be formed, within which the master and his associates, to the number of three all told, are carefully to retire. The dimensions of the circle are as follows. A piece of ground is usually chosen nine feet square, at the full extent of which parallel lines are drawn one within another, having sundry crosses and tria-angles described between them, close to which is formed the first or outer circle; then, about half a foot within the same, a second circle is described; and within that another square correspondent to the first, the centre of which is the seal or spot where the master and associates are to be placed. The vacancies formed by the various lines and angles of the figure are filled up with all the holy names of God.

The reasons assigned by magicians and others for the institution and use of circles is, that so much ground being blessed and consecrated by such holy words and ceremonies as they make use of in forming it, hath a secret force to expel all evil spirits from the bounds thereof; and, being sprinkled with pure, sanctified water, the ground is purified from all uncleanness. Moreover, the holy names of God being written over every part of it, its force becomes so powerful that no evil spirit, if such should appear, hath ability to break through it, or to get at the magician and his companions, by reason of the antipathy in nature they bear to these sacred names. And the reason given for the triangle is, that if a spirit be not easily brought to speak the truth, he may be conjured by the Exorcist to enter the same, where, by virtue of the names of the Essence and Divinity of God, he can speak nothing but what is true and right. The circle therefore is the principal fort and shield of the magician, from which he is not, at the peril of his life, to depart till he has completely dismissed the spirit.

The usual form of consecrating the circle is as follows: —I, who am the servant of the Highest, do, by the virtue of his Holy Name Immanuel, sanctify unto myself the circumference of nine feet about me, ✠ ✠ ✠ from the east, Glavrab; from the west, Garron; from the north, Cabon; from the south, Berith; which ground I take for my proper defence from all malignant spirits, that they may have no power over my soul or body, nor come beyond these limitations, but that, being summoned, each spirit may answer truly, without daring to transgress their bounds.

The proper attire, or pontifical, of a magician is an ephod made of fine white linen, over that a priestly robe of black bombazine, reaching to the ground, with the two seals of the earth, drawn correctly upon virgin parchment, and affixed to the breast of his outer vestment. Round his waist is tied a broad consecrated girdle, with the names Ya, Ya, ✠ Aie, Aiae, ✠ Elibra ✠ Elohim ✠ Sadai ✠ Pah Adonai ✠ tuo robore ✠ cinctus sum ✠. Upon his shoes must be written Tetragrammaton, with crosses round about; upon his head he must wear a high-crown hat of sable silk; and in his hands must be a Bible, printed or written in pure Hebrew. When all these things are prepared, when the circle is drawn, the ground consecrated, and the Exorcist securely placed within the circle, he proceeds to call up or conjure the spirit by his proper name.

The forms of conjuration most commonly appear in the first instance under a ferocious and frightful guise, which is evidence that, whatever their nature, they are not of a kind to be trusted, but if the intention of the Magus be consciously divested of the desire to communicate with the abyss, an infernal spirit would not usually, on the magical hypothesis, be able to disguise himself as an elementary or a mere familiar. All submundane spirits are variable and inclined to deceit, but when properly subjected are said to be frequent and officious; they more or less require certain conciliatory offerings, such as fumigations, odours, incense, and other ingredients; the bloody sacrifices which are occasionally enjoined are rites of a detestable nature, and should never be attempted. The Exorcist, in all cases, must be greatly upon his guard, and when he has completed the exorcism, and made such inquiries as he wished to obtain from the spirit, he must carefully discharge him by some form like the following :—

" Because thou hast diligently answered my demands, and been ready to come at my first call, I do here license thee to depart unto thy proper place, without injury or danger to man or beast; depart, I say, and be ever ready at my call, being duly exorcised and conjured by sacred rites and magic; I charge thee to withdraw with quiet and peace; and peace be continued betwixt me and thee, in the name," &c.

The magician must remain within the boundary of the circle until all signs of the spirit's presence have passed away. Then he may venture to withdraw, repeating the Lord's prayer; after which, concludes this ritual, he may take up the various utensils, and, having destroyed all traces of the circle, may return in safety to his proper home. According to an authority " The prevalence of the black colour in the requisites for the above ceremony shows that the elementals communicated with would be of the nature of the Earth, and of Saturn;

and consequently that they might show themselves inclined to be obnoxious to the Evocator."

As there is no complete ritual for the evocation of elementary spirits, so there is no formal treatise devoted to
the doctrine itself, with the sole exception of the *Comte
de Gabalis*. The basis of this belief is in folk-lore, and
it is there that the most information will be gathered;
but Burton's "Anatomy of Melancholy," and Heywood's
"Hierarchy of the Blessed Angels," may be both incidentally consulted.

BLACK MAGIC.

THE EVOCATION OF DEMONS.

A N exceedingly large proportion of mystical pneumatology was concerned with the devildom of
orthodox Christian theologians, and, the discreet
reticence of modern mystics notwithstanding, it is better
to face this fact. Much that passed current in the west
as White (*i.e.* permissible) Magic was only a disguised
goeticism, and many of the resplendent angels invoked
with divine rites reveal their cloven hoofs. It is not
too much to say that a large majority of past psychological experiments were conducted to establish communication with demons, and that for unlawful purposes.
The popular conceptions concerning the diabolical
spheres, which have been all accredited by magic, may
have been gross exaggerations of fact concerning rudimentary and perverse intelligences, but the wilful
viciousness of the communicants is substantially un-
touched thereby.

It is universally recognised by all the Christian
mystics and magical hierophants, that the demons are
fallen angels; and they are in substantial agreement with
orthodox theology as to the nature and cause of their
fall. Some fix it before the creation of the physical
world, some on the second day of the creation. Their
conceptions on the subject are quite as inadequate as
anything that is offered by theology. It would be
interesting to trace the demonological hypothesis from
its extreme Oriental origin to its gruesome mediæval
elaborations, to establish by philological and historical
facts the true nature of the fontal conception of demons,
and to distinguish between the demon of Socrates and
the fiend of the Black Sabbath, but the inquiry is beyond

our scope. It is sufficient to state that the word "demon" did not anciently imply, of necessity, a spirit of evil nature, and that the Doctrine of Devils passed over with the rest of a doubtful inheritance from the Jewish to the Christian systems, and the classification of the angelical hierarchies was counterbalanced by a classification of the masters and hosts of the great abyss. Agrippa affirms that the lost angels are equal in number to those who retained their first estate, and that they are also divided into nine formal hierarchies. Wierus, who was his disciple, has furnished a tabulated statement of the whole Satanic monarchy, with the names and the surnames of seventy-two princes and a myriad of smaller devils. It appears from this tabulation that the throne of Infernus has passed from the possession of the genuine and aboriginal serpent, Satan, and that Beelzebub reigns in his place, the entire disposition being made after the following manner:—

Princes and Grand Dignitaries.

BEELZEBUB, supreme chief of the Infernal Court and Empire, and Founder of the Order of the Fly.

SATAN, Leader of the Opposition.

EURONYMUS, Prince of Death, Grand Cross of the Order of the Fly.

MOLOCH, Lord of the Land of Tears, Grand Cross of the Order.

PLUTO, Lord of Fire.

LEONARD, Grand Master of the Sabbath, Knight of the Fly.

BAALBERITH, Master of Alliances.

PROSERPINE, Arch-she-fiend, sovereign princess of the perverse spirits.

Ministers.

ADRAMALECK, Lord High Chancellor, Grand Cross of the Order of the Fly.

ASTAROTH, Lord High Treasurer.

NERGAL, Chief of the Secret Police.

BAAL, Commander-in-Chief of the infernal armies, Grand Cross of the Order of the Fly.

LEVIATHAN, Lord High Admiral, Knight of the Fly.

Ambassadors.

BELPHEGOR, Ambassador in France.
MAMMON, Ambassador in England.
BELIAL, Ambassador in Turkey.
RIMMON, Ambassador in Russia.
THAMUZ, Ambassador in Spain.
HUTGIN, Ambassador in Italy.
MARTINET, Ambassador in Switzerland.

Judge.

LUCIFER, Lord Chief Justice.

ALASTOR, Commissioner of Public Works.

Royal Household.

VERDELET, Master of Ceremonies.
SUCCOR-BENOTH, Chief of the Eunuchs.
CHAMOS, Grand Chamberlain, Knight of the Fly.
MELCHOM, Paymaster.
MISROCH, Chief Steward.
BEHEMOTH,
DAGON,
MULLIN, First Valet-de-Chambre.

Masters of the Revels.

KOBAL, Stage Manager.
ASMODEUS, Superintendent of Playhouses.
NYBBAS,
ANTICHRIST, Juggler and Necromancer.

In a perfectly phenomenal work, a record of personal experiences in all species of deviltry, written in the first quarter of the present century by Alexis-Vincent Charles Berbiguier de Terre-Neuve du Thym, and quaintly entitled " *Les Farfadets ;* or, all Demons are not of the Other World," the author affirms that the Court of Hell had human emissaries and representatives in a number of great cities, and even enumerates persons, apparently his actual contemporaries, who occupied posts in the viceroyalty of eternal perdition.

Amidst the superstition, the stupidity, the malice, and

perversity of goetic experiments, we may recognise the existence of one central truth, which is of great importance in rational mysticism, the existence of a class of intelligences in the extra-mundane spheres, whose natures are gross, formless, and undeveloped, or have been developed along the lines of that intense spiritual malice which is commonly identified with the essential nature of devils. The hypotheses and the formal tabulations of the grandmasters of mediæval demonology — of Agrippa and Wierus, of Bodin, Delancre, and Delrio—have little value except from the archæological standpoint, and as otherwise unheard-of curiosities ; that is to say, they have nothing in themselves to recommend them, and as doctrinal extensions of alleged facts, they cannot be consistently resuscitated along with revived mysticism, which is concerned with the facts alone, and not with fantastic explanations.

It may be concluded from the tenour of the foregoing remarks that the holy horror of Black Magic which is entertained by the modern apostles of mysticism is in the main well-founded ; but, nevertheless, much nonsense has been written on the subject of the darker side of the transcendental art, and many exaggerated notions have been propagated concerning the infernal branch of mystic practice. Sometimes these exaggerations take the form of distinct, and, it would seem, of wilful perversions. Eliphas Lévi is the prophet of modern mysticism, one of the most finished mystics of all the Christian centuries, though probably no person who has entered into "that great magic chain which began with Hermes or Enoch, and will only end with the world," had ultimately not only a less belief, but a more profound disdain for all pneumatic theorems. Indeed he has considerably blackened the Black Art by sensational pseudo citations which do not exist in the works from which he proposes to quote.*

* It is suggested that Eliphas Lévi, as one who was acquainted with the real and awful dangers of black magic, was determined to confuse and mislead the ill-intentioned dabbler by all possible methods, including false quotations.

The "Grimorium Verum" and the "Grand Grimoire" divide with the "Grimoire of Pope Honorius" the doubtful honour of being the official text-books of mediæval black magic. Their contents are reprehensible enough, and there is no need to intensify their motive by vitiated selections, and by interpreting the recipes which they contain in an unwarranted sense.

The most noticeable feature of the Grimoires, and of the science which they represent, is their utter futility, the immense expenditure of elaborate liturgic and ritualistic energy for the smallest possible result. Black magic offers to its possessor absolutely no power with which the permissible branches of Magic are unable, by their claim, to endow him, and it is for the most part little more than an ignorant, stupid, and grossly superstitious perversion of the "white" art. Why should it be necessary to call up the devils of hell, to invoke every intelligence of the abyss, from Bel and the Dragon to Astaroth and Lucifer, merely to obtain possession of a hidden treasure? Now, the concealed money bags of dead misers represent the utmost altitude of the ambition of average black magicians. Why should the wizard barter both body and soul, and bind himself, with bloody parchments, to the infernal hierarchy simply to acquire the material riches which the less nocuous sister art pretends to dispense generously through the harmless and uncovetous hands of Gnomes and Nature Spirits? *

It would appear that in mediæval times the doctrine of Nature Spirits, partly derived from the classical mythology of Rome, partly from the aboriginal religions of the Teutons, and partly from the Arabian lore which at an early period penetrated into Europe, became confused with the orthodox doctrine concerning the lost angels. More correctly, the indiscriminate condemnation of all branches of magic by victorious Christianity resulted in the identification of the elementary intelligences with the minor hordes of devils, and this grotesque classification was accepted by

* A distinction should, however, be made between the mere sorcerer and the veritable Black Magician. The latter was ambitious of far different possessions than the miser's money bags.

the black magicians, who expected to obtain their desires with greater facility from the fiends than from other classes of invisible beings. This opinion was completely accredited by the theology of the period, for the universal diffusion of devildom, the practical omnipotence of Satan, and his extreme readiness to distribute the kingdoms of the earth, with all their pomps and vanities, to those who would fall down and adore him, were doctrines untiringly taught by the Latin church.

The orthodox views concerning demonology have lapsed into deserved discredit; the system of infernal magic erected on their foundation has sunk with them into irretrievable oblivion; rudimentary, retrogressive, and malevolent intelligences may indeed exist among the peoples of the illimitable world invisible, and with these it may be possible to communicate, but not on the lines, not with the alleged results, and not with the involved penalties of the black rituals. Were it otherwise, their reproduction at the present day, when all classes of mystical experiment are obtaining a certain credence, and exciting curiosity not unmixed with reverence, would be little short of criminal. But, unlike the beliefs and the practices connected with lawful magic, they belong to an order of ideas which has utterly passed away; they are the dead branch of the living tree of occultism, and it is only their archaic interest, and the high place to which they are entitled among the curiosities of effete superstition, that warrant their consideration in any comprehensive statement of the whole scope of esoteric science.

Many of the practices taught in the "Grimoires" are, however, comparatively harmless; on the other hand, many of the experiments contained in legitimate rituals border closely on Black Magic—those which are concerned with bloody sacrifices, a survival of Judaism and of Hellenic theurgy, being specially open to objection.

The garbage, trickery, and rubbish of the "Grimoires" is the most noticeable feature which concerns them. Filthy physical processes for the recovery of female purity, revolting recipes for procuring invisibility by devouring the boiled bones of dead black cats, directions for the composition of aphrodisiacal potions, and other refuse from the gutters of superstition, combine with grotesque and commonly impossible *formulæ* for the evocation of "the grand Lucifuge," and written compacts for the sale of the souls of men for small premiums to the tenants of perdition.

It is impossible to interpret the "Grimoires" in any serious manner; diabolical practices are invariably prefaced by long and solemn prayers which insist on the purity of the magician's intention, and on his fixed resolve to belong irrevocably to God. The most sacred rites of the church are practised as required preliminaries, and the authors are apparently guiltless of any conscious profanation in the matter. When the supreme moment of evocation at length arrives, when the masses have been said, when the long fasts have finished, when the celebrant has divested himself of all impure desires, and has preserved his body from all sexual defilement for a prescribed time, when at length he determines to invoke the devil, it is generally evident that he intends to trick the fiends; he possesses the words which master them; he can torture them with his magic wand; he can bully them into compliance with his demands; he treats them uniformly as fools. When he sells them his soul, he deceives them by an obvious play upon words; and the devil departs contented, while his evoker chuckles at his hoax, and completes his grotesque performance by a determination to devote himself to good deeds, to distribute the buried treasures he has unearthed by the fiend's help among the poor of Christ, while his familiar is put off with a paltry coin on the first day of the month. Such is Infernal Magic! Such is the art or science on which some modern mystics expend their anathemas!

Should there be anyone sufficiently imbecile to desire to revive this truly awful art, it will be well to remind him that it can only be put in practice by a believer in the Catholic church.* The belief in that system must be at once real and strong, and it is an absolutely vital condition. "The evokers of the devil

---

* That is to say, a complete materialist, believing only in the evidence of the senses, could not succeed, and a true Catholic would not try.

must before all things belong to a religion which believes in a devil who is the rival of God ; " and as all ceremonial, more especially from the magical standpoint, is ineffectual apart from faith, those who undertake to make use of rites borrowed from the Roman church, and to invoke divine names which are the property of that church, must themselves have embraced it, and that in all sincerity. When this condition has been fulfilled, which is certainly a difficult feat for the mystic of modern times, the postulant in the carnal synagogue of black magic will have to legislate as best he may for compliance with the substantially impossible directions which will be presently cited.

Black Magic in its esoteric aspect is a barbarous perversion of legitimate mystic science. The conditions of success in infernal evocations have been defined by Lévi as follows :—1. Invincible obstinacy. 2. A conscience at once hardened by crime and most subject to remorse and terror. 3. Affected or natural ignorance. 4. Blind faith in everything incredible. 5. A completely false notion of God. Stripped of its grotesque and inhuman ceremonial, and considered simply in its intention and result, the diabolising of the human soul is at once its condition and end. When the frightful transformation is completed, the abandoned operator receives, even by the terms of his science, absolutely no return. Every practical power, as we have before stated, which Black Magic can at the utmost offer to its initiates is guaranteed with tenfold additional capacity, on ten times stronger authority, and in an infinitely simpler way, by the branch which is denominated Divine. " To be a Christian is hard," said the impressed but vacillating pagan, and the heights of mystical sanctity are also laborious in the ascent, but the apex of adeptship is far more easily attained by the humanity which is called thereto, than is the diabolical condition which the Black Magic that is behind Black Magic requires of its professors.

The true nature of the pseudo-science of the " Grimoires " having been thus defined, we may proceed to a brief consideration of their archaic curiosities.

Abstinence from every species of impurity must be observed for the space of an entire quarter of the moon; a pledge must be given to the "grand Adonay," who is the master of all spirits, that the number of daily collations shall not exceed two, and that they shall be prefaced by prayer during the whole of the term prescribed. The operator, moreover, must disrobe as seldom, and sleep as little, as possible, but he must meditate continually on his undertaking, and centre all his hopes in the infinite goodness of the divine Adonay. The "Grimoires" are so full of deceptions and mystifications that it is frequently difficult to pronounce with any certainty upon their real meaning, but it would appear to be God whom they designate under his name Adonay, and not some master-fiend who is invested with the title of Deity. The invocation of Lucifer must be distinguished from his worship, which we have not found in the rituals of black magic.

According to the "Grand Grimoire," the materials required for evocation are a stone made of red enamel, and called ematille, which, it is said, can be purchased from a druggist; a virgin kid, which must be crowned with vervain and decapitated on the third day of the moon; and a forked branch of a wild hazel which has never borne fruit, and which must be cut on the day of evocation, when the sun is just rising. A piece of wood must be fashioned to a size corresponding with one end of the fork of the genuine rod, and must be taken to a locksmith that he may hoop the two little branches with the steel blade with which the victim was slain, taking care that the ends are slightly pointed when they are fitted to the wood. The whole being executed after this manner, the Magus may return home and adjust the before-mentioned hoop with his own hands to the genuine rod. Subsequently, he must obtain a piece of loadstone to magnetise the two points, at which time he must pronounce the following words :—

" By the grand ADONAY, ELOIM, ARIEL, and JEHOVAM, I bid thee be united to, and I bid thee attract all substances which I shall require through the might of sublime ADONAY, ELOIM, ARIEL, and JEHOVAM. I command thee, by the antagonism of fire and water, to separate all substances as they were separated on the day of the world's creation. Amen."

When these matters have been accomplished, the operator may be convinced that in the "Blasting Rod" (which is the name given to the instrument) he is in possession of a most priceless treasure.

The place of evocation must be a forlorn and isolated spot, and the time night. Thither he must transport the rod, the skin of the kid, the stone called ematille, two vervain crowns, together with two candlesticks and as many candles of virgin wax, made by a virgin girl, and duly blessed. He must take also a new steel and two new flints, with sufficient tinder to kindle a fire, likewise the half of a bottle of brandy, some consecrated incense and camphor, and four nails from the coffin of a dead child. The great Kabbalistic circle must be formed with strips of the kid's skin, made fast to the ground by means of the four nails. Then, with the stone called ematille, a triangle must be traced within the circle, beginning at the eastern point. In the centre of this figure the operator must take up his place; he must deposit the two candlesticks and the two vervain crowns on the right and left of the triangle. The candles should then be lighted, and a brazier, which must be in front of the operator, must be heaped up with charcoal of willowwood, and kindled with the help of a small quantity of the brandy and a part of the camphor, the rest being reserved for the periodical renewal of the fire in proportion to the length of the business.

Many conjurations are given in the rituals, and these are to be used in succession till the apparition of the spirit is obtained. The most powerful, as it is also apparently the most senseless, may be cited as a specimen of the whole.

Grand Conjuration.

(Extracted from the veritable Clavicle.)

"I adjure thee, O Spirit! by the power of the great Adonay, to appear instanter, and by Eloim, by Ariel, by

Jehovam, by Agla, Tagla, Mathon, Oarios, Almouzin, Arios, Membrot, Varios, Pythona, Magots, Salphæ, Gabots, Salamandræ, Tabots, Gnomus, Terræ, Cœlis, Godens, Aqua, Gingua, Janna, Etitnamus, Zariatnatmit, &c., A. . E. . A. . J. . A. . T. . M. . O. . A. . A. . M. . V. . P. . M. . S. . C. . S. . T. . G. . T. . C. . G. . A. . G. . J. . F. . Z. . &c."

The manifestation of the spirit is guaranteed after a second repetition of these sublime words, when the operator may demand what he requires, and enforce it by the terrors of the Blasting Rod, which tortures all Infernals when it is plunged into the consecrated flame. The demon is generally ordered to discover the nearest buried treasure, which is done on the condition that the secret is kept inviolate, that the Magus is charitable to the poor, and that he receives a gold or silver coin on the first day of every month.

If the operator was deterred by the extreme difficulty of complying with the ceremonial requirements of Black Magic, but not dismayed by the character of its proceedings, his masters in infernal knowledge could provide him with a simpler ritual at an increased personal expense. He was free to compound with perdition for a slightly less elaborate performance, if he would enter into a compact with the fiend whom he chose to evoke, and dispose of his soul in eternity for certain defined favours, invariably of a paltry character, which hell would guarantee him in time. The particulars of this process were contained in the "Sanctum Regnum," or the "True Method of making Pacts with all Spirits whatsoever."

Of the fiends who are open to this kind of negotiation with humanity, the first is the great LUCIFUGE' ROFOCALE, Prime Minister infernal. He has the power with which Lucifer has invested him over all the wealth and treasures of the world.

The second is the grand SATANACHIA, General-in-Chief; he has the power of subjecting all women and girls to his wishes, and to do with them as he wills.

AGALIAREPT, another Commander, has the faculty of discovering the most arcane secrets in all the courts and council chambers of the world. He also unveils the most sublime mysteries. He commands the Second Legion of Spirits, and has under him *Buer, Gusoyen*, and *Botis*, &c.

FLEURETY, Lieutenant-General, has the power to perform any labour during the night; moreover, he can cause hailstones in any required place. He controls a very large army of spirits, and has *Bathim, Pursan*, and *Abigar*, &c., &c., as his subordinates.

SARGATANET, Brigadier-Major, has the power to make any person invisible, to transport him to any distant place, to open all locks, to reveal whatsoever is taking place in private houses, to give instruction in all the rogueries of the shepherds. He commands several brigades of spirits, and has *Laray, Valefar*, and *Faraii*, &c., for his immediate inferiors.

NEBIROS, Field-Marshal and Inspector-General, has the power to do evil to whomsoever he will. He discovers the Hand of Glory; he reveals all the virtues of metals, minerals, vegetables, and animals both pure and impure. He also possesses the art of predicting things to come, being one of the greatest necromancers in all the infernal hierarchies; he goes to and fro everywhere and inspects all the hordes of perdition. His immediate subordinates are *Ayperos, Nuberus*, and *Glasyalabolas*, &c., &c.

"When you have determined to make a Pact with one of the Governing Intelligences," says the "Sanctum Regnum," "you must begin on the previous evening by cutting with a new and unused knife, a Rod of Wild Hazel, which has never borne fruit, and is rigorously similar to the Blasting Rod. This must be done precisely at the moment when the sun appears upon our horizon. The same being accomplished, arm yourself with the stone called Ematille, and two blessed candles. Then proceed to select for the coming operation a place where you will be wholly undisturbed. You may even make the Pact in some isolated room, or in some remains of an old and ruinous Castle, for know that the Spirit has power to transport the Treasure to any required place. This having been arranged, describe a Triangle with the Stone called Ematille. Set the two blessed candles in a parallel position on either side of the Triangle of Pacts; inscribe the holy name of Jesus below, so that no spirits can injure you after any manner. You may now take up your position in the middle of the Triangle, holding the Mysterious Rod, together with the Grand Conjuration of the Spirit, the Clavicle, the Requisition you mean to make, and the Discharge of the Spirit."

When all these conditions have been fulfilled, the Magus proceeds to the prayers and adjurations, which are closed with the ensuing—

Grand Conjuration of Spirits.

Emperor LUCIFER, Master of all the Revolted Spirits, I entreat thee to favour me in the adjuration which I address to thy mighty minister, LUCIFUGE' ROFOCALE, being desirous to make a Pact with him. I beg thee also, O Prince Beelzebuth, to protect me in my undertaking! O Count Astarot! be propitious to me, and grant that to-night the great LUCIFUGE' may appear to me under a human form, and free from evil smell, and that he may accord me, in virtue of the Pact into which I propose to enter, all the riches that I need. Oh! grand LUCIFUGE', I pray thee to quit thy dwelling, wheresoever it may be, and come hither to speak with me; otherwise will I compel thee by the power of the strong living God, of His beloved Son, and of the Holy Ghost. Obey promptly, or thou shalt be eternally tormented by the power of the potent words in the Grand Clavicle of Solomon, wherewith he was accustomed to compel the rebellious Spirits to accept his compact. Therefore, straightway appear, or I will persistently torture thee by the virtue of these grand words in the Clavicle—*Aglon Tetragram, vaycheon stimulamaton ezphares retragrammaton olyoram irion esytion existion aryona onera brasym moym messias soter Emanuel Sabaoth Adonay te adoro, et te invoco.* Amen.

Like that of the ordinary evocation, the most general object of a pact was the possession of a buried treasure, or the gratification of some unlawful desire. The condition laid down by the spirit was the possession of the soul and body of the operator at the end of twenty years. The agreement, which was to be signed with

the blood of the operator, would, however, invariably
involve some play upon words, which was designed to
impose upon the apparition, as, for instance :—"I promise the Grand Lucifuge to recompense him in twenty
years for all the treasures with which he may endow me,"
which seemed generally to satisfy the fiend without
imperilling the magician in any irrevocable manner.

In the "Grimorium Verum" the infernal hierarchy
is described at greater length than in the "Grand
Grimoire," and Lucifer, Beelzebuth, and Ashtaroth are
said to reign respectively, the first over Europe and
Asia, the second over Africa, and the third over
America, apparently with equal power.

Most modern apologists for Black Magic would be sur-
prised to find what a ridiculous concatenation of errors
Black Magic was reduced to in the Middle Ages; but
such an apologist would aver that anciently it was not
so, and that Black Magic in its true acceptation represents the prostitution of the Divine Magic to produce
material and evil results; and that too often the desire of
worldly aggrandisement and the gratification of revenge
had led aside the mediæval student from the higher
paths.

The solemn and ceremonial invocation of curses upon
another person undoubtedly formed an important part
of ancient goetic art. An instance in the life of Marcus
Crassus by Plutarch, may be here quoted. It occurred
when Crassus was leaving Rome to march against the
Parthians, notwithstanding the fact that they were
allies of Rome at the time. "Ateius, one of the
tribunes, advanced to meet Crassus. In the first place,
by the authority of his office, he commanded him to stop,
and protested against his enterprise. Then he ordered
one of his officers to seize him, but the other tribunes
interposing, the officer let Crassus go. Ateius now ran
before to the gate, and placed there a censer with fire on
it. At the approach of Crassus, he sprinkled incense
upon it, offered libations, and uttered the most horrid
imprecations, invoking at the same time certain dreadful
and strange gods. The Romans say, these mysterious
and ancient imprecations have such power, that the

object of them never escapes their effect; nay, they add, that the person who uses them is sure to be unhappy, so that they are seldom used, and never but upon a great occasion. Ateius was much blamed for his rash zeal. It was for his country's sake that he was an adversary to Crassus, and yet it was his country he had laid under that dreadful curse." The evil issue of Crassus' expedition is well known. His army was almost completely destroyed, and both himself and his son were slain by the Parthians.

The following goetic invocation of Typhōn Sēth, the Egyptian Evil Deity, is taken from the Leyden Papyrus (No. 65, col. xv.). It is Græco-Egyptian, and is of value not only as representing an antique ceremonial for invoking a curse upon a person, but also as showing the great importance attached to the correct knowledge of certain names. This is corroborated again and again in the Egyptian "Ritual of the Dead," and seems to prove that such an idea is no mere mediæval superstition. It is furthermore especially to be noted that the magical names are *not* Egyptian. Some have thought them to have been adopted from Hebrew or Chaldee.

"I invoke thee who art in the empty wind, terrible, invisible, all potent God of Gods, bringer of destruction and bringer of desolation, thou who hatest a well-established race, seeing that thou hast been cast out from Egypt and from her lands. Thou hast been named the breaker in pieces of all things, and the unconquered one. I invoke thee, O Typhōn Sēth, I perform thy magical rites, seeing that I invoke thee through thy veritable name, in virtue of which thou canst not refuse to hear :— JŌERBĒTH, JŌPAKERBĒTH, JŌBOLCHŌSĒTH, JŌPATATHNAX, JŌSŌRŌ, JŌNEBOUTOSOUALĒTH, AKTIŌPHI, ERESCHIGAL, NEBOPOŌALĒTH, ABERAMENTHŌOU, LERTHEXANAX. ETHRELŪŌTH, NEMAREBA, AËMINA; come unto me in thy complete form, and go forward, and overthrow such a man or such a woman by cold and by heat. For he or she hath wronged me, and by him or by her hath the blood of Phyōn (or of generation? or of Typhon?) been poured forth. Therefore perform I these rites." Such are the words !

E

Regarding the importance attached to the genuine name of the power invoked, see Porphyry's *Epist. Ad Anebonem*, and the answer of Iamblichus to Porphyry. Hebrew names were supposed to have great effect; but if translated into Greek or Latin they lost their power.

We may close these examples with the translation of a very ancient Accadian hymn to avert the attack of the Seven Evil Spirits.

" Seven are they, seven are they !
In the channel of the deep, seven are they !
In the radiance of heaven seven are they !
In the channel of the deep in a palace grew they up.
Female they are not, male they are not ;
In the midst of the deep are their paths.
Wife they have not, son they have not,
Order and Mercy know they not.
Prayer and supplication hear they not.
The cavern in the mountain they enter.
Unto HEA they are hostile ;
The throne-bearers of Gods are they.
Disturbing the lily in the torrents are they set.
Baleful are they, baleful are they !
Seven are they, seven are they, seven twice again are
      they.
Spirit of the Heaven, remember it !
Spirit of the Earth, remember it ! "

Although this is hardly an incantation of Black Magic, we may insert it here as showing the Accadian ideas of the evil forces.

The mystical doctrine concerning spiritual essences, and the practice of ceremonial magic to establish communication with invisible beings, having been adequately considered, we are entitled to proceed to certain general conclusions. The rejection of much of the magical hypothesis of the Spirit World is the first course which enlightened reason seems to require of the modern student. The divine character of the Hebrew alphabet, for instance, will be accepted by few persons at the present day. The supposed correspondence of its ciphers with the divine creative forces which combined for the production of the innumerable hierarchies of intelligence, as the letters of an alphabet combine for the production of an indefinitely extensible language, is, however, an important article in the creed of the Kabbalist; as is also the anagrammatical extraction of the names and offices of angels from scriptural verses arbitrarily selected. There is little in the mystical doctrine concerning demonology to distinguish it in philosophical importance from the demonology of the Christian church. The hypothesis of elementary spirits is extremely suggestive, and is an interesting contribution to folk-lore, but its classifications are by no means scientific in character. The eschatological doctrine derived by magic from Jewish Kabbalism is undoubtedly of value as a hypothesis, though there is little to confirm it in the discoveries of modern psychology.

But when point after point of the salient doctrines of magic is eliminated in this manner, the student may reasonably inquire whether the mystical basis and temple have not both melted into air. Criticism which "pumps out with a ruthless ingenuity, atom by atom," must inevitably leave us "vacuity." It should, however, be remembered that the secret which the mystics possessed was the opening of the inner eye for perception into the world called spiritual. Prophecies will become void, tongues will cease, but love, it is affirmed, will not fail. In like manner, doctrines once of authority, hypotheses once held adequate, are outgrown in the progress of the mind and in the extension of the intellectual horizon, but the facts which they seem to have been invented to explain cannot be made obsolete by time, and truths which can be verified by experiment are not left behind in evolution. Now, the experiments which were the foundation of magical doctrine and magical hypothesis are facts which are not to be evaporated by the severity of critical analysis; they are the synthesis of the experiments of the ages, and they can be verified by those who desire it.

The lucidity of the mystics exhibited, what there is, naturally, good reason to believe, namely, the existence of innumerable hierarchies of being, which, according to the fashion of the time, were duly classified and arranged, as has been already shown. In actual performance, the magician of the past was in advance of existing psychological experiment; but the new mysticism, while enlarging the circle of experiment, and seeking to surpass the Magi in the extent of its practical research, endeavours in addition to make actual in its disciples that ideal life which the Magi conceived : and it should also, in proportion to its progress, do its best to establish the foundations of a rational hypothesis of the unseen.

The ceremonial part of magic, with its direfully potent formulæ and its excess of grotesque ritual observance, was accredited in the past with an absolute value. It will be seen that an inherent virtue was supposed to reside in certain words and acts—a principle which is at the basis of all superstitious observance. Now, the actual and demonstrable value of ceremonial magic is of two kinds. It produced an exaltation in the operator which developed the latent faculties of his interior being; and the atmospheric conditions required for success in all classes of mystical experiments were produced by its perfumes and incense. As human imagination is ever open to the same classes of impressions, and as modern psychology is equally dependent for success on atmospheric and other conditions, Ceremonial Magic should be as potent in its effect to-day as at any period of antiquity.

The *Hexameron* of Torquemada; the *Tableau de l'inconstance des démons*, by Delancre; the *Pseudomonarchia Dæmonorum* of Wierus; and the *Disquisitiones Magicæ* of Delrio, are the most orthodox and exhaustive sources of knowledge on demonological doctrines and science. There is a complete cycle of mediæval Latin literature devoted to the processes for the exorcism of evil spirits. As the intervention of devils has ever been the popular explanation of all extranatural phenomena, so in all languages extranatural literature has been largely demonological in character. In English there are innumerable books, which cover all branches of sorcery and witchcraft. One of the most notable is Scot's "Discovery of Witchcraft," date 1651, with which, in the opposed interest, may be compared Glanvill's *Sadducismus Triumphatus*, belonging to the same period, and Cotton Mather's "Wonders of the Invisible World." In 1859, a "Philosophy of Witchcraft" was attempted by J. Mitchell. The "Letters on Demonology" addressed to J. G. Lockhart by the author of "Waverley," will not be confused with the "Discovery." There is also a "History of Witchcraft;" and many sermons, treatises, and displays of corporeal leagues between devils and witches, have contributed to the right understanding and illumination of the general subject. Richard Baxter's "Certainty of the World of Spirits fully evinced," 1691, is a representative work of its kind. For the practical part, or the method of communicating with demons, the *Grimorium Verum* and the *Grand Grimoire*, are said to be entirely sufficient.

NECROMANCY.

THE EVOCATION OF THE SOULS OF THE DEAD.

W E have seen in the section devoted to angelology, that after the nine choirs of celestial intelligences in the pneumatic enumeration of the Kabbalists, there is the order of beatified human souls, who exercise a beneficent and energising influence on the incarnate race of man. Their chief is said to be Moses, and by their natures they are in opposition to the souls of the wicked, who are under the tyranny of Nahema, the demon of impurity. Such a classification is, to all appearance, very arbitrary and inadequate; the formal distinction between good and bad is not substantiated by present psychological experiments. But this and other doctrinal teachings of the old mystics do not belong to that portion of esoteric wisdom which it is alone rational to revive. The student should always carefully separate the ascertainable facts of the science from the theoretical structure which overlays them. The differentiation of the soul of man into a multiplicity of separable parts (even the time-honoured and reasonable distinction between the soul and the spirit) must be properly referred to the domain of speculation to which it properly belongs. As regards the subject of this chapter, a central, fundamental, and vital fact is this—that practical magic in its investigations of extra-mundane worlds has come into communication with "those whom the living call dead," and that the ritual of such communication has been bequeathed by magicians to posterity.

Many speculations concerning Necromancy are reason-able, many hypotheses are probable, others are neither probable nor reasonable. Yet some writers appear to suppose that if we accept the fact recorded by the mystics we are bound to accept the solution which they offer.

On the other hand, it is not unreasonably urged that the men who have most investigated the psychological world have most right to an opinion about it. They have, indeed, every right to an opinion, and their opinions must have a claim on our respect, but we need not consider them final. We hold that in magic there is no authority but that of the pioneer who has preceded. Now, the pioneer may be a beacon in the darkness, but he is not a guide infallible. The mystics have penetrated far beyond ourselves into the infinite realms of the soul, but they may not have gauged the infinite, and thus we are by no means committed to any of their absolute doctrines.*

Generally speaking, the pneumatic dogmas of the middle ages were based on the lines of orthodox pneumatology; as we have seen, they admitted the distinction between pure and fallen angels and reproduced their spiritual histories point by point. The hierarchy of elementary spirits is foreign to Christian theology, and theology denounced them as demons; the psychological history of the human individual in its past-mortal condition is, on the other hand, substantially identical in both systems, and the higher the position of the mystic the nearer he gravitates in his opinions to the accredited teachings of the great religion of the day.

Once more, an important point in that branch of transcendental science which has reference to the souls of humanity consists in the possibility of establishing that the soul survives death and preserves its intelligence and its individual being in another order of subsistence, by the contrivance of an actual and conscious communication with departed men and women.

The hypotheses which have been founded on this fact are excessively numerous and are sometimes suggestive and beautiful. They all have analogies with each other as well as with the Christian scheme. When estimated at their true worth, they will deserve and repay study,

* The counter-view has been well enunciated by an esteemed *collaborateur* as follows:—"The value of psychological authority can only be gauged by equal experimental knowledge."

and are rich in reflected lights. One of the explanatory
hypotheses derived from the Kabbalah which most recommends itself to esoteric students at the present day is
concerned with the existence of a fluidic envelope of the
spirit, which corresponds to St Paul's conception of a
spiritual organism, and is termed the astral body. An
exceedingly lucid exposition of this hypothesis and of
the soul's eternal progress has been given us by Eliphas
Lévi, and it fairly represents the archaic doctrine of the
Hebraistic mystics.

In its most extended scope, this hypothesis affirms the
existence of a single substance diffused through all space,
out of which the entire Cosmos, with all its sentient
populations, was originally developed, and into which at
the close of the grand and extreme cycle it will all ultimately be resolved. It is the Great Telesma of Hermes
Trismegistus, an ambient and all-penetrating substance,
the first matter of aboriginal creation, the created Light
of Genesis. The polarisation of this substance about a
centre produces living beings, and in man it forms the
Astral Body, or Plastic Mediator. The spirit, or permanent principle of the individual, which the hypothesis
apparently distinguishes from the cosmic substance, and
refers to a divine origin, departs at the moment of death
clothed in the astral form, which in the case of a
virtuous person evaporates like a pure incense, but
which enchains the vicious intelligence.

The ministry of mystical doctrine to the spiritual
aspirations of man has a definite value of its own. The
ascent of the ladder of being, the revolutions and incarnations of the soul, are delightful poetical conceptions which
give nourishment to the loftier energies of imagination.
The legendary romances of the soul deserve to be incorporated in a volume devoted to the subject of pneumatic
speculations; they are not confined to mysticism; they
exist among all peoples both savage and civilised ; they
throw great light upon comparative mythology ; but it
must ever be remembered that ordinary psychological
theories are as much in the field of speculation as are
the North American traditions of Travels into the Land
of Souls.

The ceremonial evocation of the departed is usually termed Necromancy. This word, however, by its derivation means the art of discerning future events through communications established with the dead ; it is divination by the tenants of the tomb. The science of the mystics has enlarged the original significance, while popular superstition has perverted it. Necromancy by the interpretation of the mystics is the evocation of the souls of departed humanity, for whatsoever end it is undertaken; as it is understood by-the vulgar, it is synonymous with " Black " Magic, with obscene rites, and dark, abhorrent practices. Professed mystics, however, have occasionally authorised the second view, which is only excusable by ignorance. Eliphas Lévi, after having personally disturbed the eternal rest of Apollonius by a deliberate ceremonial evocation, indiscriminately denounced the whole art of Necromancy as the "blackest of the sciences of the abyss," when endeavouring to identify modern Spiritism with the infernal devices of sorcery.

As a fact, the evocation of the souls of the departed is one of the most important branches of practical mysticism ; it is one of the test experiments by which the mystic gospel may be said to stand or fall. If it be possible, after following for a certain prescribed period a certain method of life, calculated to exalt the intellectual faculties, to quicken spiritual perceptions, and to germinate what may be called a new sense in man; if it be possible to enter into actual and undeceived communication with beings who have departed from this our plane of subsistence ; if we can see them as they were ; if we can, to some extent, know them as they are ; and if, at the time, we are in conscious possession of our common senses, then the mystic gospel must be the truth itself.

There are important questions connected with legitimate Necromancy which cannot be discussed here. If the pathological fact be admitted, there is the problem of identity to deal with ; to establish the truth of evocations is not to explain all spiritual mysteries. In an elementary text-book, we conceive it is sufficient to indicate by what means the mystics pretend to place their disciples in communication with the invisible planes of subsistence. In the evocation of the souls of the dead, one form of procedure is, at any rate, comparatively simple, and a synthetic account, based, it is affirmed, on an ancient arcane theory, has been given by a French writer in a recent work on the secret sciences.

"Prompted by a sentiment of profound tenderness," says P. Christian, "it occasionally happens that a bereaved person will dedicate to perpetual mourning the room where a beloved being has expired. Like a holy place, the chamber is shut and sealed, to be revisited alone on the anniversaries of the joys that are dead and of the separation which is final for earth.

"The soul, notwithstanding, can be occasionally attracted by the worship of the heart; though unseen, it assists at the sacrifice of loving tears, and if it be the hour of dusk, if the departed intelligence be called on by an exalted act of faith and affection, made in the name of the Almighty, the brilliancy of its immortal essence may break forth in splendour for a moment in the midst of that restful twilight wherein nature rests after the setting of the sun.

"The affection which unites us from beyond the tomb to lamented individuals must be entirely pure in its character. They are exclusively to be considered as the transfigured tenants of a more elevated sphere, who in their new form of subsistence implore the Eternal and Almighty Being to make us worthy of one day attaining to their own beatitude. The examination of conscience is another and as indispensable condition. If we have wronged our neighbours, the injury must be repaired; if we have enemies, we must pardon them from the very depth of our hearts; if we have neglected the soul-exalting duty of adoration and prayer to God, we must cultivate regularity in worship, in accordance with the rites which we have received from our ancestors; preliminaries which are the best evidence that the evocation of the dead is not sorcery, and that it is not an unholy compact with the malicious spirits in the abysses of the world invisible. It is by these preparations alone that it is possible to enter the avenues of the unseen universe without danger to life and reason.

"The place chosen for the evocation is not an unimportant point. The most auspicious is undoubtedly that room which contains the last traces of the lamented person. If it be impossible to fulfil this condition, we must go in search of some isolated rural retreat which corresponds in orientation and aspect, as well as measurement, with the mortuary chamber.

"The window must be blocked with boards of olive-wood, hermetically joined, so that no exterior light may penetrate. The ceiling, the four interior walls, and the floor, must be draped with tapestry of emerald-green silk, which the operator must himself secure with copper nails, invoking no assistance from strange hands, because, from this moment, he alone may enter into this spot set apart from all, the arcane Oratory of the Magus. The furniture which belonged to the deceased, his favourite possessions and trinkets, the things on which his final glance may be supposed to have rested—all these must be assiduously collected and arranged in the order which they occupied at the time of his death. If none of these souvenirs can be obtained, a faithful likeness of the departed being must at least be procured, it must be full length, and must be depicted in the dress and colours which he wore during the last period of his life. This portrait must be set up on the eastern wall by means of copper fasteners, must be covered with a veil of white silk, and must be surmounted with a crown of those flowers which were most loved by the deceased.

"Before this portrait there must be erected an altar of white marble, supported by four columns which must terminate in bulls' feet. A five-pointed star must be emblazoned on the slab of the altar, and must be composed of pure copper plates. The place in the centre of the star, between the plates, must be large enough to receive the pedestal of a cup-shaped copper chafing-dish, containing dessicated fragments of laurel wood and alder. By the side of the chafing-dish must be placed a censer full of incense. The skin of a white and spotless ram must be stretched beneath the altar, and on it must be emblazoned another pentagram drawn with parallel lines of azure blue, golden yellow, emerald green, and purple red.

" A copper tripod must be erected in the middle of the Oratory ; it must be perfectly triangular in form, it must be surmounted by another and similar chafing-dish, which must likewise contain a quantity of dried olive wood.

" A high candelabrum of copper must be placed by the wall on the southern side, and must contain a single taper of purest white wax, which must alone illuminate the mystery of evocation.

" The white colour of the altar, of the ram's skin, and of the veil, is consecrated to Gabriel, the planetary archangel of the moon, and the Genius of mysteries ; the green of the copper and the tapestries is dedicated to the Genius of Venus.

" The altar and tripod must both be encompassed by a magnetized iron chain, and by three garlands composed of the foliage and blossoms of the myrtle, the olive, and the rose.

" Finally, facing the portrait, and on the eastern side, there must be a canopy, also draped with emerald silk, and supported by two triangular columns of olive wood, plated with the purest copper. On the North and South sides, between each of these columns and the wall, the tapestry must fall in long folds to the ground, forming a kind of tabernacle ; which must be open on the eastern side. At the foot of each column there must be a sphinx of white marble, with a cavity in the top of the head to receive spices for burning. It is beneath this canopy that the apparition will manifest, and it should be remembered that the Magus must turn to the East for prayer, and to the West for evocation.

" Before entering this little sanctuary, devoted to the religion of remembrance, the operator must be clothed in a vestment of azure, fastened by clasps of copper, enriched with a single emerald. He must wear upon his head a tiara surrounded by a floriated circle of twelve emeralds, and a crown of violets. On his breast must be the talisman of Venus depending from a ribbon of azure silk. On the annular finger of his left hand must be a copper ring containing a turquoise. His feet must be covered with shoes of azure silk, and he must be provided with a fan of swan's feathers to dissipate, if needful, the smoke of the perfumes.

" The Oratory and all its objects must be consecrated on a Friday, during the hours which are set apart to the Genius of Venus. This consecration is performed by burning violets and roses in a fire of olive wood. A shaft must be provided in the Oratory for the passage of the smoke, but care must be taken to prevent the admission of light through this channel.

" When these preparations are finished, the operator must impose on himself a retreat of one-and-twenty days, beginning on the anniversary of the death of the beloved being. During this period he must refrain from conferring on any one the least of those marks of affection which he was accustomed to bestow on the departed ; he must be absolutely chaste, alike in deed and thought; he must take daily but one repast, consisting of bread, wine, roots, and fruits. These three conditions are indispensable to success in evocation, and their accomplishment requires complete isolation.

" Every day, shortly before midnight, the Magus must assume his consecrated dress. On the stroke of the mystic hour, he must enter the Oratory, bearing a lighted candle in his right hand, and in the other an hour-glass. The candle must be fixed in the candelabra, and the hour-glass on the altar to register the flight of time. The operator must then proceed to replenish the garland and the floral crown. Then he shall unveil the portrait, and erect and immovable in front of the altar, being thus with his face to the East, he shall softly go over in his mind the cherished recollections he possesses of the beloved and departed being.

" When the upper reservoir of the hour-glass is empty, the time of contemplation will be over. By the flame of the taper the operator must then kindle the laurel wood and alder in the chafing-dish which stands on the altar ; then, taking a pinch of incense from the censer, let him cast it thrice upon the fire, repeating the following words :—Glory be to the Father of life universal in the splendour of the infinite altitude, and peace in the twilight of the immeasurable depths to all Spirits of good will !

"Then he shall cover the portrait, and taking up his candle in his hand, shall depart from the Oratory, walking backward at a slow pace as far as the threshold. The same ceremony must be fulfilled at the same hour during every day of the retreat, and at each visit the crown which is above the portrait, and the garlands of the altar and tripod, must be carefully renewed. The withered leaves and flowers must be burnt each evening in a room adjoining the Oratory.

"When the twenty-first day has arrived, the Magus must do his best to have no communication with any one, but if this be impossible, he must not be the first to speak, and he must postpone all business till the morrow. On the stroke of noon, he must arrange a small circular table in the Oratory, and cover it with a new napkin of unblemished whiteness. It must be garnished with two copper chalices, an entire loaf, and a crystal flagon of the purest wine. The bread must be broken and not cut, and the wine emptied in equal proportions into the two cups. Half of this mystic communion, which must be his sole nourishment on this supreme day, shall be offered by the operator to the dead, and by the light of the one taper he must eat his own share, standing before the veiled portrait. Then he shall retire as before, walking backward as far as the threshold, and leaving the ghost's share of the bread and wine upon the table.

"When the solemn hour of the evening has at length arrived, the Magus shall carry into the Oratory some well-dried cypress wood, which he shall set alight on the altar and the tripod. Three pinches of incense must be cast on the altar flame in honour of the Supreme Potency which manifests itself by Ever Active Intelligence and by Absolute Wisdom. When the wood of the two chafing dishes has been reduced to embers, he must renew the triple offering of incense on the altar, and must cast some seven times on the fire in the tripod; at each evaporation of the consecrated perfume he must repeat the previous doxology, and then turning to the East, he must call upon God by the prayers of that religion which was professed by the person whom he desires to evoke.

"When the prayers are over he must reverse his position, and with his face to the West, must enkindle the chafing-dishes on the head of each sphinx, and when the cypress is fully ablaze he must heap over it well-dried violets and roses. Then let him extinguish the candle which illuminates the Oratory, and falling on his knees before the canopy, between the two columns, let him mentally address the beloved person with a plenitude of faith and affection. Let him solemnly entreat it to appear, and renew this interior adjuration seven times, under the auspices of the seven providential Genii, endeavouring during the whole of the time to exalt his soul above the natural weakness of humanity.

"Finally, the operator, with closed eyes, and with hands covering his face, must call the invoked person in a loud but gentle voice, pronouncing three times all the names which he bore.

"Some moments after the third appeal, he must extend his arms in the form of a cross, and lifting up his eyes, he will behold the beloved being, in a recognisable manner, in front of him. That is to say, he will perceive that ethereal substance separated from the perishable terrestrial body, the fluidic envelope of the soul, which Kabbalistic initiates have termed the PERISPIRIT. This substance preserves the human form but is emancipated from human infirmities, and is energised by the special characteristics whereby the imperishable individuality of our essence is manifested. Evoked and evoker can then inter-communicate intelligibly by a mutual and mysterious thought-transmission.

"The departed soul will give counsel to the operator; it will occasionally reveal secrets which may be beneficial to those whom it loved on earth, but it will answer no question which has reference to the desires of the flesh; it will discover no buried treasures, nor will it unveil the secrets of a third person; it is silent on the mysteries of the superior existence to which it has now attained. In certain cases, it will, however, declare itself either happy or in punishment. If it be the latter, it will ask for the prayers of the Magus, or for some religious observance,

which he must unfailingly fulfil. Lastly, it will indicate
the time when the evocation may be renewed.

"When it has disappeared, the operator must turn to
the East, rekindle the fire on the altar, and make a final
offering of incense. Then he must detach the crown and
the garlands, take up his candle, and retire with his face
to the West till he is out of the Oratory. His last duty
is to burn the final remains of the flowers and leaves.
Their ashes, united to those which have been collected
during the time of retreat, must be mixed with myrtle
seed, and secretly buried in a field at a depth which will
secure it from disturbance by the ploughshare."

The conditions of necromantic evocation, it will be seen,
are somewhat elaborate; they are devised for the legitimate exaltation of the intellectual faculties, and for the
direction of the force of will; but there is nothing which
endangers the reason or beclouds the brain, and they
may be fulfilled by any person who has a little money
at command for the purchase of the requisite instruments, and has occasionally the privilege of possessing
his soul in solitude. The theurgic doctrine has made
provision in the event of a failure; it recommends the
renewal of the experiment, with additional precautions,
on the next anniversary, and affirms that the third time
will never be barren of result, unless the operator be
oppressed by an inveterate vice which has become to
him as a second nature.

It must be clear from the above ceremonial that there
is nothing repellent to the most cultivated spiritual
sense in the rites of lawful necromancy. It is otherwise,
however, with the evocations of the infernal art, with the
unhallowed necromantic practices of Black Magic, which
violate the sanctity of the sepulchre, and endeavour to
establish a vicious communion with the souls of evil men.

The rituals of infernal evocations are the outcome of
certain psychological doctrines which prevailed during
the middle ages, and are to some extent remnants of a
very remote antiquity. Persons who died by their own
hands, or who perished by a violent death, being separated from their bodies in advance of the natural time,

F

were supposed to be more or less bound to the place where the catastrophe happened, till the "radical moisture" of their corpse was entirely consumed.

Such earth-bound souls were easily attracted and abused by the sorcerers and black magicians, and many repellent and objectionable recipes for their evocation are extant. The skeleton or corpse was fumigated with mixtures of blood, milk, eggs, and other substances, and the deceased person was invoked with the usual adjurations of Black Magic, and generally for an evil purpose. These and other abuses led the Romans to the classification of Necromancy with treason, secret poisoning, and other crimes.

In a Græco-Egyptian papyrus in the British Museum, there is a curious necromantic process described for making a magical ring to bind a person in any manner desired. This ring, the papyrus goes on to say, is to be taken to the grave of a person untimely dead, and to be there buried four fingers deep in the ground, with the words, "O departed spirit, whosoever thou art, I deliver to thee such an one, that he may not do such a thing. Then having covered it up, depart. And you will do it best in the waning of the moon."

The bibliography of Necromancy is coextensive with the literature of the supernatural. For the ritual, it is unnecessary to go further than the directions which we have given. For the practice of black necromancy, the student is referred to the last division of Ebenezer Sibly's "Occult Sciences." In general literature, some information may be found in Howitt's "History of the Supernatural;" in the "Universal History of Apparitions," date 1770; and in Jung Stilling's "Theory of Pneumatology," translated in 1884. There is also some curious matter to be found in Dr F. G. Lee's "Glimpses of the Supernatural." The recent publication, by the Authorities of the British Museum, of a facsimile of the Papyrus of Ani ("The Book of the Dead"), a manuscript which scholars refer to a period fourteen centuries before Christ, will enable modern students to ascertain the nature of this celebrated work, which was intended for the use and the protection of the dead in the world beyond the grave.

PART II.

——o——

ALCHEMY.

ALCHEMY is known, and misknown, to all the world as the supposed science of transmuting the metals which the ignorance of a benighted epoch denominated base into the resplendent perfections of gold and silver. Outside the circle of Hermetic students, the possibility of such a conversion is generally derided at the present day, and if any one, by an accident, alights upon the evidence which exists for its actuality in the entombed scientific literature of the far past, he is embarrassed by its extent and solidity, but can hardly be shaken in his prejudice.

We intend in the present essay to define in a positive manner the exact theory of metallic transmutation which was professed by the alchemists, to state the ulterior possibilities which may be developed from that theory, and to expose the connection which subsists between this branch of Hermetic art and the branch that is known as Magic. As we are forced to embody in the briefest possible compass the largest available amount of compressed information, we must solicit from our readers a certain rational confidence in those statements that a narrow space forbids us to verify.

The philosophical writings which, in the fourth century, were produced under the name of Hermes Trismegistus, were the source of alchemical inspiration during the subsequent Christian centuries. The first distinct and undoubted reference to alchemy is posterior to the circulation of these books, as mysterious in matter, and as important in mystical history, as they are doubtful and suspicious in their origin. The reference in question is contained in a manuscript treatise by Zosimus the Pomopolite, which is preserved in the library at the Louvre. The first of the practical alchemists—Geber, the Arabian physician—is usually referred to the eighth century of our era. By his writings it would appear that the art was already matured, and he appeals to the authority of a line of anterior adepts and to a literature of apparent antiquity from which he extensively drew. From the eighth to the sixteenth century the doctrines and practices of alchemy continued to be propagated in the West, and, with Germany as its centre, it diffused a great light of mysticism till the eve of the French Revolution.

The avowed object of physical alchemy was such an investigation of natural secrets as would elicit a practical method for the conversion of certain substances, generally metallic, into gold and silver. This was accomplished, in the main, by means of an elixir, which, in harmony with a theory to which much Hermetic importance has been sometimes attached, could be applied to the body of the alchemist after a certain occult adaptation as well as to a metallic body, and with a strictly analogical result. In the mineral kingdom the completed process was termed transmutation; in its application to humanity it was known as the conversion or transfiguration of the individual by means of alchemy. The result, in the first place, was gold, or if the process was arrested at a certain stage, silver was the product instead. In the second case, a complete renewal of all the vital forces and the development of the physical capacities to an exceptionally advanced degree, transferred the successful magus to an advanced stage of evolution, and endowed him with powers and capacities which could be put in operation both in a material and spiritual direction.

While the uninitiated students of the Hermetic mystery exhausted their revenues and squandered their entire lives, ransacking every kingdom of nature, and experimenting with every conceivable subject from ordure to egg shells, so as at length to accomplish the extraction of the fundamental matter of the elixir, the adepts, who appear to have received the secret by oral transmission, pursued their experiments in accordance with an arcane theory which was a precious inheritance from the past. The philosophers who were participants of the theory could operate with ease, and ensure success. For them it was the work of a child or a woman. The student who was outside the select circle of the hierophants was, however, in the hands of God, and the divine science of the Hermetists might be communicated by one of those inexplicable flashes of unprefaced intuition which the God-encompassed minds of the philosophers, who rejected the fortuitous and believed in an imminent Providence, interpreted as direct revelation. A perfect master of science might also initiate a stranger after proper tests and progressive study.

The Hermetic theory was at once philosophical and practical. Its philosophical section is, for the most part, exposed in the literature of alchemy; its practical portion is preserved in symbolic language and in pictorial symbols which are capable of such diverse interpretations that their true meaning seems invariably to escape the student. By the terms of the philosophical theory, it is evident that the adepts regarded the animal creation as so many successive steps through which Nature laboriously ascended to the creation of her most perfect achievement, Man; and in every stage of production, Man was the end in view. That which the human individual was to the rest of the animal kingdoms, gold was to the world of minerals, and it was therefore affirmed, in the allegorical language of alchemy, that Nature always intended to produce gold; the existence of the inferior metals was due to arrested development at various stages of operation. Less crudely put, through the successive steps of the whole mineral kingdom Nature worked up towards gold. The foundation of the precious metal is thus to be found in its inferiors, as there is also a certain common nature between man and the animals which are below him. It was the object of alchemy to take up the work of Nature where it had been arrested by circumstances, to develop the latent perfections in lead, mercury, and antimony, and in a thousand other subjects, and to produce on the lines of her observed operations the metallic perfection which was her aim.

Possibly there is little in this hypothesis to recommend it to those who are acquainted with the facts of modern science, yet the evidence which exists for the performance of transmutations in the past is abundant and good of its kind. If the composite character of metals can be tolerated as a possibility, and the drift of scientific experiment is, we believe, in this direction, then it is conceivable that the life-long labours of so many generations of adepts, may have occasionally resulted in discovering the constituent elements of gold and in the actual composition of the metal. That success, if it were in reality achieved, was occasionally wholly fortuitous, is made evident by the fact that the operator was sometimes unable to repeat the experiment which had realised his absorbing ambition. The crudity of the explanatory hypothesis does not much undermine the evidence; there are many undoubted facts in modern physics which, even at this day, are very inadequately explained.

The philosophical theory of alchemy, which we have thus briefly exhibited, deserves more extended consideration; and as the belief in the transmutation of metals has by no means passed away; as the study of practical alchemy is said to be actually reviving, with the general resurrection of mysticism; as Figuier admits that the romantic conversion is possible and may even be ultimately performed; and as, so late as the middle of this century, Dr Christopher Girtanner, who has been described as an eminent professor of Göttingen, actually affirmed in the *Annales de Chimia* that it was destined to be generally known and practised, that every chemist and artist would be able to manufacture gold, that kitchen utensils by the close of the present age would be made of the precious metals; it seems desirable to provide the reader with a comprehensive account of the principles which, on the authority of the alchemists themselves, were involved in the art of transmutation. The substance of the ensuing pages is derived from the masonic alchemy of Baron Tschoudi, which is based on the authority of Paracelsus; wherever it seems obscure or imperfect, we have endeavoured to supplement it with side lights from the writings of other adepts.

The first study of an alchemical philosopher is research into the operations of Nature, whose end is God, as He also is her sole beginning. Now, Nature is divisible philosophically into four chief regions, the dry, the moist, the warm, and the cold, which are the four elementary qualities whence all that is must be derived. Nature is differentiated into male and female. She is compared to mercury. She is never visible, though she acts visibly, being a volatile essence which performs its office in bodies, and is informed by the universal spirit. She represents the divine breath, the central fire, which is termed by the philosophers the sulphur of matter, and is identical with that mercury of the sages which manifests itself by the gentle heat of Nature.

The investigators of Nature should be, like herself, simple, truthful, patient, and persevering. What they desire to perform should be in accordance with her, whom they should follow in every point. In seeking to achieve something more excellent than she has performed in a particular subject, they should consider by what it is ameliorated, which is invariably by its like; for example, if you would develop the intrinsic virtue of a metal beyond the natural point, you must grasp the metallic nature itself, and know how to distinguish between the male and female in Nature.

The searcher must know how to obtain the seed of metals, which is their elixir or superior quintessence, the most finished and perfect decoction and digestion of the thing itself. This seed, or germ, is produced by the four elements through the will of the Supreme Being and the Imagination of Nature.

The true and primeval matter of metals is of double essence, being an aerial warmth and moisture and a dry heat. But the student must beware how he interprets these terms in their literal sense. There are many circles within the circle of alchemical philosophy. For example, the air of the philosophers is said to be a water coagulated by fire, which produces a universal dissolvent, and even by the centre of the earth, where the elements are supposed to deposit their metallic seed, the philosophers appear to have referred in an arcane manner to

a mysterious storehouse of chaotic forces. But the
allegory and the intentional confusion are by no means
at an end here. The disciple of Hermetic art is required
to direct his attention to what is termed by the French
adepts the *point de la nature,* and this he should not seek
in the vulgar metals which are absolutely dead, while
those which are known to the hierophants are absolutely
living and possessed of a vital spirit. Now, the living
gold of the philosophers is explained by another authority to be that "fixed grain" which animates the
mercury of the sages; but as the sophic sulphur, or Red
Magisterium, is also a vivific gold, the confusion of
alchemical nomenclature is to the uninitiated of an
exceedingly embarrassing kind.

Metals were supposed to be engendered in the bowels
of the earth after the following manner. When the
circulation of the philosophical elements has deposited
the seed, it is returned towards the surface in a sublimated state. The seed of every metal is originally one, in
which the possibility of their conversion is founded;
they are differentiated by local influences acting within
the centre. Before all other study it is affirmed to be
absolutely needful that an amateur should understand
the formation of metals in the bowels of the earth.
Without this, and the faithful imitation of Nature, he
will never achieve anything successful. Nature com-
poses all metals of mercury; which, however, is a living
and feminine principle, and not the substance which
under that name is known to ordinary chemistry; and
of sulphur, which is a living male. In a matrix of
saline water, these substances are combined in a vapor-
ous condition, and a species of vitriol results, which by
the circulation of the elements is again converted into
vapour, is combined with sulphur, is transformed into a
glutinous mass, and after other complicated processes,
which it would be perfectly idle to enumerate, a metal
is evolved, that is pure or impure according to the locality of its production.

These explanations, it will be seen, offer no instruc-
tions for the discovery of the all-important seed. It is
evident throughout that the described processes refer to

the laboratory practices of the adepts, and not to cosmic evolution. Simplified and pruned as it is in this brief presentation, it will appear to the ordinary scientific reader as a raving chaos of unintelligible extravagance, out of which it would seem impossible to develop any form or harmony, could even a key be provided to the exact meaning of every figure of speech. When it must be added that the most illustrious adepts were accustomed in addition to allegorical language, insoluble cryptograms, and symbols which admitted innumerable interpretations, to fill their pages with false recipes, useless fictions, and numberless errors, so as still further to disguise from the ignorant the truth which they pretended to reveal, it is evident that the recovery of the practical process for metallic transmutation is a hopeles and insane quest; for when no reliance can be placed upon any statement, while everywhere deception abounds, progress of any kind is impossible.

That alchemical typology is nonsense and a hoax from beginning to end cannot, however, be affirmed by any person who has acquaintance with the facts of the case. In the seventeenth and eighteenth centuries, when the spread of Hermetic ideas and the increasing facilities of printing made alchemy a remunerative speculation for the bookseller, a literature which largely consisted of unadulterated imposture appears to have sprung into existence; but in anterior centuries, there was no such inducement to dishonesty. The writings of the alchemists remained in the obscurity of manuscript, and it is absurd to suppose that a laborious terminology was invented, and innumerable books were written, to gratify a purposeless passion for unprofitable and aimless deception. It is more probable that a conventional language was devised to enable the participators in a common pursuit to communicate without difficulty upon matters which it was dangerous to refer to in any open and comprehensible manner. At the same time it must be admitted that the entire problem is almost inscrutable, and it is difficult to propound any theory that can be tolerated concerning it.

It may be stated, by way of a conclusion to this portion of the subject, that the alchemists were accustomed to distinguish three kinds of gold—astral gold, whose centre is in the sun, and, like light, is communicated in its rays to all inferior beings; elementary gold, the most pure and fixed part of the elements and of all substances which are composed of them, so that all the sublunary beings of the three kingdoms of Nature contain in their centre a precious grain of this elementary gold; lastly, there is vulgar gold, the most beautiful of known metals, and perfect and unchangeable in itself.

When from the natural principles of alchemy the adepts proceed to an account of the actual process, they are less barbarous in their methods and less contradictory in their statements. The operations described have the character of serious experiments, and might be reproduced if the materials which are required could be obtained.

The profound study of Hermetic allegory has indicated to a few minds an unexpected solution which is exceedingly suggestive and curious. We have seen that the mystics regarded the successive steps of creation as all leading up to man; and, though the analogy may have nothing to recommend it, the occult doctrine of correspondence led them to regard the evolution of minerals as proceeding after a parallel method. More recently, we have seen that every mundane substance, animate or otherwise, possesses in the centre of its nature a spark of elementary gold. It is evident, therefore, that, on the one hand, the gold of the philosophers is not a metal; that, on the other hand, man is a being who possesses within himself the seeds of a perfection which he has never realised, and that he therefore corresponds to those metals which the Hermetic theory supposes to be capable of development. It has been consequently advanced that the conversion of lead into gold was only the assumed object of alchemy, and that it was in reality in search of a process for developing the latent possibilities in the subject, MAN; that the quest was pursued with success; that it led to magnificent results in the physical and spiritual orders, and to an acquaintance with facts and forces which it was unwise indiscriminately to divulge, and which resulted in the invention of a typological literature that was intelligible to the initiated alone. Without in any way pretending to assert that this hypothesis reduces the literary chaos of the philosophers into a regular order, it may be affirmed that it materially elucidates their writings, and that it is wonderful how contradictions, absurdities, and difficulties seem to dissolve wherever it is applied.

At the same time, it is equally and abundantly evident that those alchemists with whose lives we are in any way acquainted, were, in the overwhelming majority of cases, indisputably physical chemists in search of a physical secret, and ambitious of material wealth.

It may be said that as actions speak louder than words, the new interpretation, however plausible, is probably fallacious, yet outside the illumination which it casts on a large section of alchemical literature, there are other considerations in its favour which cannot be lightly set aside. There is, in the first place, this fundamental and really important fact, that those Hermetic books of Alexandrian Platonism, theurgy, and Egyptian tradition, attributed to Trismegistus, which were the ultimate, ever quoted, and infallible authority of all the western alchemists, appear absolutely devoid of any assignable connection with metallic transmutation; they are devoted to transcendental cosmology and a system of spiritual philosophy. If the alchemists were workers in metals, why did they appeal to Hermes? It is insufficient to reply that they were of opinion that the Alexandrian symbolist was delineating the processes of their metallic science in an arcane fashion. There is nothing to support the assertion, for the Golden Treatise of Hermes Trismegistus, which alone is concerned with physical transmutation, is a composition of the fifteenth century, long after the establishment of alchemical doctrines in the West, long after Hermes had been appealed to as an authority, and in all probability a product of the opinion in question, so the fact remains that there is nothing in early Hermetic literature to give colour to such an interpretation.

In the second place, it is fairly certain that the

mystics who were confessedly devoted to the development of psychic potentialities in man made use of the same symbols, of similar allegories, and of methods rigorously akin to those of the alchemists. Lastly, the mystics as well as the alchemists appeal to the authority of Hermes.

These, in a brief compass, are the most important facts of the case, and in the face of so much conflicting evidence it is exceedingly difficult to arrive at a tenable and moderate conclusion which shall bring both of these views into a harmonious and consistent relationship. We must begin by conceding that from facts which are obvious in the lives of the alchemists, and from facts in the history of chemistry, these early investigators of Nature were in search of metallic transmutation, and that in the course of their experiments they admittedly made discoveries in physics which laid the foundations of the existing science of chemistry. We must suppose that the literature of alchemy was devoted—as it claims to be devoted—to veiled instruction in the physical processes of mineral conversion. In this case, we are forced to regard what may be termed the spiritual gleams that we discover in Western Hermetics as simply lights which are diffused by a theory which is too broad for the practice. The metallic work is the threshold of a larger achievement, and the lustre of that more consummate *opus* permeates the material veils of the metallic theory with oblique and confusing rays. If we turn to the writings of the mystics, to Hermes, Trithemius, Swedenborg, Vaughan, Böhme, and the other innumerable lights which diffuse their psychic splendour on the golden ladder of the transcendental, we shall find that we have entered the field of the larger hypothesis, the grander hope, the superb, if unfinished, achievement. These men wrought upon the subject Man; his were the potencies which they endeavoured, though perhaps imperfectly, to develop and extend; his transmutation from material to spiritual consciousness, from lower to higher life, from humanity to superhumanity, was the conversion which these had in view; his regenerated perfection was the end towards which they strived. The opening of his interior faculties till he was enabled to form a correspondence with superior intelligent subsistences, and might in the end be enabled to create an intellectual union with the *Summa totius Perfectionis*, was the divine dream of the mystics. This they endeavoured, this they aspired, to accomplish by virtue of a theory of development which Hermes applied in explanation of the material cosmos, which they deemed of equal application to humanity as *minutum mundum*, the cosmos within the cosmos, the small world within the great world, and intellectually the centre of this; by the alchemists it was also appropriated because they believed that the development of a particle of matter must proceed on the same line and according to the same basis as that of the grand totality. With such an interpretation we can understand the appeal to Hermes on the part of physical and spiritual mystics alike, the identity of symbols, and the parallel in allegory between the two schools of thought.

At this point we must pause; it would be quite out of place in an elementary treatise to attempt any delineation of mystical methods in the development of the interior Sol and of its complement, the interior Luna. We believe ourselves to have established the points which we undertook at the beginning to demonstrate. We have shown that the ordinary notions concerning the Hermetic mystery and alchemy are inadequate to the scope of the subject; we have endeavoured to explain the conceptions which are at the base of the theory of transmutation, to indicate the possibilities which the mystics beheld behind it, and to expose, as was promised, the connection which subsists between this branch of transcendental experiment and that which is known as magic, for magic from the mystical standpoint was the modification of man by alchemy, or the spiritual side of *magnum opus*.

Books on the subject of alchemy in the English language are rare and expensive. The following are recommended :—" A Suggestive Enquiry into the Hermetic Mystery;"* " Remarks on Alchemy and the Alchemists,"

---

* Of all modern works this is most important to the student. Issued in 1850, it was suppressed almost on the day of publication, authoress and advisers considering that it was too suggestive to be circulated with prudence.

Boston, 1857; "Lives of the Alchemistical Philosophers, with a Selection of the most celebrated Treatises on the Theory and Practice of the Hermetic Art," 1815.

There exist, also, English translations of works by Geber, Paracelsus, Van Helmont, Helvetius, George Starkey, Eugenius Philalethes (Thomas Vaughan), Basil Valentine, Roger Bacon, Sendivogius, and Pseudo-Hermes. A considerable insight into the life and work of a physical alchemist in the middle ages may be obtained in a very pleasant manner by the perusal of "A Professor of Alchemy," which is an account of the history and adventures of Denis Zachaire, the celebrated French alchemist.

THE ELIXIR OF LIFE.

JUST as the aims of the alchemists have been interpreted in a romantic spiritual sense, so has that other department of thaumaturgic physics, intimately connected with alchemy—alchemy, indeed, under another aspect—which is concerned with the conversion, reconstruction, and complete transmutation of the present body of man. The entire transcendentalism of the West seems to have been emphatically based on the lapse of humanity from a primordial condition of grace, strength, perfection, beauty, and physical immortality, and the divine dream of its professors was to re-establish the harmony which once existed between man and his fontal source, so as to retrieve the individual at any rate from the miserable ruin of the race, and to restore him to his original condition. This, indeed, was unmistakably their patent and avowed object. A certain method of life and a certain medical regimen were the means by which it was deemed possible to secure this resplendent rehabilitation. To achieve immortality by a medicine which had the quality of renovating wasted tissues, of eliminating the germs of disease, and arresting the progress of decay, was a grand upward step, a substantial realisation of the dream; the possibility was universally admitted, the process was hoped for, longed for, toiled for, often died for; some claimed to have accomplished it, many pretended to possess the secret, a few, ravished out of sober reason by search, expectation, and desire, genuinely believed themselves to have attained to the grand way, the true path, and may have been encouraged in their sublime self-deception by the actual discovery of powerful healing secrets which are unknown to modern science. It is at any rate moderately certain that the Elixir of Life, the Universal Medicine, and the renewal of youth are conceptions which

were understood by the mystics in a literal sense, and
no modern interpretation must be accepted which does
outrage thereto. But it also becomes evident by the
study of the great transcendentalists that the double
aspect of alchemy must be extended to the life-elixir; it
was actual, it was physical, it was truly sought, there
was neither pretence, nor allegory, nor subterfuge about
it; but it included also another side, a larger scope, a
deeper search, a higher meaning.*

Eliphas Levi, ever open to the most adverse criticism,
but to whom we must always recur for quotation, says :
"To imprison a soul for ever in a mummified human
body, such would be the horrible solution of pretended immortality in the same body and on the same
earth." That may be true enough, but impossible, unworthy, gross though it may be, it was still sought
by transcendental science in the West; only the apostles
of transcendental science would have cried out against
the perverted presentation of their cherished idea;
they would have said that their great elixir renews
vitality, that it gives immortality to youth and not to a
mummy.

When we turn from these higher considerations to
the renewal of physical youth, which the mystics desired
to achieve, we are brought into the presence of much that
appears barbarous, absurd, and belonging to the awkward, clumsy, and stumbling infancy of medical science.

The entire subject of the life-elixir, the grand palin-
genesis, the universal medecine, and the perfect way of
youth-renewal, has been exhaustively discussed in an
excessively curious book published at Paris in 1716, and
entitled : *An History of those Persons who have lived more
than a century, and of those who have Renewed their Youth,*

---

* The following mystical commentary has been offered on this
point. "The arcane understanding of the Elixir of Life is in the
alchemical *Solve et Coagula,* when spirit is turned into matter, and
vice versa. When a man knows his own spirit, he cannot die,
that is, lose consciousness in the flesh. He can put off his tabernacle if he will, and if he have allowed it to become feeble. He
then disappears. If he has kept up the physical correspondence
perfectly, he can pass to another country, appearing to die in a
given place. But to do so, he must have friends with knowledge."

with the Secret of Rejuvenescence, drawn out by Arnold de Villenieuve, by M. de Longueville-Harcourt. The fifteenth chapter discusses the possibility of renewal, with the quaint illustrations that follow.

" To renew youth is to enter once more into that felicitous season which imparts to the human frame the pleasures and strength of the morning. Here it is to no purpose that we should speak of that problem so much discussed by the Wise, whether the art can be carried to such a pitch of excellence that old age should itself be made young. We know that Paracelsus has vaunted the metamorphic resources of his Mercury of Life which not merely rejuvenates men but converts metals into gold ; he who promised unto others the years of the sybils, or at least the 300 winters of Nestor, himself perished at the age of thirty-seven. Let us turn rather to Nature, so admirable in her achievements, and deem her not capable alone of destroying what she has produced at the moment she has begotten them. Is it possible that she will refuse unto man, for whom all was created, what she accords to the stags, the eagles, and the serpents, who do annually cast aside the mournful concomitants of senility, and do assume the most brilliant, the most gracious amenities of the most joyous youth ? Art, it is true, has not as yet arrived at that apex of perfection wherefrom it can renew our youth ; but that which was unachieved in the past may be accomplished in the future, a prodigy which may be more confidently expected from the fact that in isolated cases it has actually already taken place, as the facts of history make evident. By observing and following the manner in which nature performs such wonders, we may assuredly hope to execute this desirable transformation, and the first condition is an amiable temperament, such as that which was possessed by Moses, of whom it is written that for one hundred and twenty years his sight never failed him.

" The stag, eagle, and sparrow-hawk renew their youth. Aldrovandus has written on the rejuvenescence of the eagle. Among the birds of the air, we are told by Pliny that the raven and the phœnix live, each of

G

them, six hundred years. No one denies that the stag is renewed by feeding on vipers and serpents, while the apes of Caucasus, whose diet is pepper, prove a sovereign remedy for the lion, who grows young by devouring their flesh. Those who have written of the elephant maintain that his normal life is extended through three centuries, while the horse, which alone in creation participates in the natures of man, of the lion, of the ox, the sheep, the mule, the stag, the wolf, the fox, the serpent, and the hare, from each deriving three of its qualities, has occasionally survived with undiminished vigour the lapse of a hundred years. The serpent, who is instrumental in the rejuvenescence of the stag, himself renews his youth at the shedding of his scales, from all which considerations, it follows that it is not beyond belief that a like prodigy may be found in the superior order of the same productions whence man has been himself derived, for man is assuredly not in a worse condition than the beasts whom he rules."

From these considerations the writer passes to an account of those persons, male and female, who are supposed to have renewed their youth. Unfortunately, the evidence is chiefly confined to the mythic periods of antiquity. Eson, the father of Jason, was enveloped by Medea in a quantity of warm herbs and aromatics, saturated with certain liquids which extracted the potent juices of these plants and recovered the youth of the patient. A fountain is mentioned by Herodotus which restored strength to the aged. The spring of Lucaga in America is accredited by Peter Chieza with the same marvellous property. A similar fountain is located in an island of the Greek Archipelago, according to Andræus Baccius, and another in the neighbourhood of Argos was called the Fountain of Canathus. Torquemada and Peter the Martyr, Aulus Gellius and Pliny, Lovrichius, and William Postel are cited in support of the actuality of renewal, and when the historic evidence has been at length exhausted, M. de Longueville-Harcourt supplies, what is promised in his title, the "arcanum" of Arnold de Villeneuve for the operation of the grand work of renewal.

"This marvellous process for the rehabilitation of Nature," says the author already cited, "is not to be found in the folio edition of the illustrious Arnold de Villeneuve; it is preserved in an ancient Latin manuscript, which came into the hands of a certain M. du Poirier, chief physician of the general hospital at Tours, who lent it to the Abbé de Vallemont, of Pomaine," by whom it was communicated to the author, M. de Longueville-Harcourt. The rejuvenating process of Arnold de Villeneuve is supplemented by a recipe for the Universal Medicine, which is generally identified with the Elixir, but appears to be of lesser virtue. This special elaboration is the achievement of M. de Comiers, who had a doctrine that diet and sweating were certain remedies for everything. It was claimed to be the universal medicine in a liquid form, and was guaranteed to set free or preserve the partaker from every disease. The dose was from five to six drops in wine or broth, according to the nature of the illness."

According to Bernard Trévisan, a distinguished French adept, the reduction of the "philosophical stone" into mercurial water results in the alchemical elixir of life, which is the Hermetic *aurum potabile*. Its potent virtues are equal to the cure of every variety of disease and it prolongs life beyond the ordinary limits. When the perfect elixir has been elaborated to the Red, it is said to transmute copper, lead, iron, and all metals into a purer gold than that which is found in the mines, while the same elixir elaborated to the White produces an excellent quality of wholly unalloyed silver.

Several formal recipes for the composition of the Universal Medicine are given in alchemical literature. That in *Albertus Parvus* requires eight pounds of sugar of mercury as its foundation. Those who partake night and morning of one dose will find their life prolonged, their health insured; while gout, sciatica, vertigo, and every internal complaint will be entirely and speedily eradicated.

At the solemn moment of death, the illustrious Benedictine, Trithemius, who is counted among the greatest of the Christian and Catholic hierophants, formulated a

recipe which he is said to have affirmed would preserve
a good stomach, a strong mind, and a tenacious memory,
together with perfect sight and hearing, for all who
made use of it.   As it is concerned with available
materials, it deserves to be given in full :—

Pulvis Medicinalis valde celebratus Trithemii.

Calami Aromatici, Gentianæ, Cinimi, Sileris Montani, Anisi, Carvi, Ameos, Sem. Petroselini, Spicæ Nardi, Coralli Rub,	15 gram. 625 millig. of each.
Unionum sive perlarum non perforatorum,	156 gram. 250 millig.
Zingiberis Albi, Amari Dulcis, Foliorum Senae, Tartari Adusti,	19 gram. 331 millig. of each.
Macis, Cubebarum,	7 gram. 331 millig. of each.
Cariophyllorum,	27 gram. 344 millig.

Fiat pulvis.
    Dose.—5 gram. 859 millig., taken night and morning
in wine or brodium, during the whole of the first month ;
during the second month, in the morning only ; during
the third month, thrice in the week, and so continue
through life.
    Occasionally the miraculous recipe was formulated in
the terms of the alchemists. The true method of composing the divine medicine is thus imparted by Eugenius
Philalethes :—" Ten parts of cœlestiall slime ; separate
the male from the female, and each afterwards from its
own earth, physically, mark you, and with no violence.
Conjoin after separation in due, harmonic, vitall pro-

portion; and, straightway, the Soul descending from the pyroplastic sphere, shall restore, by a mirific embrace, its dead and deserted body. Proceed according to the Volcanico magical theory, till they are exalted into the Fifth Metaphysical Rota. This is that world-renowned medicine, whereof so many have scribbled, which, notwithstanding, so few have known."

In the "Doctrine and Ritual of Transcendental Magic," Eliphas Lévi informs his students that he has come into possession of Cagliostro's great secret of rejuvenescence, but his reasons for withholding it from publication will be readily understood. If it be necessary to pose as the protector of dangerous knowledge, one should at least do so consistently, but with true French fickleness, and without a word of warning, much less of explanation or defence of his change of front, he supplies the recipe in his next book, and makes evident by its nature the pure charlatancy of his previous scruples, which are wholly in character with the transcendental devices which abound in his earlier work.

By means of this preposterous regimen, which is too complicated to admit of reproduction in this place, the impostor, who was not all an impostor, pretended to have extended his life over a period of several centuries; and on the authority of Lévi, we learn that the apostles of the marvellous are convinced that the great Copt is now located in America, where he is the supreme and invisible pontiff of the grand chaos of the spirit rappers.

Aristeus, the philosophical alchemist, is supposed to have delivered to his disciples what he terms the golden key of the Grand Work, which will render all metals diaphanous, and man himself immortal. The process appears to consist in the esoteric treatment of air, but whether of the ordinary atmosphere, or of something more concealed and recondite, we have no means of judging. It is congealed and distilled till it develops a divine sparkle, and subsequently becomes liquified. It is then subjected to heat, and is reinforced by another atmosphere. After these and other treatments, the elixir or solar marvel of all the sages, should reward the alchemical worker.

An arcanum may be possibly contained in this truly philosophical explanation, but the explanation is itself an arcanum, and an exceeding great and monumental mystery. It is the concentrated centre of the incomprehensible. But the principles thus bequeathed to the elected children of Aristeus have been the subject of reflection, we are informed, among skilful artists of the *magnum opus.* The result of their pondering is the luminous conclusion that he shall not truly work in vain who composeth a medley with the veritable balm of mercury, which, treated after the methods of alchemical confection and united with the elixir of their master, will perform every possible wonder that can be expected from so supreme an achievement.

However this may be, it is certain that on the lines of the Hermetists no practical performance can be so much as attempted in the physical order, for want of the necessary materials. No investigation, however assiduous, can possibly elucidate secrets that have never been revealed, and a long and exhaustive study leaves the whole subject exactly where it was found by the tyro, in a chaos of cloud and darkness. It is exceedingly probable that some of the minor recipes which will be found in Hermetic books may contain medical secrets which are unknown to modern science, and may be recovered by careful experiment. Among so vast a mass of material—mystic therapeutics, mystic chemistry, mystic herbalism—there may well be something of value; but it will not be Raymond Lully's great Elixir, nor the true Metallic Medicine. These, if they ever existed, would appear to be beyond recovery.

The literature of the Universal Medicine, as distinct from the literature of alchemy, is not extensive. The work which we have already cited is perhaps the most complete of its kind; but one which is excessively curious, and should not be overlooked by the curious, is Salmon's *Polygraphia,* which has much information upon the Grand Elixir of the philosophers. Some of our information will be found in *Les Admirables Secrets d'Albert le Grand;* and there are annotations on potable gold in the "Infernal Dictionary," and in Migne's encyclopædic *Dictionnaire des Sciences Occultes.*

CRYSTALLOMANCY.

THOUGH properly belonging to divination, an elementary branch of occultism, the Science of the Crystal is sufficiently serious in character and sufficiently important in result to demand a separate treatment.

It was found in the past that the fixed contemplation of a transparent and radiating object dazzled and troubled the eyes, and ultimately produced in a number of subjects the condition which we denominate hypnotic.

The artificial production of the hypnotic state was thus obtained in an innumerable variety of ways, but by none more successfully than the intervention of such substances as mirrors, crystals, and precious stones like the beryl. The mirror was more largely made use of in ceremonial evocations ; the crystal, on the other hand, was deemed the most perfect instrument for eliciting supernatural revelations in visions. It was practised in two manners, each of them preceded by a formal consecration, or charging of the potent stone. Those who were personally devoid of the faculty of clairvoyant lucidity could operate by the intervention of a virgin girl or boy, born in lawful wedlock, the physical purity and spiritual innocence, which in children more closely than in others approaches the ideal of unfallen humanity, being intimately connected with success in the practice of all lawful magic, and the preponderance of intuitive over rational perception during the first period of youth being another and distinct advantage.

The imagination of the subject was impressed by the recitation of the charge, and perhaps was still further exalted by the use of a slight ceremonial. He might be draped, for example, in a mantle of violet silk and crowned with a garland of lilies. Incense would be burnt in his presences, or penetrating and delicious perfumes, such as that of syringa and magnolia, might be diffused around; his hands, feet, and forehead might be anointed with chrism, and an aromatic draught might be given him. When these preparations were over, he was placed in a subdued light in front of the magic crystal and his eyes were fixed upon its surface. Gradually, to a suitable subject, a mist would gather in the depths of the globe; the interior faculties of the mind would ex- pand like a flower, the exterior senses would be at least partially suspended, except to the voice of the operator, with whom he was in magnetic rapport, the crystal itself would vanish from the sight of the entranced being, the mist would melt or part, and he would be ravished by the apparition of a radiant being, the abiding spirit of the stone, or of some other vision which he was influenced to behold by the words or the will of the Magus.

This form of divination is undoubtedly one of the most innocent, pleasing, and successful methods of minor magical practice, and it is one which can be reproduced by an operator at the present day with considerable facility. The true crystal has been accredited with magnetic properties which assist the development of the interior sight, but it is indispensable for success that they should be of considerable size, and in shape either a perfect sphere or an egg; a good specimen is therefore expensive, but excellent imitations in glass may be easily procured, which are said to be utilised by occult students with genuine results, and can be purchased at the cost of a few shillings. The favourite medium in the past was the pale water-green beryl; a clouded crystal was preferred by some operators, and every variety of precious stone has, on occasion, been pressed into service.

Testimony to the complete reliability of many recorded results obtained by the crystal is to be found in abund- ance; things taking place at a distance having been beheld by the seer in his trance and afterwards verified in detail. By virtue of what law such occurrences are possible is beyond the scope of our present investigation; we are concerned with the facts alone; explanations may be ingenious and plausible, and many have indeed been devised, but at the present stage of psychological experiment hypothesis seems decidedly premature.

Crystallomancy in its second and more advanced form was practised without the intervention of a medium, when the Magus believed himself to possess the required faculty of clairvoyance.

In modern times, the rules for obtaining a vision have been exceedingly simplified. A practical student of the subject has reduced them to the following points:— "Keep the crystal clean. Don't be too liberal in allowing strangers to handle it, except you are going to look for them, when they ought to hold it in their hands for a few minutes. Hold the crystal between fingers and thumb, or on a table, if flat at the end. If the crystal appears hazy or dull, it is a true sign that you will see; the crystal will subsequently clear, and the forms manifest. If it be required to see events which are taking place at a distance, say, in Australia, look lengthwise through the crystal, when, if you can see at all, you are likely to accomplish your object."

But there are rituals contained in old manuscripts and books of magic which insist upon a far more elaborate ceremonial.

"Those who desire to establish communication with good spirits in the crystal," says one of these older authorities, "must lead a religious life, and keep themselves unspotted from the world. The operator must make himself clean and pure, using frequent ablutions and prayers for at least three days before he attempts the practice, and the moon must be increasing. If he choose, he may have one or two wise and discreet persons as companions and assistants, but he and they must equally conform to the methods and rules of art. The operator must be firm, strong in faith, great in confidence, and he must be careful that no portion of the ceremonies be omitted if he desire to achieve success, for on the exactitude with which the entire ritual is performed depends the accomplishment of his design. The invocant may perform the practice at any time of the year, provided the two luminaries are in a fortunate aspect, in conjunction with fortunate planets; when the sun is in his greatest northern declination is said to be the best time."

In order to prosecute his work, the operator must have a small room in a retired part of the house, such as an attic, or a low kitchen. It must be clean and neat, but with no sumptuous ornaments to distract his attention. The floor must be well scoured and quite level, so as to receive the lines of the several circles and characters which are to be traced thereon. The room must be free from intruders, from the hurry of business, and it should be locked when not in use. Every preparation belonging to the art must be made during the moon's increase. The operator must be provided with a small table, covered with a white linen cloth; a chair should be placed in the room, and the materials required for a fire, which will be necessary to enkindle the perfume proper to that planet which may govern the hour of practice. A torch, two wax candles, placed in gilded or brass candlesticks, highly polished and engraven, must be likewise provided, together with a pair of compasses, and several minor accessories, such as twine, a knife, a pair of scissors, &c. The magic sword must be made of pure steel; it must be supplemented by a wand of hazel wood, of a year's growth and a yard in length, graven with appropriate sacred characters. Every instrument, large or small, must be entirely new, and must be consecrated previous to use.

The most important adjunct of the practice is the crystal, which must be about four inches in diameter, or, at least, the size of a large orange. It must be properly ground and polished, so as to be free from specks or spots; it should be enclosed in a frame of ivory, ebony, or boxwood, also highly polished. Sacred names must be written round about it, in raised letters of gold; the pedestal to which the frame is fixed may be of any suitable wood, properly polished. The crystal, like the other instruments, must be consecrated before being used, and should be kept in a new box or drawer, under lock and key. The names to be engraved on the frame are, at the North, TETRAGRAMMATON; at the East, EMANUEL; at the South, AGLA; and at the West, ADONAY. The pedestal which supports the frame should bear the mystical name SADAY, while on the pedestals of the two candles, ELOHIM and ELOHE, must be respectively embossed.

In consecrating all the instruments and other accessories of the art, the invocant must repeat the forms of consecration while imposing his hands upon the different articles, and his face must be turned to the East.

The consecrations being ended, he may then arrange the table with the crystal thereon, together with a candlestick containing a wax candle on each side of the circle, which should be seven feet in diameter, and must enclose a mystic square, whose angles at the apex point must, in each case, impinge on the circumference. Both figures must be appropriately inscribed with sacred names and mystical characters and symbols. When the operator enters the circle with his companions, if any, it must be the day and hour of Mercury, the moon increasing, and the operations must be prefaced by an earnest invocation of VASSAGO, who is the genius of the crystal.

If the conjurations be often repeated, if the operator be patient and constant in his perseverance, and not disheartened or dismayed by reason of any tedium or delay, the spirit, it is affirmed by the ritual, will at last appear, when he must be bound with the Bond of Spirits, after which he may be conversed with freely. "That this is a true experiment, and that the spirit hath been obliged to the fellowship and service of a magic artist heretofore, is very certain," says the same authority; " but as all aërial spirits are very powerful, it will be well for the operator not to quit the limits of the circle till a few minutes after the apparition has been formally licensed to depart."

It seems clear that the intelligences which manifest to the Magus through the graceful medium of the crystal are members of an elementary hierarchy, and it will be discerned by the intelligent reader that the force which controls them is the will of the operator, rendered magnetic by the discipline of the ritual, and dilated as well as directed by the elaborate, if grotesque, ceremonial. He will probably conclude that the so-called divine names, which are frequently barbarous perversions of dead tongues, or are . simply chaotic, are

impotent symbols in themselves till they are vivified
by the intelligent and measured desperation of the
operator, and that the whole *modus operandi* is calculated to work upon the interior faculties of the man,
not upon the fears of the spirit. If the will and the
imagination of the operator be sufficiently strong, and at
the same time sufficiently governed to dispense with
ritual formalities, an effect may be produced without
them. Paracelsus, relying upon the force of the concealed *magnes* in the arcane man, denounces the ceremonial of magic with the violence of the mediæval
hierophant. At the same time, if the rites be observed
at all, they must be observed *in toto*, for the smallest
deflection will react on the will of the operator, and, as
Eliphas Lévi indicates, it will produce apprehension and
embarrassment which may stultify the whole process.

Among the many persons who in recent years have
conducted experiments with the crystal, one of the most
successful was the late Frederick Hockley, who devoted
his life to the collection and transcription of works on
the secret sciences, and who was also a practical student
of several branches of magic. He was not himself a seer
in the ordinary sense of the term, and his dealings with
the spirits of the crystal were conducted by the media-
tion of clairvoyantes. When his extraordinary library
was dispersed, a long series of communications obtained
through the crystal, and extending to several volumes,
written in his own hand, was a centre of interest to the
collectors of occult manuscripts. The success which was
obtained by Mr Hockley in this as in other departments
of magic art, had considerable evidential value, as it was
achieved by a private gentleman who never posed as a
mystic, who pursued his experiments in secret for his
personal satisfaction only, who never published the results of his researches, and was neither seeking notoriety
nor pecuniary gain.

THE COMPOSITION OF TALISMANS.

THE English Platonist, Joseph Glanvil, author of *Sadducismus Triumphatus*, a formidable discovery of witchcraft, of a "Key to the Grand Mysteries in Relation to Sin and Evil," and of other tracts and treatises, was an important mystic of his period, but he is now known only by one anecdote and one pregnant sentence. The anecdote is that of the Scholar Gipsy, who renounced his Oxford studies to lead a nomadic life and to discover an arcanum possessed by the Bohemians, whereby they could strangely influence the will of others. Which of us is unacquainted with the imperishable beauty of Matthew Arnold's elegy founded on this anecdote? As transcendentalists, we should be grateful to the sweet singer who has indirectly perpetuated the memory of the dead mystic. But Glanvil is immortalised also by a sentence which Poe disentombed, and has placed as the central idea of one of his wildest narratives. "And the Will therein lieth, which dieth not. Who knoweth the mysteries of the Will, with its vigour? For God is but a great Will pervading all things by nature of its intentness. Man doth not yield himself to the angels nor to death utterly, save only through the weakness of his feeble will." The anecdote and sentence are both taken from the "Vanity of Dogmatizing," a title which may be respectfully recommended to the attention of many persons at the present day. This single sentence is, in effect, the sum of magic, for the seat of the power of the soul is said to be in the Will of the man, which is the great magical agent, the instrument in the development of all interior faculties, the life of conscious act, and the sole informing principle of mystic rites and ceremonies.

As the will of a strong man can influence a weaker

mind, as it can bid the magnetic patient sleep, and the clairvoyant see, so it was believed in the past that it could endue an inert substance with an occult force transferred from the inmost individuality of the operator by a grand mental projection; and this was Talismanic Magic. The principle was debased by the unintelligence and superstition of the past; the virtue was divorced from its connection with the operating mind, and was referred to the methods, and to the substance of the talisman, or to the blind observation of times and seasons. The life of the belief departed, and the vivid realisation of the absolute power of man over all things animate and inanimate was replaced by a slavish veneration of occult forces which exercised a fatal and undiscerning tyranny over men and the magus.

At its best, talismanic magic seems to rank as one of the curiosities of esoteric science which are chiefly archæological in interest. We may recognise the principle which it involves as a reasonable part of mysticism. This principle is concerned with the communication of human magnetism to inert objects, which in an inferior kingdom of nature is paralleled by the transference of a similar and equally mysterious virtue from the loadstone to iron. Beyond this, and beyond the part which is played by the talisman in the ceremonies of evocation, it is a branch of mysticism which has little to warrant its revival at the present day. It encourages intellectual weakness, and directs the attention of the student to the frivolities of transcendental art. The talisman has been tersely defined as an astrological character engraven upon a sympathetic stone in correspondence with the constellation or star which was represented by the character in question. Its name is derived from a Greek word which signifies a symbol, image, or figure. It is a sign which stands as the nominal equivalent of a force or influence. The emblem must be engraved upon the substance of the talisman by an operator who is at any rate philosophically acquainted with the nature of the influence which it signifies, who can concentrate his entire attention and his undivided will upon the work, while his mental powers are isolated from all sources of distraction and all thoughts which are unconnected with the matter in hand.

The doctrines and practice of talismanic magic, as it flourished amidst the christianity of the West, are derived from the Kabbalah, which in turn was indebted to Chaldea, Egypt, and Babylon; for if the talisman be less old than religion, it is as old as superstition and as wide in the sphere of its influence.

The seal of Solomon is the most famous of all talismans, and nothing was believed to be impossible for those who possessed it, as it had power over all spirits, which is equivalent to saying that it represented a strong psychic force. The five-pointed star of the microcosm, which is the Star of Bethlehem, the star of the Magi, and the mystic sign of humanity, as the double triangle of Solomon was the symbol of the universe, the macrocosm, or the great world—man being *minutum mundum* —this emblem was of equal repute and, in the human sphere, of even greater power than the seal of the mythic monarch of transcendental Judaism. With the single point, or horn, in the ascendant, it represented White Magic; reversed, it was the emblem of sorcery, witchcraft, and the grotesque extravagances of the "Sabbath."

Occasionally, talismanic influence has been accredited with a broader range. Five varieties are enumerated by Elihu Rich :—1. The astrological, having the characters of the heavenly signs or constellations. This branch was developed by Paracelsus, who refers talismanic virtue to the seven genii of the seven planets. 2. The magical, engraved with symbolical figures, and the names of unknown angels. The mystical designs which are found upon Gnostic gems may be referred to this branch. 3. The mixed, engraven with celestial signs and barbaric words. 4. The *sigilla planetarum*, composed of Hebrew numeral letters, or their equivalents in Roman and Arabic ciphers. 5. Hebrew names and characters. This classification is, however, exceedingly arbitrary. The majority of talismans are sufficiently composite in design to embrace all of these varieties. Within the historical period, they were all formed under appropriate planetary influences, and to this, if no further, extent, were of distinctly astronomical character. A more accurate distinction, though one originating in superstition, may be based on the difference between artificial talismans composed by the science of the Magus and substances which were accredited with a natural talismanic virtue, as in the case of precious stones.

The virtues which were attached to the talisman were usually of a practical character, and an important position was assigned them in the mysteries of the healing art. As in modern mesmeric therapeutics, the health-giving power of the physician is supposed to be transmitted to a patient at a distance by means of a magnetised water, or other suitable medium, so it would appear that the power of the magus had entered into the talisman by the penetrating force of will, and could exercise a similar influence over a sick person when it had been composed for a healing purpose. But the talisman would be more potent than the magnetic water of the unilluminated mesmerist. The science of the Magus enabled him to combine with the force of his own will and intelligence the most favourable influences of the whole sidereal world. The genius of the predominating planet of the moment—which, in other words, was the specific influence and destiny which it was astrologically supposed to radiate—entered into the act of composition; the talisman was informed by his genial and benevolent potency, which was superior to that of the Magus (whose participation was practically forgotten from the moment that the composition was over), and the consecrated object became the talisman of that planet under which it was made and consecrated. The alleged value of planetary influences will be appreciated in a subsequent portion of this book; here it is sufficient to observe that the belief in intervention on the part of the astral world largely assisted talismanic healing by its effect on imagination, which by its natural therapeutics can accomplish what is impossible to medicine, and is the chief agent in all so-called miraculous cures— magnetic, magic, talismanic.

The Doctrine of Talismans supposes that the influence

of the Seven Planets which were known to the astronomy of the ancients, is never more strong and conspicuous than when it acts through the intervention of the Seven Metals of alchemy, which are each in correspondence with one of these celestial bodies. The metals, which are to be severally referred to each of the several planets, are said to have been ascertained by the sublime penetration of the Kabbalists. However this may be, it is certain that, from the magical standpoint, gold was the metal of the Sun, and of the first day in the week; silver of the moon, and of Monday; iron of Mars, and of Tuesday; quicksilver of Mercury, and of Wednesday; pewter of Jupiter, and of Thursday; copper, or brass, of Venus, and of Friday; and lead of Saturn, and of Saturday.

From Christian's *Histoire de la Magie*, from the curiosities of the "Little Albert," and similar authorities, we may gather an intelligible notion of the most important astral talismans. It should, however, be remarked that, as in other ceremonial matters, there is little unanimity on this subject among writers on magic. A variety of pentacles are attributed to each of the planets in the so-called "Keys of Solomon" which differ altogether from those which are described by Paracelsus, while, among modern authors, Eliphas Lévi has developed a system of his own.

I. The TALISMAN OF THE SUN must be composed of a pure and fine gold, fashioned into a circular plate, and well polished on either side. A serpentine circle, enclosed by a pentagram must be engraved on the obverse side with a diamond-pointed graving tool. The reverse must bear a human head in the centre of the six-pointed star of Solomon, which shall itself be surrounded with the name of the solar intelligence PI-RHÉ, written in the characters of the Magi. This talisman is supposed to insure to its bearer the goodwill of influential persons. It is a preservative against death by heart disease, syncope, aneurism, and epidemic complaints. It must be composed on a Sunday during the passage of the moon through the first ten degrees of Leo, and when that

H

luminary is in a favourable aspect with Saturn and the
Sun. The consecration consists in the exposure of the
talisman to the smoke of a perfume composed of
cinnamon, incense, saffron, and red sandal, burnt with
laurelwood, and twigs of dessicated heliotrope, in a new
chafing-dish, which must be ground into powder and
buried in an isolated spot, after the operation is finished.
The talisman must be afterwards encased in a satchel
of bright yellow silk, which must be fastened on the
breast by an interlaced ribbon of the same material, tied
in the form of a cross. In all cases the ceremony should
be preceded by the conjuration of the Four, to which
the reader has already been referred. The form of consecration, accompanied by sprinkling with holy water,
may be rendered in the following manner :—

In the name of Elohim, and by the spirit of the living
waters, be thou unto me as a sign of light and a seal of
will.

Presenting it to the smoke of the perfumes :—By the
brazen serpent before which fell the serpents of fire, be
thou unto me as a sign of light and a seal of will.

Breathing seven times upon the talisman :—By the firmament and the spirit of the voice, be thou unto me as a
sign of light and a seal of will.

*Lastly, when placing some grains of purified earth or salt
upon the pentacle :*—In the name of the salt of the earth
and by virtue of the life eternal, be thou unto me as a
sign of light and a seal of will.

II. The TALISMAN OF THE MOON should be composed
of a circular and well-polished plate of the purest silver,
being of the dimensions of an ordinary medal. The
image of a crescent, enclosed in a pentagram, should be
graven on the obverse side. On the reverse side, a
chalice must be encircled by the duadic seal of Solomon,
encompassed by the letters of the lunar genius PI-JOB.
This talisman is considered a protection to travellers,
and to sojourners in strange lands. It preserves from
death by drowning, by epilepsy, by dropsy, by apoplexy,
and madness. The danger of a violent end which is

predicted by Saturnian aspects in horoscopes of nativity, may be removed by its means. It should be composed on a Monday, when the moon is passing through the first ten degrees of Capricornus or Virgo, and is also well aspected with Saturn. Its consecration consists in exposure to a perfume composed of white sandal, camphor, aloes, amber, and pulverised seed of cucumber, burnt with dessicated stalks of mugwort, moonwort, and ranunculus, in a new earthen chafing-dish, which must be reduced, after the operation, into powder, and buried in a deserted spot. The talisman must be sewn up in a satchel of white silk, and fixed on the breast by a ribbon of the same colour, interlaced and tied in the form of a cross.

III. The TALISMAN OF MARS must be composed of a well-polished circular plate of the finest iron, and of the dimensions of an ordinary medal. The symbol of a sword in the centre of a pentagram must be engraved on the obverse side. A lion's head surrounded by a six-pointed star must appear on the reverse face, with the letters of the name EROTOSI, the planetary genius of Mars, above the outer angles. This talisman passes as a preservative against all combinations of enemies. It averts the chance of death in brawls and battles, in epidemics and fevers, and by corroding ulcers. It also neutralizes the peril of a violent end as a punishment for crime when it is foretold in the horoscope of nativity.

This talisman must be composed on a Tuesday, during the passage of the moon through the ten first degrees of Aries or Sagittarius, and when, moreover, it is favourably aspected with Saturn and Mars. The consecration consists in its exposure to the smoke of a perfume composed of dried absinth and rue, burnt in an earthen vessel which has never been previously used, and which must be broken into powder, and buried in a secluded place, when the operation is completed. Finally, the talisman must be sewn up in a satchel of red silk, and fastened on the breast with ribbons of the same material, folded and knotted in the form of a cross.

IV. The TALISMAN OF MERCURY must be formed of a circular plate of fixed quicksilver, or according to another account, of an amalgam of silver, mercury, and pewter, of the dimensions of an ordinary medal, well-polished on both sides. A winged caduceus, having two serpents twining about it, must be engraved in the centre of a pentagram on the obverse side. The other must bear a dog's head within the star of Solomon, the latter being surrounded with the name of the planetary genius, PI-HERMES, written in the alphabet of the Magi. This talisman must be composed on a Wednesday, when the moon is passing through the ten first degrees of Gemini or Scorpio, and is well aspected with Saturn and Mercury. The consecration consists in its exposure to the smoke of a perfume composed of benzoin, macis, and storax, burnt with the dried stalks of the lily, the narcissus, fumitory, and marjolane, placed in a clay chafing-dish which has never been devoted to any other purpose, and which must, after the completion of the task, be reduced to powder and buried in an undisturbed place. The talisman of Mercury is judged to be a defence in all species of commerce and business industry. Buried under the ground in a house of commerce, it will draw customers and prosperity. It preserves all who wear it from epilepsy and madness. It averts death by murder and poison ; it is a safeguard against the schemes of treason ; and it procures prophetic dreams when it is worn on the head during sleep. It is fastened on the breast by a ribbon of purple silk folded and tied in the form of a cross, and the talisman is itself enclosed in a satchel of the same material.

V. The TALISMAN OF JUPITER must be formed of a circular plate of the purest English pewter, having the dimensions of an ordinary medal, and being highly polished on either side. The image of a four-pointed crown in the centre of a pentagram must be engraved on the obverse side. On the other must be the head of an eagle in the centre of the six-pointed star of Solomon, which must be surrounded by the name of the planetary genius PI-ZÉOUS, written in the arcane alphabet.

This talisman must be composed on a Thursday, during the passage of the moon through the first ten degrees of Libra, and when it is also in a favourable aspect with Saturn and Jupiter. The consecration consists in its exposure to the smoke of a perfume composed of incense, ambergris, balm, grain of Paradise, saffron, and macis, which is the second coat of the nutmeg. These must be burnt with wood of the oak, poplar, fig tree, and pomegranate, and placed in a new earthen dish, which must be ground into powder, and buried in a quiet spot, at the end of the ceremony. The talisman must be wrapped in a satchel of sky-blue silk, suspended on the breast by a ribbon of the same material, folded and fastened in the form of a cross.

The talisman of Jupiter is held to attract to the wearer the benevolence and sympathy of every one. It averts anxieties, favours honourable enterprises, and augments well-being in proportion to social condition. It is a protection against unforeseen accidents, and the perils of a violent death when it is threatened by Saturn in the horoscope of nativity. It also preserves from death by affections of the liver, by inflammation of the lungs, and by that cruel affection of the spinal marrow, which is termed *tabes dorsalis* in medicine.

VI. The TALISMAN OF VENUS must be formed of a circular plate of purified and well-polished copper. It must be of the ordinary dimensions of a medal, perfectly polished on both its sides. It must bear on the obverse face the letter G inscribed in the alphabet of the Magi, and enclosed in a pentagram. A dove must be engraved on the reverse, in the centre of the six-pointed star, which must be surrounded by the letters which compose the name of the planetary Genius SUROTH. This talisman must be composed on a Friday, during the passage of the moon through the first ten degrees of Taurus or Virgo, and when that luminary is well aspected with Saturn and Venus. Its consecration consists in its exposure to the smoke of a perfume composed of violets and roses, burnt with olive wood in a new earthen chafing-dish, which must be ground into powder at the end of the operation and buried in a solitary spot. The talisman must, finally, be sewn up in a satchel of green or rose-coloured silk, which must be fastened on the breast by a band of the same material, folded and tied in the form of a cross.

The talisman of Venus is accredited with extraordinary power in cementing the bonds of love and harmony between husbands and wives. It averts from those who wear it the spite and machinations of hatred. It preserves women from the terrible and fatal diseases which are known as cancer. It averts from both men and women all danger of death, to which they may be accidentally or purposely exposed. It counterbalances the unfortunate presages which may appear in the horoscope of nativity. Its last and most singular quality is its power to change the animosity of an enemy into a love and devotion which will be proof against every temptation, and it rests on the sole condition that such a person should be persuaded to partake of a liquid in which the talisman has been dipped.

VII. The TALISMAN OF SATURN must be composed of a circular plate of refined and purified lead, being of the dimensions of an ordinary medal, elaborately polished. On the obverse side must be engraven with the diamond-pointed tool which is requisite in all these talismanic operations, the image of a sickle enclosed in a pentagram. The reverse side must bear a bull's head, enclosed in the star of Solomon, and surrounded by the mysterious letters which compose, in the alphabet of the Magi, the name of the planetary Genius REMPHA. The person who is intended to wear this talisman must engrave it himself, without witnesses, and without taking any one into his confidence.

This talisman must be composed on a Saturday when the moon is passing through the first ten degrees of Taurus or Capricorn, and is favourably aspected with Saturn. It must be consecrated by exposure to the smoke of a perfume composed of alum, assa-fœtida, cammonée, and sulphur, which must be burnt with cypress, the wood of the ash tree, and sprays of black hellebore, in a new earthen chafing-dish, which must be reduced into powder at the end of the performance, and buried in a deserted place. The talisman must, finally, be sewn up in a satchel of black silk and fastened on the breast with a ribbon of the same material, folded and tied in the form of a cross. The talisman of Saturn was affirmed to be a safeguard against death by apoplexy and cancer, decay in the bones, consumption, dropsy, paralysis, and decline; it was also a preservative against the possibility of being entombed in a trance, against the danger of violent death by secret crime, poison, or ambush. If the head of the army in war-time were to bury the talisman of Saturn in a place which it was feared might fall into the hands of the enemy, the limit assigned by the presence of the talisman could not be overstepped by the opposing host, which would speedily withdraw in discouragement, or in the face of a determined assault.

The names of the presiding planetary intelligences which are given in the foregoing pages purport to be Egyptian in origin. In the Teraphim, which were the talismans of mediæval Kabbalistic rabbis, these names were replaced by Michael, Gabriel, Samael, Raphael, Zachariel, Anael, and Oriphiel.

Talismanic theories and practice are almost exclusively confined to the operations of White Magic; but we learn, on the authority of Christian, that the seven celestial talismans had also their infernal complement; there was the white and the black talisman. It was possible for the perverted Magus to infuse into the material of the metals the poison of his vitiated will, and to combine it with the diabolical influence of the seven demons who corresponded in eternal opposition to the seven planetary angels. To the angel of Saturn was opposed the demon Nabam; to that of Jupiter, the demon Acham; to the angel of Mars, the demon Nambroth; to the Genius of Venus, the demon Lilith or Naemah; to that of Mercury, the demon Astaroth or Tharthae; to the angel of the Moon, the demon Satan.

The talisman was always an accessory of considerable

importance, and was invariably an indispensable adjunct, in all classes of evocation, but occasionally in the ancient rituals it figures as the chief condition of the practice. This is especially the case with the talisman called Almadel, which is described in the earliest work on magic that is known to have been printed in English. By the intervention of this instrument, SOLOMON, the father of Jewish mysticism—in the sense that from the altitudes of theurgic experiment to the lowest science of the abyss, all kabbalistic arts are gratuitously fathered upon him— is affirmed to have attained his great and sublime wisdom from the chief angels that govern the four altitudes of the world, "for you must observe," says this curious ritual, "that there are in the world four altitudes, which represent the four corners of the world —East, West, North, and South, these being twelve times subdivided, three to every part." The angels of each of these altitudes have their particular virtues and powers.

The mysteries of talismanic magic have exercised the erudition of most writers on the practical branches of mysticism. Paracelsus is the prince of authorities; but there is a fund of information in the "Occult Philosophy" of Cornelius Agrippa. "The Magus," by Francis Barrett, is an accessible book which summarises the anterior literature. *Secrets Merveilleux de la Magie Naturelle et Cabalistique du Petit Albert* contains also talismanic secrets.

DIVINATION.

THE circle of each of the physical sciences is surrounded with a fringe of light, easy, and pleasing
experiments which in themselves are exceedingly
trivial, but are as so many thresholds of the deep things
of knowledge, and are to be valued for that which they
lead to, and not for what they are. The profundities of esoteric science have also their light, fantastic
borderland where the tyro may amuse himself, and
where the vacuous interest of the modern *dame de société*,
who describes herself as " very occult," finds sufficient
nourishment to sustain a shallow and sentimental interest
in the mysteries of psychic force. Such are the methods
of divination which abound in old books, and in the
folk-lore of all European peoples. They are preliminary
and trivial experiments with the powers of the interior
man ; if the conditions which are indispensable to the
manifestation of these powers in any of their phases are
fulfilled, they are successful, they excite wonder, and
nourish credulity ; if the ignorance and stupidity of the
operator, or the inanity of a particular method, should
render a result abortive, the entire science is condemned.
Yet physics, as much as psychology, though each in their
own way, depend for success on conditions. The friction
of silk and sealing-wax may produce an elementary
phenomenon of magnetism, but the friction of cloth and
clay will be barren of any such result, and without any
blame to magnetics.

It should be definitely laid down at the beginning that
all forms of divination are simply methods of exercising
the intuitive faculties ; they are calculated to produce
that temporary suspension of the outer senses which is
known as the hypnotic condition. In some varieties the
phenomena of complete trance are elicited in a suitable

subject. On the other hand, the several forms of carto-
mancy are simply designed to awaken a dormant quality
of psychic perception. Those which are exclusively concerned with the performance of a barren rite, and produce no impression on the interior nature, are either
worthless impostures, or foolish, superstitious practices.

Considerable futility is mixed up with divination ; it
is essentially trivial in character ; in itself it can be productive of no valuable results ; the student of discrimination and sense will not squander his time and his powers
on the little marvels of magic art ; he will win entrance
into the larger field of achievement.

The word divination is occasionally used in a broad
philosophical sense which places a different complexion
upon it. Its significance is extended till it includes the
sublime dream of astrology, spiritual visions, and the
gift of inspired prophecy. According to the vulgar
meaning of the term, to divine is to conjecture what we
do not know, says Lévi, but its true significance is
ineffable in its sublimity. To divine (*divinare*) is to
exercise divinity. To be a diviner in all the force of
the term is therefore to be divine, and something still
more mysterious. In a popular and elementary work,
we have judged it advisable to make use of the word
divination in the popular and narrower sense. The
art in itself is anterior to any historical period, and is
therefore supposed to have descended from primitive
tradition. "That in the first ages of earth," says the
Rev. Henry Thompson, " some means of communication
between God and man, with which we are now unacquainted, existed, appears from the history of Cain
and Abel; and the same circumstance instructs us that
these means were connected with sacrifice, an extensive
source of divination in later ages. After the degeneracy
of mankind had banished those real tokens of the
divine interest with which they had been originally
favoured, they no less endeavoured to obtain counsel
and information by the same external observances; but,
finding them no longer efficient, they invented a multitude of superstitious ceremonies, which, in the progress of
religious corruption, and beneath the influence of idolatry,

became the hydra Divination." Evolutionists who are also mystics, and mystics who are men of reason, will discountenance definite opinions on the origin of religious beliefs and practices of the pre-historic period. It is sufficient for our purpose to know that divination flourished in Egypt, Chaldea, and Assyria, among the Babylonians and Ethiopians, and that in the most distant regions of the globe we find a striking similarity, descending even to details, among its practised methods.

Upwards of one hundred recorded forms of divination are known to the magic of the West. Those which are in use in the East, and among barbarous nations, are probably innumerable. In selecting the following varieties for the information and use of the student, it is just to observe that they are gleaned from several sources, from Latin, French, and English writers, and are reproduced with but slight adaptation in the words of the originals.

ÆROMANCY.

This is the art which, sometimes under an alternative appellation, Meteoromancy, is concerned with the prediction of things to come by the observation of atmospheric variations and the different phenomena of the air, particularly those of thunder, lightning, and fiery meteors. It is by virtue of this divination that the apparition of a comet has been supposed to portend the death of a great man. In his vast work upon magic, François de la Torre-Blanca, who follows Psellus, affirms that the veritable æromantic art is the prediction of the future by the evocation of spectres in the air, or the pictorial representation of things to come, by the aid of demons, in a cloud, as in a magic lantern. On this supposition it would be simply a branch of ceremonial magic; on the other, it may be supposed that the observation of tremendous atmospheric phenomena, of sunset pageantries, auroral lights, of peaceful midnight splendours, of stars and storms and lightning, the merely prolonged contemplation of "the magical, measureless distance," would profoundly excite the imaginations of sensitive persons, and transform the

dome of the empyrean into a veritable " glass of vision."
" It is the same with star-groups as with points in geo-
mancy," says Éliphas Lévi, "and with the card-medleys
of modern fortune-telling.   They are all pretexts for self-
magnetization, and mere instruments to fix and determine natural intuition.   The imagination is exalted by
a long contemplation of the sky, and then the stars
respond to our thoughts accordingly as the soul is disturbed or serene, the stars scintillate with menaces, or
sparkle with hope.   Heaven is thus the mirror of the
human soul, and when we think that we are reading the
stars, it is in ourselves we read."

ALECTROMANCY.

From the standpoint of magical folk-lore, the cock
is a bird of much interest and many virtues.   It is
endowed with the remarkable power of putting to flight
the infernal hosts, and as according to Peter Delancre
in his *Tableau de l'inconstance des Démons*, the devil, who
is the lion of hell, will vanish the moment that he hears
the voice of this domestic fowl, it is popularly supposed
that the natural lion, who is the king of beasts, can be
subdued and put to flight thereby.   The entire fantas-
magoria of the Black Sabbath disappears when the cock
crows, and to prevent him from sounding his clarion
during the night-hours, and routing the whole assembly,
the sorcerer, instructed by the devil, anointed his head
with olive oil, and twined a collar of vine leaves about
his neck.   But while his voice was inimical to the midnight mysteries of the wizard world, his flesh was
supposed to be possessed of valuable virtues in sorcery,
and, in particular, an ancient and venerable method of
divination was practised by the instrumentality of this
bird of the gods and of Æsculapius.   The *modus operandi*
is as follows.   A circle must be traced on the ground
in a spot which shall be free from observation, and it
must be divided into twenty-four equal spaces, which shall
be inscribed with the letters of the alphabet, rejecting J
and U, which are usually represented in ancient writings
by their correspondents, I and V.   A grain of wheat

or barley must be placed over every letter, beginning with A, and during this operation the depositor must repeat the verse "*Ecce enim veritatem tuam*," &c. The most favourable time for the divinatory performance is when the sun or moon is in Aries or Leo. Set in the centre of the circle the cock, who is the chief agent in the occult rite. The bird should be wholly white, and, according to some authorities, he should be deprived of his claws, which he should, moreover, be forced to swallow, together with a little scroll of lambskin parchment, inscribed with Hebrew characters. Then the diviner, while his grasp is still upon the cock, should repeat, "*O Deus Creator omnium, qui firmamentum pulchritudine stellarum formasti, constituens eas in signa et tempora, infunde virtutem tuam operibus nostris, ut per opus in eis consequamur effectum.*" Subsequently, in the act of placing the bird within the circle, he must repeat these two verses from the Psalms, "*Domine dilexi decorem domûs tuae et locum habitationis tuae. Domine Deus virtutum, converte nos, ostende faciem suam, et salvi erimus.*" All that remains for the operator, after these preliminaries, is to note very carefully from what letters the bird picks up the grains, which should be invariably replaced by others till his meal is over. From the assemblage of letters thus obtained, the ingenuity of the anagrammatist can generally extract an oracle which will give information on the desired subject. It will be seen that this form of divination is wholly fortuitous; instead of appealing to the interior faculties of a clairvoyant subject, it makes use of an indiscriminating instrument, and, as such, the entire rite is a rank and unmixed superstition.

ALEUROMANCY.

This divinatory method was practised by depositing small strips of writing, rolled into balls, in a heap of flour. The whole was well mixed, and the inquirers, who should be several in number, received each an equal share. Subsequently each of them unrolled the strips that had fallen to his lot, and extracted from the assemblage of words and phrases the information of which he was in search. Diviners have foreborne to inform us what should be written on the scrolls, and the method, on the whole, is worthless, and less curious, than that which is concerned with the cock.

ALPHITOMANCY.

This form of divination is sometimes considered of importance and is accredited with great antiquity, but it is superstitious and worthless from the transcendental standpoint. When several persons were accused or suspected of a certain crime, and when it was desired to discover the true culprit, each of them was forced to swallow a morsel of hard bread. Those who could do so without difficulty were dismissed without a stain upon their character. Those who were nearly choked in the act were held to be guilty. When the test could be successfully passed by all, it may be concluded that the esoteric detectives went further afield for the criminal. The pellet of bread was denominated the corsned, or morsel of execration, and it has originated the common vindication, "If I deceive you, may my next mouthful of food choke me." The practical method was as follows :—Pure barley flour, unmixed with leaven, was kneaded with salt and milk, baked in the ashes in a covering of greasy paper, and finally rubbed over with vervain leaves. The composition became exceedingly hard, and as incipient strangulation in swallowing an unmasticated lump could only be averted by a miracle, many guilty persons were naturally discovered by its means. In the neighbourhood of Lavinium, there is said to have been a sacred wood where a variety of this idiotic process was practised as a test of virginity. A dragon, otherwise a serpent, was kept in captivity by the priests of the place, and, on certain occasions, young females were commissioned to feed him. Their eyes were bandaged, they were led into the grotto, bearing cakes of honey and barley flour, and those whose contributions were refused, by the discriminating reptile, were supposed to have contracted dishonour.

AMNIOMANCY.

Divination was practised by the Greeks with the caul of a new-born child. The superstition was exceedingly simple and excessively silly, being simply an inspection of the colour which the membrane chanced to exhibit. A fortunate future was predicted for the possessor of a ruddy-tinted caul, and sinister omens were drawn from the presence of a livid hue.

ANTHROPOMANCY.

From gross superstition divination occasionally passed to foul and revolting practices. Auguries were drawn from the examination of the entrails of disembowelled men and women; under the name of anthropomancy this rite is one of considerable antiquity. It is mentioned in Herodotus, who informs us that Menelaus, when detained in Egypt by contrary winds, sacrificed the native children to his barbarous curiosity, and sought information on his destiny from the signs in their stomachs. The nature of the signs, and the manner of their interpretation, have, fortunately, not been recorded. Similar but unaccredited stories are narrated of Julian, the apostate, who, in his necromantic operations and nocturnal sacrifices, is said to have immolated many children in order to consult their intestines. When in his last expedition, he tarried at Carra, in Mesopotamia, he is affirmed to have retired, with some accomplices, into the Temple of the Moon, and, when their impious occupations were over, they left it locked and sealed with a guard round about it to keep away all comers till their return. Julian died, however, in the war, and when the temple was opened, in the reign of the Emperor Jovien, a woman was found hanging by her hair, her hands outstretched, her stomach cut open, and the liver torn out. But the memory of the Emperor Julian has been calumniated by partisans, and the reports of his enemies should be received with uncommon caution.

ARITHMOMANCY.

The mystical properties of numbers were developed by Pythagoras and Plato, and the science of esoteric mathematics passed from the Greeks to the Kabbalists, who transmitted it to the western mystics, Louis Claude de St Martin being one of the last and most distinguished of its initiates. The powers, and virtues, and mysteries, which were attributed by the ancients to numbers are similar to those which have been already described as the properties of the occult alphabet of the Hebrews. " In estimating these doctrines," says Elihu Rich, "it must be remembered that all movement, proportion, time, and, in a word, all idea of quantity and harmony, may be represented by numbers: hence, whatever may be attributed to the latter, may also be expressed by numbers, as the signs of occult virtues and laws. It is known to philosophers that the movements of nature are rhythmical; physicians have observed this in the periodicity of diseases; and the appointment of the seventh day as a Sabbath, has added a religious obligation to this law of nature. The *three*, the *ten*, and the *twelve* are also numbers of well-known import, and *one* is the most divine of all, as expressing the unity of God, and the comprehension of all things in perfect harmony. The use of numbers in divination has assumed many curious forms. It may suffice to mention here the *Gematria*, or first division of the Cabbala, which teaches how to cast up the letters of particular words as numerals, and to form conclusions from the proportion between the sum of one text and the sum of another. This method converts the Bible into a book written solely by numbers, and some curious results are obtained, probably as near the truth as the rabbinical astrology. Some curious properties of perfect, amicable, and other numbers have been elucidated by the English Platonist, Thomas Taylor, in his 'Theoretic Arithmetic.' The most valuable remains of antiquity connected with this subject are contained in the 'Chaldean Oracles of Zoroaster.'"

In was the custom of the Greeks to examine the number and value of the letters in the names of two combatants, and the predominant number, it was held, would be victorious in conflict. By virtue of this science certain diviners predicted that Hector would be over- come by Achilles. The Chaldeans divided their alphabet into three parts, which they attributed to the seven planets, and extracted their omens accordingly. It is evident that such calculations must produce totally opposite results in different languages, and unless nation- ality enters as a determining element into destiny, it is difficult to look upon these numerical arts as anything but ingenious curiosities.

ASTRAGALOMANCY

This was a form of divination with a pair of ordinary dice, which might be cast together or singly. If it be de- sired to obtain information on any subject by this method, including the mysteries of the future, the question must be written upon paper which had been passed through the smoke of a fire of juniper wood. The writing must be placed face downward on the table, and the dice must then be thrown. The result of each cast must be converted into its literal equivalent, and carefully noted. If both the dice are used, the process must be continued till the numbers from 2 to 12 have been all obtained, when the intuition of the operator must be concentrated on the as- semblage of letters. If the order in which they are evolved should result in an intelligible message, he will have cause to be gratified. If no sense can be extracted he must seek in another rite for the required revelation. The alpha- betical equivalent of the numbers has been thus given:— 1 = A ; 2 = E ; 3 = I or Y ; 4 = O ; 5 = U ; 6 = B ; 7 = C, K, or Q ; 8 = D or T ; 9 = F, S, X, or Z ; 10 = G or J ; 11 = L, M, or N ; 12 = R. As most of the numbers may signify any of three letters, the calculation will be some- what embarrassing. The letter H is omitted as it is as unnecessary to successful divination as to the speech of the cockney. The laws of destiny are independent of those of orthography, says one sententious writer. Whatever may be thought of the mystic notary art, it is unlikely that common numerical divination, more especially when

I

restricted to the spots on the cubes of the gambler, will provide the student with any reliable result.

AXINOMANCY.

This method was employed for the discovery of hidden treasures and the detection of criminals. In the first case the method is of a singularly fatuous kind. A round agate must be carefully balanced on the edge of a red-hot hatchet. If the balance be preserved for a certain time there is no treasure in the neighbourhood. If it fall, remark the direction in which the ball will roll, and perform the operation in all three times. If the direction taken by the agate be the same in each case, it will not be vain to dig ; should it vary, it will be well to conduct your experiments in another place. The second method would be discreditable to the intelligence of the Sandwich Islanders. To detect a thief or other criminal the blade of the hatchet must be buried perpendicularly in the earth, with the handle protruding in a perpendicular position. The rest of the performance consists in a circular dance around the hatchet till the soil is torn up, and the hatchet falls flat on the ground. The direction assumed by the handle will indicate that quarter of the physical cosmos in which search should be made for the criminal. It will be well for the operator to remember that he has before him the magical, measureless distance ; that he has eternity, if need be, for the quest, and that as Macdonald, the poet, remarks, "There is plenty of room for meeting in the universe."

BELOMANCY.

Under this name, divination with arrows was long practised in ancient military expeditions. A number of darts were selected, favourable and unfavourable answers to the given question were written indiscriminately upon them ; they were then shuffled after the manner of cards, and one of them drawn at random. The reply which chance thus provided was considered the voice of destiny and the will of the gods. The operation is supposed to have been practised so far back as the time of the Chaldeans. It is a point to be noticed that the more ancient the method, the more gross is the superstition which it involves, a fact that may be commended to the consideration of some over-zealous believers in the wisdom of the far past. There was another method of Belomantic divination, which consisted in casting certain arrows into the air, and the course of the inquirer, whether an individual or an armed host, was directed by the inclination of the weapons.

BIBLIOMANCY.

Occasionally the forms of divination exceeded the bounds of superstition, and passed into the region of frantic madness. There was a short way with sorcerers which was probably the most potent discoverer of witchcraft which any ingenuity could devise. A large Bible was deposited on one side of a pair of weighing scales. The person suspected of magical practices was set on the opposite side. If he outweighed the Bible he was innocent; in the other case, he was held guilty. In the days of this mystical weighing and measuring, the scales may be truly said to have fallen from the eyes of a bewizarded generation, and to have revealed "sorcery and enchantment everywhere."

Bibliomancy, however, included a more harmless practice, and one of an exceedingly simple character. This was the opening of the Bible with a golden pin, and drawing an omen from the first passage which presented itself. Books like the Scriptures, the "Following of Christ," and similar works, abound in suggestive and pertinent passages which all men may apply to themselves, and the method was consequently much in vogue. St Augustine denounces the practice in temporal affairs, but declares that he had recourse to it in all cases of spiritual difficulty. The appeal to chance is, however, essentially superstitious.

CAPNOMANCY.

This was a method of divination by smoke, and frequently, it may be judged, must have ended in that whence it first originated. The concentration of an impressionable mind upon fantastic wreaths of vapour might, however, produce a hypnotic condition as success-fully as another method. The shapes which imagination gave to the ascending fumes were interpreted in an oracular manner, and omens were drawn from the direction in which they passed off, the latter being wholly superstitious. Two methods were followed. In the one, seeds of jasmin, or poppy, were cast on burning coals, and the form of the fumes examined; in the other, the smoke was inhaled by the operator, and was supposed to impart a prophetic gift. A powerful effect would undoubtedly be produced by the smoke of strong narcotics, but the visions which originate in poppy heads are not to be counted among the infallibilities of magian art.

CEROSCOPY.

Divination with wax has long been replaced by divination in tea leaves and coffee grouts, but it has the advantage of superior antiquity over these methods, and is further removed from the commonplace. Wax of the purest quality was melted in a brazen vase and stirred into a liquid of uniform consistence. It was then poured into another vase filled with cold water, but slowly, and in such a manner that it congealed in tiny discs upon the aqueous surface. A variety of figures were thus presented to the eye of the seer, and inter-preted according to the impulse of his intuitive powers. This is an exceedingly harmless practice, which might be productive of clairvoyant results in a suitable subject.

CLEIDOMANCY.

The key which shuts and opens is a favourite symbol with all mystics, and is founded on a natural analogy, which has a quality that is rare in analogies, being perfect in its own way. The suggestiveness of the symbol reacted on the material instrument, and divination by means of a key was long practised after various manners. Each method, it is said, should be practised when the sun or moon is in Virgo. One is for the discovery of the name of a suspected person, or in any case where a name is required. The latter should be written on a key, the key should be tied to a Bible, and both should be suspended from the ring finger of a young virgin, who must repeat in an undertone the words, "*Exurge Domine, adjuva nos et redime nos propter nomen sanctum tuum.*" The operator meanwhile must repeat the supposed or suspected name with a few sentences of appropriate prayer. If any oscillation of a marked character is visible in the book and key, it may be concluded that the name has been correctly divined, and proceedings may be taken accordingly. On the other hand, if they remain stationary, it is certain that the inquiry has been pursued upon a wrong track. Occasionally more elaborate forms of prayer are used, such as litanies and the seven penitential psalms, when the guilty person was accustomed to develop a miraculous impression of the mystic key upon his body; he was also liable to be deprived of one of his eyes, a possibility which gave rise to the proverb, "*Ex oculo quoque excusso hodie fur cognoscitur.*" The second method was a solemn superposing of the key upon a certain page of a book. When the Bible was used for this purpose, it was opened at the fiftieth Psalm.* The volume was then closed with the key inside, and tightly secured with a cord, which was, if possible, a woman's garter, but in such a manner that the ring of the key protruded. The book was then suspended from a nail in the wall, or from the finger of the inquirer, when it was positively certain that it would perform as complete a revolution, as the nature of the case would permit, at the name of the person who had committed that deed which was the subject of occult investigation. By a third, but less common method, two persons suspended the volume between them, holding the ring of the key by their two forefingers.

Cleidomancy is said to be still performed in Russia

---

* Even at the present day, divination with the Bible is said to be in general use among the uneducated classes of the dissenting persuasion.

for the discovery of hidden treasures, the index finger of
the right hand being placed in the ring of the key, and
the names of likely places are repeated over it in turn.

A variety of these entertaining but fatuous practices
was divination by means of a sieve suspended from a
thread, or by shears which were hung from the finger.
The choice of instruments might be varied indefinitely,
and the use of a consecrated pulley would be probably a
useful improvement, which may be commended to the
modern magician. If divinatory rites, however superstitious and grotesque, are possessed of the potency
ascribed to them in the remote ages of faith, we
may confidently look forward to the time when they
will be utilised in our Courts of Justice, when the
godless skill of the common detective shall have perished
with the reign of reason, and the unbounded resources
of magic will enable an illuminated humanity to prove
and disprove anything. Then may the enemies of the
initiates look forward to an evil time. Sacred and
beautiful science of the Magi, last word to humanity,
first and final revelation, harmony of the whole universe, universal synthesis, science of Barrett and of
Solomon,

> " *Dies venit dies tua,*
> *In qua reflorent omnia !* "

DACTYLOMANCY.

Who is not aware of the virtues of the ring in magic ?
Equally powerful for binding and loosing, it is more important than the ring in expousals. Of a truth, says
Chispa, there is more in marriage than the wedding
ring, but there is nothing that is greater, worthier, or
more wondrous, than is the great, worthy, wondrous, and
altogether mystical ring of the occult art. The ring of
Fastrada, the ring of Gyges, the ring of Solomon, they are
better than the bells of Fairyland, better than the cap of
Fortunatus. The chain of Mesmer was a magnetic ring ;
the séance circle is a living, palpitating, universal ring of
humanity ; the magic circle is truly a ring also. Ye
who would unearth treasures, secure the magic ring !

Ye who would be adepts of the "divine science," learn
its many - sided mysteries! Ye who would fascinate
woman, wear it invisibly on your persons, and invisibly
shall you enter into the penetralia of woman's affection, and be sure she will then entertain you as an unseen god! Ye who would divine truly, divine only by
the ring! ·Compose it under a benign constellation,
enchase it with mystic characters, suspend it by a thread
or a hair over a tumbler, and it will oscillate with the
celerity of a pendulum, and once for YES and twice for
NO, just as you choose to determine, it will respond to
your questions with delicious, musical vibrations awakened
in the sides of the glass. Inscribe on the edge of a circular table the symbols of the alphabet, and the intelligent·
instrument, passing over certain letters, will compose
you a definite answer, and reveal you the mysteries you
are in search of, with the precision of the spirit-rapper's
table. It is well to perform the operation with religious
observances; the diviner should be clothed in white
linen, his head shaven; he should bear in his hand a
branch of vervain, a beneficent plant provided by Nature
to drive away evil spirits; and the ring should be consecrated solemnly with adjurations and vows. The
power is indefinitely increased by the due constellation
of the rings under the influence of the planetary genii.
The ring of Saturn should be of lead, enchased with
onyx or garnet, which should be engraved with a stone
writhen about by a serpent. The ring of Jupiter should
be of brass, enchased with a topaz, sapphire, or amethyst,
engraven with the image of an eagle holding a pentagram
in his beak. The ring of Mars should be of iron, enchased with ruby, red jasper, or hematite, engraven with
the symbol of a serpent devouring the point of a sword.
The ring of the Sun should be of gold, enchased with
hyacinthus or chrysolite, engraven with a crowned and
lion-headed serpent. The ring of Venus should be of
copper, enchased with an emerald, engraven with the
Indian lingam. The ring of Mercury should be composed of an alloy of brass, lead, and fixed quicksilver,
enchased with cornelian or alectorine, engraved with
the symbol of the caduceus, which is a sceptre interlaced

by two serpents. The ring of the Moon should be of silver, enchased with crystal or moonstone, and engraven with the image of a sphere intersected by two crescents.

The use of constellated rings involves a more elaborate ceremonial. The day and time of constellation regulates the use of the rings. Should it take place on a Tuesday that of Mars should be selected, and the inquiry conducted during the first, eighth, fifteenth, or twenty-second hours, which are consecrated to the Genius of that planet. The circular table already mentioned, must be engraven with the signs of the Zodiac, and of the seven planets. A number of discs of the metal proper to the period, and having the symbols of three alphabets, should be cast indiscriminately on the table, a prayer should be addressed to the Genius, the ring should be suspended by a thread above the table, and the priest, or the pythoness, should set fire to the thread with a torch consecrated to Hecate, the goddess of enchantment. The ring will then fall upon the table, and the letters over which it rolls, and those by which it pauses, must be carefully noted. This operation should be repeated seven times, and then the intuition of the diviner must collect the sense of the oracles from the assemblage of letters contained. Now, the faculty of intuition, which is possessed to an extra ordinary degree by persons of certain temperaments, can be, doubtless, as successfully exercised on a fortuitous heap of letters as on the grouts of coffee, and herein is the extent of the value which inheres in divination with rings.

GASTROMANCY.

This is a method of divination which induces clairvoyance in suitable subjects, and might lead to very interesting results. Several circular glass vessels filled with clear water are placed between a number of lighted candles. The intelligences of the spiritual world are invoked in an undertone, and a virgin boy or girl is then introduced, and is directed to concentrate their gaze on the surface of the vessels, when the answer of the oracle becomes visible to the magnetised faculties in fantastic figures produced by refraction of the light within the vessels.

There is another gastromantic method, which is more in correspondence with the significance that belongs to the term—divination from the belly, which was either the exercise of ventriloquism or the result of some form of possession.

HYDROMANCY.

The art of divination by water is simply a branch of clairvoyance, which has been successfully practised in all ages and nations, though, as the demonologist Delrio truly remarks, *nulla fœcundior imposturis.* Several varieties are distinguished by authorities on this interesting subject :—

1. When at the conclusion of invocations and other magical ceremonies, the names of persons or other information required are seen written upside down in the water. 2. When a ring is suspended by a thread above a glass of water, and when vision begins after the sides of the vessel have been smote a certain number of times during the course of oscillation. 3. When three small pebbles are successively, and at short intervals, cast into clear and tranquil water, and when the circles which form on the surface, and the intersections which they happen to make, are interpreted as omens. 4. When the innumerable movements and agitations of the waves of the sea are attentively examined and clairvoyant conclusions are drawn. 5. When an interpretation is placed upon the colour of water, and upon the figures which are seen therein. The traditions of the ancients invested certain streams and springs with special qualifications for this form of hydromancy. 7. When water was poured into a glass or crystal basin and a little oil added which was supposed to increase the visionary power of the seer. 8. When the twists and turns, together with the noises, made by rivers and torrents when they plunged into gulfs or seethed in whirlpools, were interpreted as fatidic utterances. This method was much in vogue among the primitive germanic peoples. There are also some minor species of hydromantic divination of a more distinctly superstitious character. One which is native to Italy was used for the discovery of thefts.

The names of suspected persons were written upon pebbles and cast into water. That of the guilty person remained ineffaceable. Another device consisted in filling a glass or cup with water and pronouncing mystic words above it. On certain occasions the water was supposed to bubble and pour over the brim, but under what circumstances we are unable to state. Lastly, the ancient Germans are supposed to have made use of a barbarous and stupid perversion of hydromantic art. When they doubted the fidelity of their wives and desired to ascertain if a new-born child were lawfully or otherwise begotten, they cast it into water. If the infant floated, the mother was held to be stainless, if it sank, the child was accounted illegitimate.

"Hydromancy," says Elihu Rich, "is, in principle, the same thing as divination by the crystal or mirror, and in ancient times a natural basin of rock kept constantly full by a running stream, was a favourite medium. The double meaning of the word *reflection* ought here to be considered, and how, gazing down into clear water, the mind is disposed to self-retirement and to contemplation, deeply tinctured with melancholy. Rocky pools and gloomy lakes figure in all stories of witchcraft— witness the Craic-pol-nain in the Highland woods of Laynchork; the Devil's Glen in the county of Wicklow, Ireland; the Swedish Blokula; the witch mountains of Italy; and the Babiagora, between Hungary and Poland. Similar resorts in the glens of Germany were marked, as Tacitus mentions, by salt springs; for this again there was an additional good reason, which would carry us far from the present subject to explain.

"It was really only another form of divination by the gloomy water pool that attracted so much public attention, . . . when Mr Lane, in his work on 'Modern Egypt,' testified to its success as practised in Egypt and Hindostan. That gentleman having resolved to witness the performance of this species of sorcery, the magician commenced his operations by writing forms of invocation to his familiar spirits on six slips of paper; a chafing-dish with some live charcoal in it was then procured, and a boy summoned who had not yet reached the age of puberty. Mr Lane inquired who were the persons that could see in the fluid mirror, and was told that they were a boy not arrived at puberty, a virgin, a black female slave, and a pregnant woman. To prevent any collusion between the sorcerer and the boy, Mr Lane sent his servant to take the first boy he met. When all was prepared, the sorcerer threw some incense and one of the strips of paper into the chafing-dish; he then took hold of the boy's right hand, and drew a square with some mystical marks on the palm; in the centre of the square he poured a little ink, which formed the magic mirror, and desired the boy to look steadily into it without raising his head. In this mirror the boy declared that he saw, successively, a man sweeping, seven men with flags, an army pitching its tents, and the various officers of state attending on the Sultan." The rest must be told by Mr Lane himself. " The sorcerer now addressed himself to me, and asked me if I wished the boy to see any person who was absent or dead. I named Lord Nelson, of whom the boy had evidently never heard; for it was with much difficulty that he pronounced the name after several trials. The magician desired the boy to say to the Sultan, ' My master salutes thee, and desires thee to bring Lord Nelson; bring him before my eyes that I may see him speedily.' The boy then said so, and almost immediately added, ' A messenger has gone and brought back a man dressed in a black (or rather, a dark blue) suit of European clothes; the man has lost his left arm.' He then paused for a moment or two, and looking more intently and closely into the ink, said: ' No, he has not lost his left arm, but it is placed to his breast.' This correction made his distinction more striking than it had been without it; since Lord Nelson generally had his empty sleeve attached to the breast of his coat; but it was the right arm that he had lost. Without saying that I suspected the boy had made a mistake, I asked the magician whether the objects appeared in the ink as if actually before the eyes, or as if in a glass, which makes the right appear left. He answered that they appeared as in a mirror. This rendered the boy's description faultless.

Though completely puzzled, I was somewhat disappointed with the magician's performances, for they fell short of what he had accomplished, in many instances, in presence of certain of my friends and countrymen. On one of these occasions, an Englishman present ridiculed the performance, and said that nothing would satisfy him but a correct description of the appearance of his own father, of whom he was sure no one of the company had any knowledge. The boy, accordingly, having called by name for the person alluded to, described a man in a Frank dress, with his hand placed on his head, wearing spectacles, and with one foot on the ground and the other raised behind him, as if he were stepping down from a seat. The description was exactly true in every respect; the peculiar position of the hand was occasioned by an almost constant headache, and that of the foot, or leg, by a stiff knee, caused by a fall from a horse in hunting. On another occasion, Shakespeare was described with the most minute exactness, both as to person and dress; and I might add several other cases in which the same magician has excited astonishment in the sober minds of several Englishmen of my acquaintance."

"It may be worth adding," says Elihu Rich, "that in a case of hydromancy known to the writer, the boy could see better without the medium than with it, though he could also see reflected images in a vessel of water. This fact may be admitted to prove that such images are reflected to the eye of the seer from his own mind and brain; how the brain becomes thus enchanted, or the eye disposed for vision, is another question; certainly there is no proof that the recollected image in the mind of the inquirer is transferred to the seer, evidence can be shown to the contrary."

LITHOMANCY.

Few particulars are forthcoming concerning the method of divination by stones. It was performed by striking a number of pebbles together, and concluding from the nature of the sound emitted the will of the supreme gods. The interrogation of a magnet which had been washed in spring water was supposed to evoke from that substance an intelligible response in the feeble tones of a small child. The amethyst is also possessed of lythomantic properties; the events in the womb of the future are supposed to be laid bare in dreams to those who are in the habit of wearing this stone upon their persons. A mystic variety of the ophite stone is mentioned in the so-called Orphic hymns under the name of "the true and vocal sideritis." Its appearance is rough and hard, it is heavy and of a black colour, and it is all writhened with wrinkled veins. It was given by Apollo to Helenus, who, for the space of ten days, abstained from the nuptial couch, from the bath, and from animal food. "Then washing this intelligent stone in a living fountain, he cherished it as a babe in soft clothing; and having propitiated it as a god, he at length gave it breath by his hymn of mighty virtue. Having lighted lamps in his own purified house, he fondled the divine stone in his hands, bearing it about as a mother bears her infant; and you, says the oracular writer, if you would hear the voices of the gods, in like manner, provoke a similar miracle, for when you have sedulously wiped and dandled the stone in your arms, on a sudden it will utter the cry of a new-born child seeking milk from the breast of its nurse. Beware, however, of fear, for if you drop the stone upon the ground, you will raise the anger of the immortals. Ask boldly of things future, and it will reply. Place it near your eyes when it has been washed, look steadily at it, and you will perceive it divinely breathing. Thus it was that Helenus, confiding in this fearful stone, learned that his country would be overthrown by the Atridae."

The possession of a similar treasure is ascribed to a physician, named Eusebius, who obtained it by an impressive intervention of celestial phenomena. "One night, actuated by an unaccountable impulse, be wandered out from the city Emesa to the summit of a mountain dignified by a temple of Minerva. There, as he sate down fatigued by his walk, he saw a globe of fire falling from the sky and a lion standing by it. The

lion disappeared, the fire was extinguished, and Eusebius
ran and picked up a bætulum. He asked it to what god
it appertained, and it readily answered, to Gennæus, a
deity worshipped by the Heliopolitæ, under the form of
a lion in the temple of Jupiter. During this night
Eusebius said he travelled not less than 210 stadia,
more than 26 miles. He never became perfectly master
of the bætulum, but was obliged very humbly to solicit
its responses. It was of a handsome, globular shape,
white, a palm in diameter, though sometimes it appeared
more, sometimes less ; occasionally, also, it was of purple
colour. Characters were to be read on it, impressed in
the colour called tingaribinus. Its answer seemed as if
proceeding from a shrill pipe, and Eusebius himself interpreted the sounds." While some authorities consider
the animating spirit of this mysterious stone to be divine,
others refer it to an elementary influence. It is said to
have been frequently found on Mount Libanus, and a
parallel has been established between it and the black
stone Elagabalus, as well as the monument anointed by
Jacob at Bethel.

PYROMANCY.

The purest, most powerful, and most exalted elementary intelligences were those who inhabited the fire ;
sacred and consecrated flame was the most perfect
method of mystic purgation ; a bright and clear fire was
not less effective in driving off evil spirits than in scaring
wild beasts from the hunter's camp at night. Lights
have been used in all religious ceremonials from time
immemorial ; it would be strange, indeed, if it were
wholly unconnected with the mysteries of divinatory art.
Pyromancy, however, is comparatively obscure as it
is also essentially superstitious. Some handfuls of
powdered resin were cast into a fire ; and if a bright
flame leaped up, a good omen was drawn from it ; a slow
and smoky combustion prognosticated misfortune.
When a victim was burned, the future was occasionally
predicted by observing the colour of the flame. Occasionally, also a sick person would be set in front of a large
fire, when if the shadow cast by the body was straight

and at right angles to the furnace, his speedy cure might be confidently expected ; if it fell upon the ground at an oblique angle, it was a certain sign of death. The observation of lighted torches was also practised in antiquity. Three torches were arranged in a triangle, all of them being composed of fine wax. The vacillation of the flame from right to left foretold approaching migrations; the manœuvres of secret enemies were signified by a spiral curl ; a fitful rising and falling presaged dangerous vicissitudes. A preponderating brilliance in a single torch was the sign of unforeseen fortune ; sparkling and crackling were considered a warning to be prudent and a menace of reverses and treachery. The formation of an extremely brilliant point at the extremity of a wick announced a permanently increasing success; the sudden extinction of one or more of the torches was considered especially disastrous for the subjects of consultation as well as for the consulter himself.

MYOMANCY.

When Halton II., surnamed Bonose, the usurper of the archiepiscopal seat of Mayence, refused, about the year 1074, to give food to the poor during a famine, and persisted so far in his sin that he is accredited with burning a house full of importunate bread-seekers, he is said to have been visited by a heavy judgment of heaven. He fell sick in a castle which was situated on a small island in the Rhine where he was devoured by a multitude of rats. A similar fate is traditionally recorded of a Polish king. Common domestic vermin besides being the ministers of Divine retribution are otherwise of a certain importance in supernatural history. It is a good omen to encounter an albino rat, as it is also a sign of destruction when these intelligent animals bodily desert a ship. Mice, on the other hand, are of evil augury, and the harmony of suspicious circumstances during the consultation of an oracle would be permanently upset by their cry. Out of these superstitions divination by rats and mice apparently originated, but the actual nature of the operation has not come down to us.

ONOMANCY.

The evolution of Shakesperian criticism has been elaborated to such a degree that his writings are sometimes regarded by persons of adequately advanced vision as a complete course of initiation into the mysteries of occult philosophy, and into the general history of the soul. This is one of the profundities of hypothesis which in a well-regulated world would, of course, have been true, but it is extravagance within the limits of space of three dimensions. A veritable Kabbalistic Magus would never have penned that proverbial question, "What's in a name?" It is a doctrine inherent in all Kabbalistic Magic that nothing happens fortuitously, that the name which is inherited by a child is inherited in virtue of eternal law, and that even his prenominal designation, though apparently arbitrary, and depending on parental taste and whim, or upon other considerations, is not a product of chance, but must also be referred to the workings of an arcane principle. Thence it is a step to affirm that the name is in itself the expression of a destiny to come, or that the events of futurity can be discerned in the letters of a name, and thus Onomancy arises, which is the art of divination by names, and was in high favour throughout the Pagan world. The adherents of the Pythagorean philosophy were accustomed to maintain that the talents, activities, and good fortune of men were in conformity with their destiny, their genius, and their name. The esoteric significance of the title Hippolytus proclaimed that its bearer would be torn in pieces by horses; it was equally predetermined that Agamemnon would for years be encamped without the walls of Troy, and that Priam would be ransomed from slavery. It matters not that there was more than one Hippolytus and that they were by no means identical in destinies. The patronymic had also its influence, and a second prenominal designation would act also on the life of its bearer. Now, the science of onomantic divination had two leading rules. An even number of vowels in a man's name signified something amiss in the left side; an uneven number indicated a similar imperfection on the right.

The causation of course is not clear; but God is all knowing. It was no less emphatically certain that a name with the majority of letters would give advantage over a rival whose progenitors had less copiously supplied him with alphabetic resources. It was not by sword or buckler that Achilles triumphed over Hector; it was by the superior length of his name; the mischances of modern warfare, and competition of every species, may be definitely referred to the neglect of this wisdom of the ancients. Happy is the modern bookmaker who falls across this volume, metaphorically or otherwise, and is constrained by his genius to glance at this page. A permanent fortune will be secured him in the possession of the mystic tips. It will be scarcely less suitable to ladies in a choice between two suitors, as the only sure guide to fortune in the lottery of the marriage market. Old times are changed, old manners gone, but there is no reason to suppose that the virtue has departed from a divination which was successfully practised in the past. What is more excellent than the authority of Cælius Rhodigunis? Has he not informed us that Theodotus the Goth practised peculiar and original Onomancy on the recommendation of a Jew, who was doubtless a king-initiate? "The divine advised the Prince, who was on the eve of a war with Rome, to shut up thirty hogs in three different styes, having previously given some of them Roman and others Gothic names. On an appointed day, when the styes were opened, all the Romans were found alive, but with half their bristles fallen off; on the other hand, all the Goths were dead; and from this prognostic the Onomantist forbode that the Gothic army would be utterly destroyed by the Romans, who, at the same time, would lose half their own force."

It appears on the authority of the French archæologist, Count de Gebelin, that this method of divination was found susceptible of unheard of developments by the "divine" Cagliostro, who foretold to masonic illuminés in solemn conclave, the most important events of the French revolution by the names, birthplaces, and other natal circumstances, of the chief participators therein. Inde-

pendent of esoteric philosophy, the ingenuities of the
modern intellect have extracted from the names and
titles of modern celebrities sentences apposite to their
destinies or characters by the art of the anagram.

ONYCHOMANCY.

Divination by the nails of the fingers would appear to
be a trivial invention, but for some unexplained reason
it has been dignified by the title of the observation of
the angel Uriel. "Upon the nails of the right hand of
an unpolluted boy or a young virgin, or the palm of the
hand, is put some oil of olives, or, what is better, oil of
walnuts mingled with tallow or blacking." Tallow was
occasionally the sole ingredient and wax was sometimes
a substitute. The nails, when they had been thus anointed,
were turned towards the sun and resolutely considered by
the seer. The ends of the inquiry determined the time of
observation. The search after money or articles buried
in the earth must be pursued with the face towards the
East, and was thus of matutinal character, as the full blaze
of sunlight must invariably fall upon the prepared nails of
the medium. The occult investigation of crimes, and con-
sultations prompted by affection, were pursued with the
face to the South, which also served for murder, while the
West was for robbery. It was requisite that the child
should repeat the seventy-two verses of the Psalms, which
the Hebrew Kabbalists collected for the Urimm and Thum-
mim; and which are preserved in a treatise entitled *De
Verbo Mirifico*, and in Reuchlin's Rabbinical collection.
"In each of these verses occurs the venerable name of four
letters, and the three-lettered name of the seventy-two
angels, which are referred to the inquisitive name *Schema-
hamphores* which was hidden in the folds of the lining of
the tippet of the high priest." The hypnotic condition
may be produced in such a variety of ways that even
the anointed nail should not be too rigorously excluded
from the category of possible instruments. There is,
however, an eternal fitness which forbids the anti-climax
whether in act or speech, and it has definitely relegated
such methods to the limbus land of bathos.

OOMANCY.

The domestic egg is redeemed from irretrievable commonplace by its symbolic value, its suggestion of hidden possibilities, and of a world in miniature. Divination by eggs may be therefore permitted to pass, if only by reason of its quaintness. The ancients were wont to discern in the exterior shape and in the interior construction of the egg the most impenetrable arcana of futurity, an art which is supposed to have originated with the divine Orpheus. If a pregnant woman should be anxious to ascertain the sex of her future child, she must carry an egg in her bosom at the proper temperature. When under the influence of the natural warmth, a chick is at length brought forth, its sex will determine the infant as either male or female. Divination, however, has of late been more usually practised with the whites of eggs, and this method was in favour with the celebrated Mademoiselle Lenormand. " Take a glass of water, break a fresh egg slowly into it, and from the figures assumed by the white let the presages of the future be collected by the intuitive skill of the seer." This is by no means a modern method ; it is referred to in the following terms by a *Grimoire* of comparative antiquity. "The operation of the egg is to ascertain what will befall some person who is then present in the company. An egg of a black pullet must be broken and the germ extracted therefrom. A large glass, very clear and clean, must stand ready, being filled with pure water. Therein must the germ be placed, and subsequently the vessel must be exposed to the mid-day sun of summer, with many prayers and conjurations, the water also being much stirred with the finger to circulate the said germ. When this has been done sufficiently, it is allowed to rest still for an instant, and is gazed at without touching. Something relating to the inquirer and the object of divinatory research will then be visible in the water."

In addition to the methods of divination which we have enumerated above, there are many of a minor character, and many which are confined to certain localities and more properly belong to folk lore.   A brief reference to a few of the former class will complete this exhaustive notice.

GYROMANCY was a kind of divination practised by perambulating a circle inscribed with the alphabet. When fatigue was succeeded by giddiness and giddiness by utter collapse, when the operator dropped to the ground, the letter upon which he fell was the first in the response of this oracle.   If after an appropriate pause, he was sufficiently recovered to recommence, he might, in the same manner, obtain a second letter, and so on till he evolved an intelligible sentence, or till death or madness intervened.   This is an interesting instance of mystic practice which may be commended to modern agility in advanced thaumaturgics and to the far behind followers of the eastern howling dervish.   HIPPOMANCY was a Celtic divination by the neighing of white horses, set apart for the purpose, and fed at the public expense in consecrated forests where the trees were their sole shelter.   They were made to tramp behind a sacred chariot, the priest and king followed and observed their every movement, drawing auguries therefrom with an absolute and unfailing confidence founded on the conviction that the animals participated in the great arcanum of the gods.   The Saxons also drew omens from the movements of a sacred horse fed and housed in a temple whence it was driven before war was declared against an enemy.   If it stepped forward right hoof first, that was a favourable augury ; in the other case, they renounced their enterprise.   ICHTHYOMANCY, like all divinations of incredible grossness, is of venerable antiquity, and may be commended to the Wisdom Religion, and the apologists of a spoliated past.   It was performed by the inspection of the entrails of fish.   An Apollonian fountain of prophetic fish was preserved at Mirea and was consulted by the grand Apuleius, who was initiated by Ceres into the many folded mysteries of the rose. KEPHALONOMANCY is an interesting practice involving diverse ceremonies with the boiled head of a donkey. The ass is a sacred, prophetic, divinatory, mystic, and essentially divine animal.   By reason of its auricular elongations, it is kindred to Baphomet and to universal

Pan. This is a very interesting, innocuous, and creditable operation which Delrio refers to the mediæval Jews. But it seems to have been practised by the ancients, who deposited the head upon some live coals, recited superstitious prayers, pronounced the names of suspected persons about whom they desired information, and listened for a cracking and convulsive movement of the jaws of the decapitated beast. The name which was pronounced at this crucial moment by the intelligent operator was that of the guilty person. LAMPODOMANCY was a form of divination by observing the shape, colour, and various movements assumed by the flame of a lamp. The art of divination by pearls was denominated MARGARITO MANCY. The precious stone was set by a fire and covered with a glass vessel. The inquiry was conducted for the recovery of stolen goods; it consisted in the repetition of the names of suspected persons, repeated in a loud voice. When that of the guilty party was pronounced by the speaker, the pearl was supposed to leap up to the top of the glass, which it occasionally shivered with its force. This is another entertaining and simple device which can easily be tested by the possessor of the stone in question, and in the event of its success, would be a good instance of divining power, and the production of wonderful effects without causes. By means of a simple ceremonial, PARTHENOMANCY guaranteed to ascertain the presence or absence of virginity. The girth of the girl's neck was measured with a thread, and on the repetition of this operation, after a reasonable period, an unfavourable conclusion was drawn from an increase in its size. SCIAMANCY was performed by the evocation of the shades of the dead. It differed from necromancy and psychomancy as it was neither the soul nor body of the deceased person which responded to the appeal of the Magus, but a kind of mysterious simulacrum, most probably an astral shell. SPODANOMANCY has a definite advantage over most forms of divination as the devil is occasionally supposed to interfere personally in its behalf. "It is performed," says Grand Orient, "by scattering ashes thickly in some place exposed to the air, and writing therein with the end of the finger any question

about which information is needed.   The inscribed
ashes are then left for the night, and on the following morning the letters that remain legible are made
use of as oracles, for which purpose they may be placed
in their natural order, when if they form an intelligible
word, it may be considered to contain the mystic sense
of the oracle and an answer to the question proposed.
Otherwise the insight of the contriver must be used to
extract an appropriate answer from the assemblage of
letters arranged after any fashion." Innumerable and
beautiful alike are the varieties of divinatory mysticisms.
By SYCOMANCY the leaves of the fig-tree are transformed
into suggestive oracles.   Interrogatory remarks upon
any subject about which information is desired are inscribed thereon.   If the leaves wither quickly, that is an
evil sign; if they preserve their freshness for a considerable period, the sign is fortunate.   Last in the long list
but first in importance is the Kabbalistic THEOMANCY of
the Jews, a research into the inner mysteries of Divine
Majesty and into the resources of sacred names.   Those
who are in possession of this tremendous science have
broken the seals of futurity, may command nature, and
control both angels and devils.   They have also the Key
of miracles.   A considerable amount of information on
subjects connected with Theomancy has been embodied
in the first section of the present book.

We have treated the methods of divination at such
length, that it will be almost superfluous to make reference to sources where more extensive information will
be found.   *Les Devins, ou Commentaire des Principales
Sortes de Devinations*, by Gasper Peucer, date 1584, is a
quarto of nearly 700 pages, and may be considered to
exhaust the subject.   Works in the English language
are few and unimportant.

THE DIVINING ROD.

THOUGH essentially a method of divination, and naturally, as such, to be included in the section which bears that name, the interest which has so long been attracted by the magnetic wand, its extraordinary history, and the very large number of witnesses who have testified to its genuine potency, demand its separate treatment as in the case of the magic crystal.

Our readers have already become acquainted with the mystic properties of the rod in necromantic and in black magic. But the ordinary divining rod, which is known by reputation to everybody, which is still made use of in remote country places, is an instrument of natural magic and not of pneumatic art. This is substantially equivalent to saying that if its curious properties are really established fact, they are unappreciated phenomena of ordinary science and belong, like the loadstone, to the domain of magnetism. They have, however, been variously explained, for the subject has been seriously treated in large volumes and has originated a literature of its own; sometimes the mystery was solved by help of a "corpuscular hypothesis" and sometimes by that of sub-surface electricity. But the agency of the devil was of course the grand explanation, the ubiquitous court of infernus being the supreme fact of the age.

The divining rod was and is a forked branch of the wild hazel, the beech, or the apple-tree. It answers best if it be a shoot of one year's growth, and, on the whole, it is safer, to minimise variations in results under conditions that appear to be identical, to cut the rod with some solemnity. The directions which are given in the "Great Grimoire" and in the "Red Dragon" are similar to those which have been detailed for the *verendum* of black magic. The wild hazel is recommended, the branch to be seized in the left hand and severed with three blows of a knife held in the opposite hand. This must be performed at the moment of sunrise, and the following recitation should be made :—" I gather thee in the name of Eloim, Mutrathon, Adonay, and Semiphoras, that by their power thou mayest possess the virtues of the rod of Moses and Jacob for the discovery of all that I desire to know." The experiments should be invariably accompanied by a short aspiration, the rod being held lightly in both hands by the two ends which form the fork :— " I command thee in the name of Eloim, Mutrathon, Adonay, and Semiphoras to make known to me "—here name the special object of your experiment.

As a rule, the rod is made use of independently of magical ceremonies, independently of prayers or formulæ, as a natural curiosity which produces singular practical results. In this case, the power of turning it is a gift which, like mediumship, belongs to exceptional persons, and to those, it would seem, alone. The operation is simple in the extreme ; it consists in holding in each hand one of the upper ends of the rod and walking leisurely over the ground. When you approach the object of your quest, the rod turns of itself in the hand, and the indication is held to be infallible.

The instrument, as will be seen later on, was originally used for the purposes of direct divination, for obtaining an omen or pressage, for discovering a thief, or unearthing a buried treasure. In Europe, and especially in England, these applications of its powers became exploded upon the discovery that numerous as they may have been in a number of directions, not even excepting alchemy, the divining rod had a wider range of sympathy with the old world element of water than with any other material substance, or with any human delinquent, whether robber or witch, and henceforth it was generally utilised for the indication of subterranean springs. The testimony already referred to has reference exclusively to this aspect of its occult virtues.

The discovery in question is ascribed to Jacques Aymar, who obtained notoriety at Lyons in 1672, by the performance of a variety of wonders which included the detection of assassins, of sorcery, of thieves, of wells underground, and of obliterated boundaries. It is curious to read in a book of the seventeenth century that the sensitive who was master of the rod was invariably subject to the same species of facial contortions, of violent nervous quivering, and of pulse elevated to fever point, which are characteristic of thought-readers and mediums at the present day. It is noticeable also, murders being common in those days of comparative violence, that whenever the psychological bloodhound was conducted by his rod or otherwise to the scene of a murder, he always experienced a painful sensation of the heart, accompanied by oppression and occasionally by sickness.

Previously to the celebrity of Aymar, this instrument of divination, as apart from its use in the practice of magical evocation, was devoid of any special celebrity. His prodigies brought him to the notice of the Prince de Condé, but his operations when he was under the patronage of this nobleman at Paris were of an equivocal kind, and he is alleged to have acknowledged that he was an impostor, that the rod had no potency of its own, and that he had recourse to the device of divining for the reasons which most commonly influence the needy rogue in his exploits of trickery. These exceedingly likely admissions notwithstanding, the fame of the divining rod increased, and its professors multiplied. Boys and women became proficient in this by way of detective skill. Books which were ponderous in its praise and were fortified into folios by big bundles of true and circumstantial relations; books in exposure of the shallow and charlatanic pretence; books that explained it by purely natural considerations; books that insisted on its miraculous character; books that ascribed it to the devil —an entire literature arose. An avocation which had originated in folk-lore became fashionable for a moment, for a century, and it returned whence it came, to the peasantry who have created folk-lore, and among whom it has been real and has lived.

The divining rod, on an impartial survey of its history, would appear to have been used, as was naturally most probable, in both good and bad faith, and in each case indifferently much the same results were obtained, for trickery is rigorously imitative, and in the production of bogus effects is seldom designed to surpass the original and genuine model. Apart altogether from mysticism, independently of magic and mediumship, the divining rod is capable of explanation by facts in animal magnetism which are now generally admitted. Psychometry, which is a part of clairvoyance as clairvoyance is a higher part of mesmerism, has many authenticated results, and offers some analogies with the wonders of the filbert wand. What the disc is to the eye in hypnotism, the rod was to the hand in rhabdomancy. The mineral applied to the forehead of the sensitive awakes an instinct, or an inner sense of sight, or some other potential faculty, into transient life, and the subject sees—sees, it is averred, the past history of the object almost from the dawn of evolution. Now, there is a correspondence, it would seem, between the eye of sense and the eye of mind, but the activity of the mind's eye can be sometimes developed by sensations from the sense of touch, and the discoveries accredited to the divining rod are often a form of clairvoyance in which the operator at the right moment sees what he is required to discover, the instrument being merely a pretext for the development of interior vision, acting much after the manner of the crystal where the eye is concerned, and producing some hypnotic or abnormal condition. Though one quality of wood may be said to be better than another, the rod itself can possess no occult virtue. The effect, whatever it may be, acts possibly through the rod, but it is the individual who is affected, as is evident from his nervous excitement.

Experiments with the divining wand have undoubtedly an element of interest and in one sense a practical utility, but they belong to the curiosities of the secret sciences, and have no value from the standpoint of true mysticism. An earnest inquirer, who, in the language of mystical allegory, is in search of Diana Unveiled and of the Way of the Light should abstain from the trivialities of the practice; he is seeking his soul; let him surrender the quest after little marvels to the wonder-stricken

weaklings who follow in the train of the mystics, and
are content with milk for babes.

The element of interest to which we have just referred,
as distinguished, for the moment, from its practical
utility, is the fact that the search after water is still
pursued after this old method of magic. It is one of the
few survivals of the antiquated faith in the sympathy
and antipathy of things, and though the citation of cases
is, generally speaking, beyond the scope of the present
work, the two following testimonies to the persistence
and the success of this divinatory method in the dawn of
the twentieth century will show that in even the byways
of mystic art there is occasionally a real and recoverable
power and truth. The accounts in each case are drawn
from the newspapers which commemorated the occurrence within a short period of its date.

"The question as to the magical or the 'scientific'
value of the 'divining rod,'" says the *Manchester
Examiner* of February 17, 1886, "has just been re-
opened by the success which has attended its use at the
Flelton Wagon Works of the Midland Railway Company in reference to the discovery of a permanent supply
of water. The required diurnal volume of water was
about five hundred or six hundred gallons, and the well
on the premises only yielded half that quantity. It was
necessary, therefore, to supplement the supply either by
the sinking of other wells or by the construction of an
expensive system of piping from Peterburgh. The
former plan was preferred, and two new wells were sunk
to no purpose. The services of a gentleman of the district, who bore the reputation of being skilled in the art
of discovering water by means of the 'divining rod,'
were then called in. This wizard or expert employed
for his purpose a forked hazel twig, holding one prong
of the fork in each hand, the point being directed to
the sky. After walking about the premises for some
time, the point of the fork suddenly began to bend down,
purely, as the best evidence goes, of its own accord, and
to turn towards the earth. The wielder of the wand
declared that in the spot indicated there would be found
a plentiful supply of water. The same phenomenon was

repeated at another spot, where the twig snapped from the violence of its spontaneous and sympathetic motion, and the same confident assertions were made with reference to the presence of water—assertions which the results obtained, by actually sinking wells, amply justified, the quantity of water to be obtained being apparently inexhaustible. Other persons essayed to use the wand, but it rebelled against the usurpation of its owner's functions, and remained contumacious and irresponsive."

In the same year a correspondent of *Farm and Home* gave the following account of experiments conducted, under his direction, on one of the largest estates of Yorkshire:—

"We are obliged here to provide a supply of water for a large colliery population, and although we have made large reservoirs we are deficient in gathering ground, the coal pits having taken away the supply in most directions. The past season having been dry, my employer was advised by several other gentlemen—members of Parliament, magistrates, and others—to employ the man with the 'divining rod' to prospect the ground about the reservoirs, and if possible find a better and more permanent supply of water in order to ensure the filling of them in dry seasons, it being suggested that if the man could find water in August, after all the other wells and springs had gone nearly dry, the supply was likely to be a good one.

"With that object, 'John Mullins, Waterspring Discoverer by means of the Divining Rod, Colerne, Chippenham, Wilts,' as his card sets forth, was sent for, and arrived here about ten o'clock at night. I found him to be a plain, working mason, who has been employed most of his life on the same gentleman's estate. There was no pretence of quackery or jugglery about him in any sense. He comes for a moderate fee and his expenses, and he undertakes 'to find' water if it be in the ground; the best guarantee for his sincerity is that he contracts to sink and build the wells himself on the spot where he says the water exists.

"To make a long story short, I took him in hand

early next morning, starting him at one end of a long
walk with a fresh, hard twig, cut by myself. I asked
him to find water anywhere within the next hundred
yards. I followed behind him, he stepping steadily
forward, partly bent, with the twig held in both hands,
the twig being of a ∠ shape, with the point held down-
wards. When he got about two-thirds of the way, it
turned up; he made a mark on the ground, proceeded
to the end of his journey, then came back again, the
twig turning up again violently at exactly the same
spot, directly over an old buried well I had covered in
with flags and earth deeply, and made a walk over, some
fifteen years ago. We were afterwards joined by my
employer, the Vicar, our engineer, and the superintendent of our waterworks, and prospected the estate over
in one direction, Mullins finding water in several places,
but no very strong springs. We dug the day after at
some of the places, and found water; and when he left,
the only water running into the reservoir was from a
spring he found not far from it. In one place a pit
about ten feet deep was hollowed out, breaking through
a rocky pan, and the water rose about eight feet in the
hole during the night.

"The best proof of the man's gifts, however, was the
fact that he set out correctly every running drain or
pipe under the ground that he was put to, by simply
going over the surface with his twig by himself. The
Vicar, an avowed sceptic, took the man into his flower
garden, the rest of the party remaining outside, and
asked him to make two or three casts with his twig
across his lawn and through his shrubs, which he did,
pegging the water out as he proceeded; and it was afterwards found that he had set a main running drain out
correctly from the first peg to the last, the whereabouts
of which no one knew but the Vicar himself, and of
which there were no signs whatever above ground. The
Vicar turned to the man and said, 'I give in; you have
beaten me.' I was myself as disbelieving as any one,
but interested and open to conviction. I had much conversation with the man afterwards, during the two days
he was here, and was greatly amused by some of his

tales about certain clever and scientific sceptics he had
met with. . . . I have given a plain statement of facts,
and offer no opinion on the subject. The man was
tested when here, and in the fairest manner, he being
perfectly willing to satisfy us as far as he possibly could.
On several occasions the Vicar held one end of the
forked twig, and I the other end, the man's hands holding each limb firmly between our hands and the bottom
of the ⌄. We took care that the ends of the two limbs
did not move; but the point of the ⌄ twisted up irre-
sistibly till the bark wrinkled and creaked, and sometimes till it broke. The movement of the twig is rapid;
it hangs down till it comes over water, when it whirls
round like lightning."

It should be added to these narratives that modern
Spiritualism has discovered a new application of the
Divining Rod, which is made use of as a means of communication on the part of the invisible intelligence. It
is placed in the hands of the medium, or of a sitter at a
séance, and is held over the letters of the alphabet
arranged in a circle or line. After preliminary sway-
ings, it is said to indicate a variety of letters with considerable rapidity, leaping from point to point, and by
this simple process the wisdom of the World Beyond is
conveyed to the interrogators of the wand in intelligible
words and sentences.

While in magic the rod was used chiefly either for the
control of visible spirits worked by the power of certain
words and ceremonies which formulated the will of the
magician, or else for the discovery of hidden springs of
water, it should not be forgotten that it was used for the
purposes of direct divination. So far back as the time
of Hosea, we know that the people sought counsel of
their stocks, and that their staves declared unto them.
In the days of Grecian augury it was the custom to
erect two staves, over which mystic verses and incantations were pronounced in an undertone, till the staves,
influenced by the *daimons*, were suddenly cast to the
ground. The direction of the fall regulated the nature
of the augury. The rods of the Hebrews were peeled
on one side, and an omen was drawn from the manner

in which they fell. In the days of the witch fever it was devoted to a more serious, and, at the same time, more abhorrent purpose. It had long been made use of in the discovery of fugitive thieves ; it was supposed to have virtues for the detection of secret spell-makers and casters of the evil eye ; then it developed a more unerring and awful power, for it was affirmed that the V-shaped rod obtained from a shrub now called the witch-hazel, would infallibly turn in the direction in which a witch was to be found. Believing in the truth of the adage that a thief should be set to catch a thief if you wish to track him, they made use of what the ignorance of the time would have denominated witchcraft to expose the witches. On being led into the presence of a company of women, the professional witch-hunter would balance his rod, and the direction in which its forked portion might chance to turn, or might be secretly made to turn, indicated the guilty person, who was persecuted, or who perished accordingly.

The actual nature of the connection between the rod and the water which it indicates has not been made clear by the numerous writers who have devoted their attention to the subject, and have given us the result of their researches. Whether it is impossible to utilise it for the discovery of precious stones and precious metals has not been discussed by theorists, nor has it been attempted in experiment. But though the mystic rod may be influenced by nothing that is denser than water, though the attention of the alchemists was concentrated on the creation of gold and silver in a manner so completely exclusive that they had no leisure to elaborate a process for their discovery in the natural form in mines, the byways of magical art have not deserted the needy seeker. This notice may be fitly concluded by putting him in possession of an exceedingly curious method for the detection of concealed treasures, which is so far connected with the subject now under notice, that it involves the use of a vervain rod, or branch.

" When by natural indications, or by those which are considered supernatural, as, for instance, by a revelation made in a dream, you have reason to believe that a treasure has been deposited in a certain place, you must begin your operations by burning over it the perfume proper to the day on which you have determined to dig. Next, you must plant with your right hand a branch of green laurel, and with your left a branch of vervain, and between these two branches you must begin turning the soil. When the foss has attained the level of your own stature, the branches must be twined into a chaplet and placed around your hat, with a talisman above it which must be composed of a circular plate of refined pewter, made in the day and hour of Jupiter, during a propitious celestial aspect." On the obverse side must be engraven the figure of a Fortuna poised with one foot upon a small sphere and moving with both hands above her head a long veil which conceals with its floating drapery the central portion of her otherwise unclothed form. Out of a cloud at her left an arm is thrust which bears in its hand a heart, and has the following inscription about it—

relactanti
Eriam ferana—

words to which we are unable to ascribe any certain significance or origin, but they may belong to the unknown tongue. On the reverse side two portentous expressions must be written in characters whose size shall be indicative of their importance,

OMOUSIN ALBOMATATOS.

If several persons should assist in the operation of delving, each must be in possession of this talisman, and must wear the garland that has been described. Should the work occupy more than a day, the perfume proper to each day must be invariably burned. These precautions are required to avert the malice of the Gnomes, who are the guardians of treasures, and well qualified to give assistance in your enterprises.

Paracelsus remarks in his "Treatise on Occult Philosophy," that in order to obtain reliable indications of hidden wealth and treasure, careful attention should be bestowed on those places where spectres and phantoms are addicted to appearing in the still hours of the night; particularly on Fridays and Saturdays. " Where wandering fires are visible, where tumults and strange brawling are heard, or any kindred manifestations, it may be reasonably conjectured that in such places there is a concealed treasure.

"But a prudent man will not rest satisfied at this point; he will take precautions to prevent being deceived by the reports of strangers, by the deceptions of mendicants, and by the chimeric visions in which weak and silly women engage many serious persons. The search should be undertaken on the evidence of trustworthy persons alone, and the operator will do well to conduct it without assistance, and to make his abode for the time in the immediate neighbourhood of the place.

" Those who would devote themselves to search after a treasure supposed to be concealed in a certain place, should examine the nature of the place, comparing its present situation with the accounts which may be discoverable concerning it in old histories. Now, there are two kinds of hidden treasures. The first is the gold and silver which is found in the penetralia of the earth by the virtue of the stars in combination with particular qualities resident in the ground itself. The second is gold or silver which has been coined into money, or wrought by the art of the goldsmith, and has been afterwards buried to preserve it in times of war or pestilence, or for any reason whatsoever. This second species of treasure is most commonly met with among the debris of mansions and castles, and in the vicinity of old churches and chapels; it is perfectly unheeded by the Gnomes, unless those who have buried it invoked their protection by means of perfumes and talismans adapted to the purpose.

" The magical search after hidden treasures should not be undertaken by persons who are subject to fear, for, to fascinate the imagination of the seeker, it is a common device on the part of the earth spirits to evoke hideous visions and appearances. If subterranean noises should increase as the work advances, repeat the perfumes, and recite in a loud voice the mystic prayer of the Salamanders, which will prevent the spirits from decamping, treasure and all, as their attention will be concentrated on the mysterious words. Their abstraction will be a good opportunity for redoubling your own efforts.

"It has occasionally happened that the Gnomes have transmitted the precious metals into filthy or worthless substances, and thus have deceived those who were unacquainted with their trickeries. But the sage and prudent delver when he finds in the bowels of the earth some matters which are foreign to the place, and could not have come there in any natural manner, will carefully collect them, and will subject them to the test of a fire of laurel wood, fern, and vervain ; the charm will be broken by this means, and the metals will revert to their original nature. One of the most common indications of these fantastic changes is the apparent deposition of vile and sordid substances in vessels of baked clay, hewn stone, or brass—substances which cannot, it would seem, be subjected to the trickeries of Gnomide transmutation."

The testimony to the virtue of the Divining Rod is scattered through many works which are but partially devoted to the subject, and much information will be found up and down the mazes of periodical literature, treasuries of folk-lore, etc. For all ordinary purposes, it will be sufficient to consult " Jacob's Rod," a curious work on the art of finding springs, mines, and minerals by means of the hazel rod. It is a translation, by Thomas Welton, of a rare French book published in 1693.

ASTROLOGY.

ONE of the most ingenious and plausible defences of the science of astrology has been made by Eliphas Lévi, in a passage sufficiently brief to admit of quotation. "Nothing is indifferent in Nature; a pebble more or less upon a road may crush or profoundly alter the fortunes of the greatest men and even of the greatest empires; much more then the position of a particular star cannot be indifferent to the destinies of the child who is being born, and who enters by the fact of his birth into the universal harmony of the sidereal world. The stars are bound together by attractions which balance them and cause them to perform their revolutions with regularity in space, the network of light extends from sphere to sphere, and there is no point on any planet to which one of these indestructible threads is not attached. The precise place and moment of birth should therefore be calculated by the true astrological adept; then, after an exact computation of the starry influences, it remains for him to reckon the chances of condition, that is, the opportunities or obstacles which the child must one day meet with in his state of life, in his relatives, in the disposition he inherits, and, consequently, in his natural aptitude for the fulfilment of his destinies. Human liberty and enterprise must also be taken into account, should the child come to be truly a man and to extricate himself by a bold will from blind influences and from the chain of fatality. It will be seen that we do not allow too much to astrology, but what we leave it is incontestable, it is the scientific and magical calculus of probabilities."

It may be at once admitted that there is nothing indifferent in Nature; it may be admitted that a stone upon a road may modify the destiny of any person, and, indirectly, of any people; it may also, and not less, be allowed that the aspect of the starry universe at the moment of birth, the other considerations being granted, cannot be indifferent to the child; all this is suggestive; all this is, at any rate, practically reasonable; but while the stone upon the road, in the event of its producing an effect upon the person who is passing, will produce an effect that can be calculated, the influence of the stars on a nativity is one that by ordinary methods cannot be appreciated, and is appreciated by astrology in a completely *empirical* manner, so far as can be judged from the standpoint of an outside impartiality, and it is at any rate quite certain that the *calculus of probabilities* which is described in the paragraph above is impossible to carry through, and has never been attempted by astrology.

In discussing the claims of this, the least occult of the secret sciences, which is, notwithstanding, so venerable by its antiquity, so majestic in its associations, and so sublime in its general theory and object, one would like to be as lenient as possible, and to find a way to believing what every one must wish should be true—that day unto day uttereth speech, and night unto night showeth knowledge, while it is possible to translate the magical language of the stars into intelligible prophecies of the unfulfilled. The distant music of the spheres has found an interpreter, the splendid pageantry of "worlds revolving unceasingly" assumes a new significance; through all the depths and heights of the "magical, measureless distance," we behold intelligence everywhere; the planets are prophets, the stars are seers, mind rules the universe; one dreams of Chaldean lore, of the clear sight and the patient study of the wise workers of old. Astrology, it is clear, if we have regard to the eternal fitness, ought to be a true instrument of knowledge.

But those who are mystics must remember that astrology, though it passes for a secret science, is scarcely a branch of mysticism. If it be capable of producing really genuine results, it must be considered to some extent as standing alone among the sciences called magical, because while it cannot be classified as unimportant, its best results can contribute nothing to the science of the soul. However sure in its results to him, it should be no more than a collateral study, and if he set it entirely aside, it will perhaps be the better for his success in spiritual researches.

Astrology proceeds upon methods which are said to be the result of many ages of accumulated experiment. The aspect of a certain planet at the moment of birth is supposed to have a definite effect upon the life of the "native," because it has been observed in the past that it actually has that effect, and it is thus that the science has been built up. Its assumptions are therefore of a strictly à *posteriori* kind ; it asks no faith of the student, and each person is open to test its value by experiment of his own, after which he may reasonably appraise it. It is useless therefore to condemn astrology till it has been honestly weighed and found wanting. It is impossible in an elementary handbook to provide our readers with the means of examining the truth of astrological claims. If they wish to pursue the subject, they must have recourse to the voluminous authorities which exist. They must study Placidus de Titus and Junctin de Florence, Ptolemy, Lilly, and Partridge.

The writers who, under the names of "Raphael" and "Zadkiel" issue "text books" and "guides" to the science, now divide between them what honour or profit is to be derived from the teaching of Astrology in the England of our own day. Miss Rosa Baughan has, in a recent book, made Astrology the basis of another "occult" science, viz., that of Palmistry.

Avoiding the responsibility of deciding between the rival systems of Placidus and Ptolemy of Horary and Genethliacal Astrology, we proceed to give a summarised version of the theory on which all systems of Astrology must rest.

At the moment of the birth of a child whose horoscope it is required to ascertain, or on the day of a given occurrence whose results are required to be traced, the astronomical astrolabe must be consulted to determine the constellations and planets which are then governing in heaven, so as to define the results which must follow from their virtues, qualities, and functions. If three signs of the same nature are found in the sky, as, for instance, the Ram, the Lion, and the Archer, these three form the trine aspect, because they divide the empyrean into three parts, and are separated one from the other by three other constellations. Such an aspect is good and favourable. When those who divide the sky by six meet in the hour of the operation, as the Ram with the Twins, the Bull with the Crab, the sextile aspect is formed, which is of a middle quality. When those which divide the sphere into four, as the Ram with the Crab, the Bull with the Lion, the Twins with the Virgin, meet in the hour of operation, they form the quartile aspect, which is distinctly a bad one. When those which belong to the opposite parts of the sky, as the Ram with the Balance, the Bull with the Scorpion, the Twins and the Archer, &c., are found similarly placed, the contrary aspect is formed, which is wicked and malevolent. The others are in conjunction when two planets are united in the same sign and in the same house; they are in opposition when they are situated at two opposite points.

Each sign of the Zodiac occupies a place which is called the Celestial House or the House of the Sun, and the twelve houses consequently divide the Zodiac into twelve parts; each house occupies thirty degrees, and each was represented by the astrologers of old by numerical symbols within a square or circular figure twelve times divided.

The first house is that of Aries, which is called the Orient Angle in the language of star-gazers. This is the house of life, because those who are born under its dominion enjoy considerable length of years. The second house is that of Taurus, which is called the Inferior Gate. It is the house of wealth, and of the way to fortune. The third house is that of Gemini, and it is called the Abode of the Brethren. It is the house of inheritance and of solid patrimony. The fourth house is that of Cancer, which is called the Foundation of Heaven, the Earth's Angle, and the Abode of Parents. It is the house of treasure, and of the emoluments of patrimony. The fifth house is that of Leo, and it is the abode of children; it is that also of legacies and donations. The sixth house is the house of Virgo; it is called the Love of Mars; it is the house of sadness, disease, and reverses. The seventh is that of Libra, which is called the Western Angle; it is the house of marriage and bridals. The eighth house is that of Scorpio, which is called the Superior Door; it is the abode of terror, alarms, and death. The ninth house is that of Sagittarius; it is called the Love of the Sun; and piety, religion, travels, and philosophy are contained therein. The tenth house is that of Capricornus, which is called the Centre of Heaven, and crowns, dignities, and responsible offices are referred to it. The eleventh house is identified with Aquarius, which is called the Love of Jove; it is the house of friends, benefactions, and fortune. The twelfth house is that of Pisces, which is called the Love of Saturn. It is the most baleful and fatal of all; it is the house of poisonings, of wretchedness, of envy, of evil temper, and of violent death.

The Ram and the Scorpion are the houses affected by Mars; the Bull and the Balance are referred to Venus; the Twins and the Virgin to Mercury; the Archer and Fishes to Jupiter; the Goat and Water-bearer to Saturn; the Lion to the Sun; and the Crab to the Moon.

The position of the planets in respect of the constellations must be carefully marked, and as the rapid revolution of the earth causes changes every moment in the disposition of the stars, so the actual instant of nativity should be ascertained from the midwife, if an accurate horoscope is to be insured. When Mars is in agreement with Aries at the moment of birth, it gives longevity, courage and pride; if it be in agreement with Taurus, riches and courage result. Broadly, the influence of Mars augments that of the constellation with which it agrees, adding strength and value. Saturn, who inflicts penalties, miseries, and disease, augments the evil and stultifies the good influences; Venus, on the contrary, increases those which are good while it weakens the power of those which are evil. Mercury augments or enfeebles influences according to the nature of its conjunctions. In agreement with Pisces, its good effect is diminished; with Capricornus it is extended. The

Moon adds melancholy to fortunate constellations, and sadness or insanity to others. Jupiter, giving honours and riches, increases all favourable influences and almost destroys bad ones. The Sun in the ascendant gives the favour of princes, and its effect upon influences is akin to that of Jupiter; in the descendant it foreshadows reverses. Gemini, Libra, and Virgo give beauty in a superlative degree; Scorpio, Capricornus, and Pisces give beauty in a middle degree; the others more or less of ugliness. Virgo, Libra, Aquarius, and Gemini endow the native with a pleasant and melodious voice; Cancer, Scorpio, and Pisces give one that is ordinary or disagreeable, while the others are devoid of influence in this respect. If the planets and constellations are found in the East at the time of the horoscope, their influence will be experienced at the opening of the life or the enterprise; if they are seen in the zenith the effect will be postponed till the middle, and till the latter end if they appear in the West.

These general notions may be supplemented by an account of the properties of the seven planets, compiled by Elihu Rich, from a number of ancient authorities. Saturn is cold and dry, melancholy, earthy, malevolent, solitary, and when "ill-governed" produces the most malignant qualities; the Buddhists represent him as crowned, and of a black colour. Astrologers consider him as the "greater infortune." Jupiter, the "greater fortune," is the author of temperance, modesty, sobriety, and justice; he rules the lungs and blood, and the last month in gestation; he is represented of a golden colour, riding upon a lion. The colours under him are sea-green, blue, and purple. Mars, the "lesser infortune," is choleric and fierce, author of quarrels, dissensions, strife, war, and battle; his colours are red and white; he is depicted riding on a peacock, with a crown on his head; fierce animals, blood-coloured stones, &c., are under his influence, and he is the cause of all fevers. The Moon is feminine, neither fortunate nor unfortunate in herself, but having an influence in accordance with the aspect of other planets; her metal is silver; her colours white, pale green, and pale yellow; when well dignified she gives a timorous, imaginative, engaging disposition, and a fondness for change and travelling. She is represented crowned, and riding on an elephant. Venus, the "smaller fortune" is the author of mirth and conviviality, the queen of pleasure and the mistress of refinement; her colours are white and light blue; the Buddhists depict her crowned, riding upon a bull; when ill-governed, she disposes to lewdness and profligacy. Mercury is the author of the most pointed wit, ingenuity, and invention; when well dignified he produces a subtle imagination and retentive memory; otherwise his tendency is to all kinds of charlatany, empty boasting, and tale bearing. His metal is quicksilver, his angel is Raphael, and his colours are black and azure. He rides on a buffalo and is painted dark blue. He is masculine or feminine according to his conjunction with other planets. The Sun, if well dignified, is always equal to one of the fortunes; in some respects, his influence is equal to that of Jupiter, but magnanimity is his predominant characteristic. The diamond, the ruby, the carbuncle, pure gold, and all yellow metals are under him; he is represented riding on a horse.

In addition to the direct influence which is exercised by the celestial universe on the destinies and dispositions of men, there is an influence of an indirect nature on life and fortune through the control which is assigned to the planets and the stars of the twelve constellations over the several members of the human body. The head, which is the seat of intelligence, is assigned to the providence of the sun, which is the root and source of the influences diffused from the entire planetary system; the Moon governs the right arm; Venus has dominion over the left; Jupiter presides over the stomach; the energies of the sexual organs are directed by the powerful spirit of the ruddy-coloured Mars; Mercury dominates the right foot, which is said to be the seat of speed; the left is assigned to Saturn. In the astrology of the twelve constellations, Aries governs the head, Taurus the neck, Gemini the arms and shoulders, Cancer the heart and breast, Leo the stomach, Virgo the womb, Libra the

loins and back ; Scorpio the generative members, Sagittarius the thighs, Capricornus the knees, Aquarius the
legs, Pisces the feet.

The pneumatic hypotheses of angelology have assigned
to the ministers of Heaven the government of empires
and cities, but the science of the stars has discovered
that the responsibility of the spiritual hierarchs is shared
by the great constellations, and it has been decided by
German adepts in the mysteries of celestial influences that
Frankfort is ruled by the Ram, Wurtzburg by the Bull,
Nuremberg by the Twins, which should therefore be the
sign of the Rosicrucian Fraternity ; Magdeburg by the
Crab, Ulm by the Lion, Heidelberg by the Virgin,
Vienna by the Balance (which to-day has a certain pro-
priety as it is there that the peace of Europe is held
in an oscillating equipoise) ; Munich by the Scorpion,
Stutgart by the Archer, Augsburg by the Goat, Ingol-
stadt by the Water-bearer, and Ratisbonne by the Fishes.

An authority more venerable than German astrologers,
the mythical messenger, Hermes, has placed the seven
openings in the head of humanity under the special
directions of the seven planets, and has referred Saturn
and Jupiter to the ears, Mars and Venus to the nostrils,
the Sun and Moon to the eyes, and Mercury to the
mouth. Leon the Israelite, in his Kabbalistic "Philosophy of Love," explains that the sun and moon are
appropriately referred to the eyes, as those luminaries
are the eyes of the superior world ; while Mercury, the
messenger, the revealer, the veritable Hermes, the Lord
of the Logos, has a natural providence over speech.

The enumeration is by no means exhausted. Saturn
has power over life, over changes, buildings, and the
circle of the sciences ; Jupiter over honour, ambition,
wealth, and cleanly habits ; Mars over war, prisons,
marriages, and animosities ; the Sun over hopes, happiness, emolument, inheritances ; Venus, over friendship
and love ; Mercury over diseases, losses, debts, commerce,
and the fountains of fear which exist in the soul of man ;
the Moon over sores and wounds, over dreams and
thefts. Such is the division laid down in Albertus
Magnus, to wit, in the "Admirable Secrets" which,

though their antiquity is great in their original black-letter form, are undoubtedly falsely ascribed.

The planets have also a presidence over the seven days of the week, a fact which is too commonly known to need more than a passing reference; but as the emblems which astrology has ascribed to the planets with which it was acquainted are continually recurring in Hermetic science, and especially in physical alchemy, it will be as well to reproduce them here for the benefit of initial inquirers.

Saturn,	♄	Venus,	♀	Quartile,	□
Jupiter,	♃	Mercury,	☿	Trine,	△
Mars,	♂	Sun,	☉	Opposition,	♊
Moon,	☽	Sextile,	✳	Conjunction,	♂

There is a simplified form of astrology which, like most simplifications in occultism, is vague and unsatisfying in its results. This is the method of foretelling the destiny of an individual from the position of the constellations at his birth. It considerably limits the varieties of human disposition and reduces the scope of fortune within exceedingly narrow bounds. Astrological computations have the interest of curiosity alone, and well-balanced minds will be indisposed to review the observations which follow in anything but an antiquarian light.

The Signs in the Heavens, and the Prophetic Significance Involved in them.

1. THE RAM.—The power or influence of Aries is hot and dry. It rules in the heaven from the 21st of March to the 23rd of April. Those who are born under its influence are irascible, prompt, lively, eloquent, inclined to study, but violent, untruthful, and inconstant. They are seldom faithful to their word and quickly forget their promises. The native receives from the constellation a dry, lean, and spare body; he is strong and large-boned, has piercing eyes, sandy or red hair, and a swarthy complexion. His chief dangers will be from horses, and he will be fond of fishing and hunting.

The woman who is born under Aries will be vivacious, inquisitive, and pretty. She will be fond of gossip, will have a proclivity to falsehood, and a taste for good cheer. She will be subject to fits of passion, and in old age will be slanderous and a severe critic of her own sex. She will marry soon, and will be the mother of many children. The presence of Jupiter or Venus in this sign at the hour of birth will impart to it a better influence; Saturn or Mars will intensify its malignant qualities. Aries rules the head and face, produces small-pox, epilepsy, apoplexy, headaches, hypochondriasis, baldness, ringworm, &c. The colour which corresponds to it is white mingled with red.

2. THE BULL.—The influence of Taurus predominates from the 22nd of April to the 21st of May. It is cold, dry, earthy, melancholy, feminine; it imparts to the native a broad brow, thick lips, a rather brutal and melancholy temperament, slow to anger, but violent and difficult to be appeased when once enraged. From these observations it is plain that it imparts also the lower class of courage as well as the physical strength. The person born under its influence will make enemies but will be able to prevent them from injuring him. He will enjoy a certain kind of happiness, and will travel into far countries; his life will be long and he will be subject to few diseases.

The woman who is born under this constellation is endowed with strength and courage. She will have great energy but will be violent and easily carried away. At the same time, she will be able to bend to her duty, and will prove an obedient wife. Much judgment and much good sense will characterise her, but she will be somewhat over-talkative. She will be more than once a widow; she will bear children, to whom she will leave fortunes. The colour corresponding to Taurus is white mixed with citron.

3. THE TWINS.—The power or influence of Gemini is hot and moist, like a fat, rich soil. The native will be fair and tall, of straight body and sanguine complexion, rather dark than clear. The arms will be long, the hands frequently short and fleshy, the hair and eyes generally a dark hazel, the looks wanton, the under-standing skilful in business. This constellation is rich in

the gifts of friendship; those who are born under its influence will be strong of heart, elegant in figure, full of spirit, prudence, and generosity. Its fortunate influence prevails from the 22nd of May to the 21st of June. The native, it may be added, will be confident, fond of the chase and of travelling, with more of the spirit of adventure than of fortune-seeking, but, as commonly happens with the indifferent, he will never be actually poor. He will be animated, subtle, and pleasure-loving, and will have some taste for the arts.

The woman who is born under Gemini will be affectionate and beautiful, with a gentle and simple heart, but somewhat neglectful of domestic duties. The fine arts, more especially music and drawing, will exercise great fascination over her mind.

The diseases which belong to the sign are those of the arms, shoulders, and hands, also frenzies, fevers, blood poisoning, disorders of the brain, and insanity. The colour corresponding to Gemini is white mixed with red. The constellation governs from the 22nd of May to the 21st of June.

4. THE CRAB.—This sign foments squabbles; it is cold and moist, like a marshy and moorish land. It rules in heaven from the 22nd of June to the 21st of July. The native who is born under its influence is fair and pale, of an undersized and small stature, the upper part of the body being large in proportion to the lower, the face round, the hair brown, the eyes grey; the disposition will be phlegmatic and heavy, the constitution effeminate, the voice weak. Men under its influence will be sensual; their life will be chequered with lawsuits and quarrels, from which, however, they may often emerge successfully. Their chief perils will be on the sea. Moreover, this horoscope commonly gives a tendency to gluttony, though occasionally prudence, wit, and a spice of modesty.

Women who are born under this constellation will be inclined to have many children; they will be very fairly good looking, active, hasty, but soon appeased. They will have no tendency to excessive corpulence. They will find pleasure in helping others, but will be timid and a little deceitful.

All diseases of the breast and stomach are peculiar to this sign, as also indigestion, cancer, consumption, asthma, &c. The colour which is in harmony with it is green or russet.

5. THE LION.—The dominion of Leo endures from the 22nd of July to the 21st of August. It is fiery, hot, dry, masculine, choleric, barren, but commanding. It gives to the native a large masculine body, with broad shoulders, an austere countenance, hair inclining to yellow, eyes piercing, looks sprightly, voice strong, and countenance of a ruddy or sanguine oval. The character which it will impart is courageous and resolute, brave, audacious, magnanimous, proud, eloquent, and self-sufficient, the mind aspiring, the heart generous, the disposition open and courteous. Such a person will love banter, will be frequently surrounded by danger, but his children will be his consolation and happiness. He will be continually abandoning himself to passion, and will as continually repent his excesses. Honours and dignities will be showered on him, but, in the first instance, he will long have sought them.

The woman who is born under this constellation will be vivacious, hasty, and brazen. She will nurse ill-feeling; she will talk much, and her speech will be frequently bitter. For the rest, she will be good-looking, though with a large head. She must beware of boiling water and of fire. She will be subject to pains in the stomach, and will have few children. This constellation produces all the passions and affections of the heart, as also convulsions, violent fevers, plagues, and pains in the back. The colour is red or green.

6. THE VIRGIN.—This sign of the celestial sphere governs from the 22nd of August to the 21st of September. It is earthy, cold, dry, barren, and feminine; the native related thereto has a well-composed, slender body, rather above the middle stature; his complexion is brown, his hair lank, his voice thin and shrill; he is also witty and studious, generous, sincere, intelligent, fond of distinction, but he will be unable to keep either his own

secrets or those that may be confided in him; he will be proud, elegant in language and carriage, a profitable friend, and compassionate towards others in their distresses.

The woman who is born under the dominion of this constellation will be chaste, honest, retiring, full of intelligence and foresight; she will love both to do and to speak good; she will have becoming pride, but she will ever be willing to serve others. Her anger will be neither dangerous nor long continued.

Diseases of the intestines are referred to the sign of the Virgin. Black speckled with blue are the colours which correspond to its influence.

7. The BALANCE rules in the celestial sphere from the 22nd of September to the 21st of October. The sign is volatile in character; it is sanguine, hot, moist, and masculine. Men who are born under this sign have a tall and well-proportioned body, a handsome countenance, a complexion which in youth is ruddy, and in age florid and pimply; the eyes are grey, the hair yellow or flaxen. According to one account, for accounts differ, the disposition is friendly and courteous, the character distinguished for rectitude; according to another it is commonly quarrelsome and pleasure-loving. Success may be chiefly expected in maritime enterprise, though it is attainable in any species of commerce; the native, in either case, is certain to undertake long voyages. His manners will be easy, his speech fluent, his promises faithless; his good fortune will be greater than his prudence, and he will be the heir of many. He will love his first wife, and will not have many children. His chief dangers are from the malice of the incendiary and from boiling water.

The woman who enters life under the auspices of this constellation will be amiable, cheerful, agreeable, sprightly, and sufficiently fortunate. Her manners will be good, her speech persuasive, her disposition susceptible and quarrelsome. She will be married either at seventeen or at twenty-three, and must beware of the same dangers as the male native.

The Balance is responsible for certain diseases of the

abdominal viscera. Black, swarthy, or dark crimson are the colours which are in sympathy with its influence.

8. The SCORPION is feminine, phlegmatic, and cold. It governs in heaven from the 22nd of October to the 21st of November. Those who are born under its influence will be robust and corpulent, of middle stature, broad visage, with brown complexion and black curly hair, the neck will be short, the legs thick, the body hairy. The authorities differ about the disposition. By some it is defined as simply reserved and thoughtful; others depict it at greater length, and with contrary qualities. According to them it will be impudent, brazen, fawning, crafty, concealing malice under an amiable exterior. The native will speak one thing and think another, and will be generally underhand and prone to dissimulation. He will be naturally changeable, will judge evilly of others, will nourish ill feeling, will be talkative, but subject to fits of despondency. When he laughs, it will be chiefly at the expense of others, yet he will have some friends and will prevail over his enemies. He may expect substantial legacies. Among indispositions, he will be chiefly subject to the disorders of the stomach.

The woman who is born under the influence of this constellation will be deceptive and subtle; she will behave better to her second than to her first husband; her words will be milder than her feelings; she will be sensuous, vivacious, a great laugher, though also at the expense of others. She will be inconsequential in act, loquacious in speech, and evil in her thoughts towards all.

The diseases which are ascribed to the constellation are similar to those of the last, but include scurvy. The colour which is in correspondence is dark brown.

9. The ARCHER is a fiery, dry, masculine sign. It can endow the person who comes into the world under its auspices with a well-formed body, a little exceeding the medium height, with a somewhat long but withal comely countenance, with chestnut hair, which, however, will be inclined to baldness, a ruddy complexion, and an active, intrepid, and careless habit. The influence of

the sign will make him a good sportsman and one fond of equestrian exercises. The predominance of Sagittarius extends from the 22nd of November to the 21st of December.

The constitution of the native will be robust, and his mind studious; he will have a passion for sea voyages, which will be the means of his advancement. He will make friends, but will squander their money, yet, on the whole, he will be just, secret, faithful, hard-working, companionable, while his high spirit will be equal to his self-love.

The woman who is born under the influence of this constellation will have a restless, active mind, and will be fond of work; her soul will be easily open to the influence of pity; she will have a taste for travelling, and will never stay long in one place. She will be rash, but at the same time endowed with several advantageous qualities alike of mind and heart. She will be married either at nineteen or at twenty-four years old, and will be a good mother.

The diseases which are caused by the Archer are sciatica, gout, rheumatism, sores, disorders consequent on intemperance, and on falls from horses. The colour which is in correspondence is yellow or sanguine green.

10. The power of the GOAT extends from the 22nd of December to the 21st of January. Its nature is earthy, cold, dry, melancholy, and feminine. The person who is born under its influence will be slender in build, and of dry constitution, with a thin visage, a scanty beard, dark hair, narrow chest and small chin. Opposite accounts of his disposition are given by different commentators on the fortuities of simplified astrology. By some it is described as collected, witty and subtle, talented and upright. By others he is endowed with an irascible, trivial, and suspicious character; he is said to be addicted to quarrels and litigation; he will be fond of work, but also of bad company, and will be made ill by his excesses. Nothing can be conceived more inconstant than the nature of this man if his birth takes place in the night. He will be cheerful, active, and sometimes will do good. The

M

influence of his star will ensure him good fortune on the sea. He will be temperate in speech, will have a small head, and sunken eyes. He will become wealthy and avaricious during the latter part of his life. It will be well for him to recollect that in all his diseases he will derive much benefit from the bath.

The woman who enters life under the auspices of the GOAT will be vivacious, volatile, but at the same time so timid in her youth that she will blush at the smallest trifle. As she advances in age, her character will, however, develop sufficient firmness and courage. While endeavouring to conceal it she will expose the jealousy that will rule her. She will speak much and will act inconsequently; she will love travelling, and will not be remarkable for beauty.

The diseases which are chargeable on this constellation are those which are caused by melancholy, hysteria, sprains, and leprosy. The colours which are in correspondence with the sign are black or russet.

11. The WATER-BEARER.—This sign is aerial, hot, moist, rational, humane, sanguine, and masculine. It endows the native with a well set, thick, robust body, a long visage, a pale and delicate countenance, a clean and sanguine complexion, and bright sandy or dark flaxen hair. The man who is born under the influence of this constellation will be amiable, intelligent, cheerful, curious, quick at scheming, boastful, and volatile, though not by any means wanting in discretion. He will covet honours and distinction, will be long-lived, being poor during the first part of his life and afterwards moderately well off. He will run many dangers, will contract several diseases, and will be especially subject to fever. His children will be few in number.

The woman who is born during the dominion of the Water-Bearer will be constant, generous, sincere, and liberal. She will be a prey to sadness, will have struggles with adversity, and will undertake long voyages.

The diseases which are ascribed to the influence of this sign are affections of the legs and ankles, dislocations, gout, and putrefaction of the blood. The colours in correspondence are azure or light blue. Its dominion extends from the 22nd of January to the 21st of February.

12. The FISHES.—This sign is watery, cold, moist, idle, effeminate, sickly, phlegmatic, and fruitful. It rules from the 22nd of February to the same date in March, and it endows the native with a short stature, a pale complexion, a fleshy and ill-shaped body, light hair and eyes, thick shoulders, a large face, and an awkward carriage of the head.

The man who is born under its influence will be officious, lively, a lover of sport, of a good temper, and outside his own house he will be fortunate. In his youth he will not be rich, and when he has got into easier circumstances, he will take little care of his fortune, and will fail to profit by the lessons of experience. He will be also presumptuous, and will be caused some trouble by indiscretions in his speech.

The woman who is born under the rule of the Fishes will be good in looks, but her youth will be full of troubles and weariness. She will love doing good, will be sensible, discreet, economical, judicious, and will avoid the world. Her health will be feeble up to the age of twenty-eight, then it will become fairly robust, though she will occasionally suffer from colic.

The sign of the Fishes governs the feet and toes, and produces all the pains which are incidental to those extremities, as also ulcers and pimples. The colour in correspondence is that of glistening light.

Could anything be more futile than chiromancy and card prognostication, it is probably the zodiacal astrology which has been just described, and which limits the varieties of human destiny, disposition, and physical appearance to twelve kinds.*

Astrological students should be made aware of the palmary importance of two ancient and voluminous treatises, which contain the whole theory and practice of the starry science, elaborated with the most perfect

---

* It has been suggested in this connection that as most people belong to mixed types, the twelve kinds are multiplied indefinitely.

precision. The first is the *Speculum Astrologiæ* of Junctin de Florence, 2 vols., 1581 ; the second is the *Matheseos, Libri viii.*, 1551. The foundation of the vast treatise of Junctin de Florence is a rare Greek treatise of Ptolemy of Pelouse, one of the last of the grand succession of oriental initiates who glorified the Alexandrian school of philosophy. The original manuscript enunciated the Hermetic traditions of Egyptian oriental magic, while the commentary of Junctin de Florence contains the result of its author's life-long researches among the profundities of Chaldaic Astromancy, Jewish Kabbalism, and Arabian Theurgy. Julius Firmius Maternus also drew from the work of Ptolemy the foundation of his astrological methods, producing, in a smaller compass, an absolutely practical manual. Junctin de Florence was an illustrious doctor of theology, the almoner of François de Valois, the youngest brother of Henry III. of France. Julius Firmius Maternus was a Sicilian priest of the fourth century. The fortunate possessor of these works may soon place himself in possession of the secret code of Astrology, but the substance of both are embodied in Christian's "Histoire de la Magie," 8vo, Paris, 1870. This disciple of Eliphas Lévi gives a general theory of the Horoscope and the Keys of Astrological Science, which he denominates almost infallible.

KABBALISM.

A S in other departments of magical literature, there
are two views current concerning Kabbalism.
There is that of incredulous criticism which considers it to be, historically, a flagrant forgery, and, in
itself, barbarous and unintelligible jargon ; and there is
that of uncritical credulity which accepts it as " the key
of things kept secret from the foundation of the world."
The truth, as in other cases, would appear to lie between
these two extremes. Before attempting to appreciate
the science, it is necessary, in the interests of the unad-
vanced inquirer, to make a few preliminary explanations.

Kabbalism is an art or a science which is derived from
the Kabbalah, a term which signifies " reception," in the
sense of an heirloom which is handed down from father
to son. It is used to denote a considerable body of
esoteric or mystical literature belonging to the Jews.
Its most important divisions are the Bahir, which is
said to be the most ancient book of rabbinical literature,
but which seems to be wholly unknown to a number of
occult students at the present day ; the Zohar, or book
of splendour ; the Sepher Sephiroth, or book of emanations ; the Sepher Jetzirah, which treats of the thirty-
two paths of the Absolute ; and the Asch Metzareph.
The philosophical doctrines developed in these works
are affirmed to have been perpetuated by the secret
method of oral tradition from the first ages of humanity.
" The Kabbalah," says Dr. Ginsburg, when explaining
the story of its birth, " was first taught by God Himself
to a select company of angels, who formed a theosophic
school in Paradise. After the Fall the angels most
graciously communicated this heavenly doctrine to the
disobedient child of earth, to furnish the protoplasts with
the means of returning to their pristine nobility and

felicity.   From Adam it passed over to Noah, and then
to Abraham, the friend of God, who emigrated with it
to Egypt, where the patriarch allowed a portion of this
mysterious doctrine to ooze out.   It was in this way
that the Egyptians obtained some knowledge of it, and
the other Eastern nations could introduce it into their
philosophical systems.   Moses, who was learned in all
the wisdom of Egypt, was first initiated into the Kabbalah in the land of his birth, but became most proficient
in it during his wanderings in the wilderness, when he
not only devoted to it the leisure hours of the whole forty
years, but received lessons in it from one of the angels.
By the aid of this mysterious science the law-giver was
enabled to solve the difficulties which arose during his
management of the Israelites, in spite of the pilgrimages,
wars, and frequent miseries of the nation.   He covertly
laid down the principles of this secret doctrine in the
first four books of the Pentateuch, but withheld them
from Deuteronomy.   Moses also initiated the seventy
Elders into the secrets of this doctrine, and they again
transmitted them from hand to hand.   Of all who formed
the unbroken line of tradition, David and Solomon were
the most deeply initiated into the Kabbalah.   No one,
however, dared to write it down till Schimeon ben
Jochai, who lived at the time of the destruction of the
second.   After his death, his son, Rabbi Eleazar, and
his secretary, Rabbi Abba, as well as his disciples, col-
lated Rabbi Simon Ben Jochai's treatises, and out of
these composed the celebrated work called Z H R,
Zohar, Splendour, which is the grand storehouse of
Kabbalism."
    This version of the history of Jewish transcendental
literature is accepted at the present day by a number of
mystical thinkers not in themselves illiterate, but whose
veneration has blunted their critical faculty.   Their
imaginations are overwhelmed by the grandiose speculations of the Jewish mystics, and, naturally inclined to
credulity, they believe in the antiquity of the Kabbalah
not actually for the reason which prompted the stormy
faith of Tertullian—*Credo quia absurdum*—but because it
is a large idea, just as they believe in the antiquity of

the Rosicrucian Society, and in the connection of the Masonic Brotherhood with the splendid order of the Temple and with the vague wonders of Eleusinian mysteries. The student who is in search of truth must, however, be fortified against the glamour of romance, and he will do well to realise that this supposed history of Kabbalistic origines is almost wholly fabulous, and no evidence worthy of the name can be adduced to support it. It is possible that a certain amount of secret doctrine and a certain number of secret exegetical methods were perpetuated by tradition in Judea, and that they were ultimately incorporated in the Kabbalah, but this is the sum total of its claim to antiquity, while, on the other hand, there is practically no doubt that the most prized, the most voluminous, and, philosophically, the most suggestive and valuable section of Kabbalistic literature is a work of the thirteenth century.

In his essay on "The Kabbalah; its Doctrines, Development, and Literature," Dr Ginsburg enters into a detailed examination of the facts and arguments which have satisfied the most eminent authorities that the "Zohar" is of modern origin. It would be beyond the scope of our purpose to enumerate them in these pages in any exhaustive manner, but it may be briefly remarked that this treatise provides a mystical explanation of the Hebrew vowel points which were introduced at the close of the sixth century, that it cites an author who is known to have lived and died during the eleventh century, that it mentions the Crusades, and records events which transpired in the year A.D. 1264. It was some few years previous to 1291 that copies of the Zohar first began to be circulated by a Spanish Jew named Moses De Leon, who pretended to be in possession of an autograph manuscript of its reputed author R. Simon ben Jochai. The value of this pretension was made evident after his death, when the wealthy Joseph de Avila promised the destitute widow of Moses de Leon, "that if she would give him the original MS. of the *Zohar* from which her husband made the copies, his son should marry her daughter, and that he would give them a handsome dowry. Whereupon the widow and daughter declared, that they did not possess any such MS., that Moses de Leon never had it, but that he composed the *Zohar* from his own head, and wrote it with his own hand."

In the same way, the consensus of authorities refers the book of Creation, attributed to the patriarch Abraham, to " the ninth century of the Christian era, when it first became known," and the rest of this curious literature to a variety of periods ranging between the eighth and the thirteenth centuries. So early as the beginning of the fifteenth century, it may be added, the suspicious character of the Zohar was exposed by a learned philosophical Israelite of the University of Padua.

The mysticism of the Mishna and the Talmud must be carefully distinguished from that of the Kabbalistic writings. Of the comparative antiquity of the two former cycles of Jewish literature there can be no reasonable doubt. What antiquity belongs to the doctrines which are developed in the latter must be traced to the Alexandrian school of theurgic magic which, post-Christian as it was, may be admitted to have been the heir of many antique traditions.

Having established, as far as may be possible in a short summary of the latest results of independent criticism, the actual antiquity of the chief books comprised in the Kabbalah, it is necessary to say a few words with regard to its claims upon the modern student of mysticism. It is clear that its philosophical value is not depreciated by its modern origin; that is completely independent of its position in history. It is said by its admirers to be an absolute guide to knowledge in all the most profound problems of life. It indicates the nature and attributes of God, the Supreme Being, whom, however, it does not attempt to define. It indicates the origin and evolution of the cosmos; it describes the creation of angels and of men, the nature possessed by both, with the nature of demons, and of the intermediate and elementary beings which fill the universe. It affords a satisfactory solution of the grand mysteries connected with the soul of man, expounds the interior significance of the written law, and contains the infallible keys of many other mysteries. Truly, this is an extensive philosophical programme, and if so inclusive a claim can be substantiated, it is obvious that the student of occultism may profitably confine his attention to the Kabbalah, and may, without detriment, ignore all that is unconnected with it. On examination, however, it proves that with all this splendour of promise, the Kabbalah is simply a series of dogmatic hypotheses ; it is not a guide to knowledge ; it is a body of positive doctrine, based on a central assumption which is incapable of proof, and enunciated in a singularly barbarous and unintelligible form. "This tradition," says Eliphas Lévi, "wholly reposes on the single dogma of magic—that the Visible is for us the proportional measure of the Invisible." And again : "The religion of the Kabbalists is at once all hypothesis and all certitude, for it proceeds by analogy from the Known to the Unknown." In other words, there is a correspondence between the seen and the unseen, and it is possible to reason from the one to the other. Pseudo-Hermes has given another and axiomatic presentation of the same notion : "That which is above is in proportion with that which is below, and that which is below is in proportion with that which is above." You can reason up from man to God, from earth to heaven, from body to spirit. This argument from analogy is something like the argument from design ; it is not satisfactory, it is not reliable, and yet it is difficult to dispense with it. We fashion the World Beyond in the likeness of the world about us, because we are unable to imagine a wholly different order of subsistence from that with which experience has acquainted us. At the same time, the limitations of our own nature cannot certainly, nor, indeed, reasonably, be upheld as the measure of eternity, and a philosophy which invests this limitation with an absolute value may be bold, as it also may be ingenious, but there is no obvious or irresistible reason for accepting it as a sober guide.

The Kabbalistic evolutions of the Macroprosopus, and the revolutions of the soul of man, are very interesting

efforts of the human mind to account in an original
manner for the mysteries which encompass us, but they
are merely speculations, they have no claim on faith,
and when we turn from such modern interpretations of
the Kabbalah as are provided by Eliphas Lévi to the
grotesque and unmanageable typology of the original
works, and become acquainted with the extent of their
crudity, their inadequacy, and their arbitrariness, it will
become more than doubtful whether they will repay the
exceedingly painstaking study which will be required
to master them.   They may be read indeed for their occasional touches of sublimity, for their occasional bits of insight, at times even for their poetic suggestiveness, and,
of course, they have their place in the history of philosophy and in the history of Jewish letters.   Whatever is
undertaken in excess of this we cannot believe will be
profitable.   The investigation of the numerical value of
words; of the effects which result from beheading them,
from curtailing them, from substituting new letters;
and the mysteries which are concealed in the shapes of
alphabetical symbols, are not subjects in reality more
serious than any other intellectual gymnastics achieved
in the world of puzzles.   In the paper on the evocation
of angels at the beginning of this book, we have given
some extensive specimens of Kabbalistic investigations
conducted in the transcendental region of pneumatology
by means of curious calculations.   Their value is on
their surface, it is easily estimated, and it is really too
late to attempt any serious resuscitation of this sort of
occultism.   The best lesson we can learn from it is the
necessity—on which we have continually insisted—of
scrupulously separating the experimental knowledge of
the mystics from their bizarre fields of speculation.

We may add in conclusion that it is mainly to the Kabbalistic combinations of the Divine Names that mediæval
magic is indebted for the terms in its rituals, as it was
thence also that it derived the belief in a resident virtue
in sacred names and in numbers.

The *Kabbala Denudata* of Baron de Rosenroth is the
most complete synopsis of Kabbalistic theosophy.   It is,
however, in Latin, and the English reader must content

himself, as best he can, with a portion of one of its divisions, which has been translated by Mr. S. Mathers, and recently published in London, under the title of the "Kabbalah Unveiled." The more advanced student will find in Maimonides' "Guide of the Perplexed" an ingenuous and suggestive unveiling of the interior sense of scripture according to the Kabbalistic laws of interpretation.

PART III.

——o——

THE MYSTICS.

THE reader has been already made acquainted with the defined end of mysticism, and with the broad division of the mystics into two classes—physical and spiritual. The physical mystics worked in accordance with Hermetic mysticism in the world of metals and minerals ; the labours of the others were devoted to the development of the secret possibilities which reside in the subject Man. For all practical purposes, the history of the alchemists proper begins with Geber, an Arabian, whose life is enveloped in an obscurity which has given a romantic warrant to a number of magnificent fables. He flourished most probably in the eighth century of the Christian era. The first ascertainable reference, in Western literature, to the transmutation of metals, occurs, as already stated, in a writing of Zosimus, the Pomopolite, who belongs to the fifth century; but the origin of the great experiment has been very imperfectly investigated. There is a literature of Oriental alchemy existing in Arabian manuscripts, now scattered and practically entombed in the public libraries of Europe, by a study of which the origins of alchemy can be elucidated. But we are in want of a history of chemistry as it was known to the ancients. We are in want, in particular, of an exhaustive catalogue of all chemical subjects known to the ancient Egyptians, Greeks, and Romans, and Jews. That would determine the actual nature of the materials of which a knowledge was inherited by the followers of the Arabian Geber. It would settle the debateable point how far these men in reality contributed to the foundation and extension of exoteric chemistry. Existing histories of this interest-

ing science occasionally enumerate the substances which
are mentioned for the first time in alchemical writings,
but there is no evidence to show that the information
was obtained first hand from the authorities quoted, and
as most of these histories, at least in England, and
undeniably as regards their earlier portions, are of the
most meagre and unsatisfactory character, it is difficult
to believe them the result of any adequate inquiry.
Thirdly ; we are in need of a history of chemical development among the Hermetists, which could be compiled
from a study of their voluminous writings in historical
order.   These matters must be necessarily handed over
to an inner circle of specialists, working to some extent
in common ; but they are of undoubted importance to all
students of mysticism, because they will determine the
true place of alchemy in the history of the sciences,
and will manifest a plain line of demarcation between
alchemists proper and the spiritual mystics, with whom
they are too completely identified by the wonder-
mongering theories of an uncritical transcendentalism.
     From the period of Geber to that of Paracelsus, the
literature of physical alchemy appears to have been
sufficiently material, and the methods pursued in the
achieved or attempted performance of the Great Work,
were simply so much wading through an enormous variety
of processes which frequently dissipated the fortunes and
squandered the existence of the workers without any
definite good being attained.   When the erratic splendour of the mind of Paracelsus rose comet-like over
the intellectual horizon of Germany, a change came.
He was the first to import into the Hermetic experiment
an element which was of a magical character ; he admitted that gold might be made by the mundane process
of common chemistry, but this he denounced as in-
efficient and poor, when compared with the result which
might be produced by an exercise of the arcane potencies
of the human soul.   There are certain operations in
which one is fain to believe that something of the nature
of the worker passes into the manipulated substance.
The cook, like the poet, is born and not made, and
under the influence of the culinary mission something

from the other world passes into the viands which he
digests over his furnaces, and that something is transmitted direct from his soul—a process which constitutes
the unteachable nature of his art. Now, the alchemist
is the cook of mineralogy, and the digestion of meats
and minerals is described in the French language by the
same term. Yet it is eminently difficult to understand
how a projection of vital fluid can accomplish metallic
transmutation. Skill, genius, and will-power can modify
forms and vary combinations, but it cannot change
natures, whence one is disposed to believe that the substance produced by the psycho-chemistry of Paracelsus
was simply a refined sophistication—a modified form, a
substance as to appearance changed, but as to radical
nature the same. On the other hand, a discriminating
criticism might discern in this magical psycho-mineralogy
and pneumatic metallurgy an agreeable manner of dis-
tinguishing between the alchemical methods of a man
of parts who infuses genius into his operations, and the
barren stupidities of the unimaginative and gross-minded
souffleur. However this may be, it is certain that
Paracelsus achieved an immense reputation, and created
a school of chemistry, which subsequently produced the
damask-like wealth and richness of that "mysterious
flower" of allegory, the Rose-Cross. More completely
than ever the science of alchemy became involved in
mysticism and centred in religion. It was a work which
to the unregenerate was impossible; it was one of the
secrets of God—*magnalia Dei et Naturæ*—and the intensification of this idea more completely obscured it with
mystery, for *sacramentum Regis abscondere bonum est.*
From the psychic manufacture of gold, it is but a step
to the conversion of the metallic subject into an allegorical idea, and men began to attribute to the philosophers
of old an aspiration less sordid than the search after
wealth unbounded, and to accredit them with a spiritual
intent. Some of the writings of Khunrath, a professed
alchemist, have nothing in common with the metallic
experiment—they are advanced text-books of Christian
theosophy expressed in the terminology of the *turba
philosophorum,* and from beginning [to end the entire

theory of the Hermetic practice was transcendentalized by Jacob Boehme. Side by side with this new school, the followers of the physical work continued to multiply their initiates till the beginning of the eighteenth century, when for historical purposes it expired with the mysterious Archimandrite Lascaris, a revival attempted by Cagliostro, some fifty years later, being probably fraudulent.

Fascinating as is the history of alchemy and the men who pursued it, there can be no comparison between its interest and the history of the larger *opus* of the spiritual mystics. It is at this point that one feels the want of a history of Christian mysticism in its relation to universal mysticism, a work which would reward and require a lifetime of labour and study.

One definition of mysticism has already been given in the course of this work. There is another which, with less appearance of precision, is also good. We must remember that mysticism is a science, a *moyen de parvenir*, a way of attainment; it endows the human mind with an instrument of knowledge; it is, in the words of an encyclopædist who has treated the aspiration with a tolerable amount of respect—it is the endeavour of the human mind to grasp the divine essence or ultimate reality of all things, and to enjoy, while in this life and in this body, the blessedness of an immediate communion with the Highest. It recognizes the totality of finite existence as a theophany—a "circle which ever returneth in to the self-same spot," to that point "which hath no parts and which hath no magnitude"—God being the beginning and the end of all, universalism being implicitly included in the terms of the proposition, the law of the universe necessitating beatitude, as the end of all that is conscious, namely, all that is philosophically capable of a permanent subsistence, and thus definitely determining the nature of

> "that far-off, divine event
> To which the whole creation moves."

As in practical alchemy, so in spiritual mysticism, Paracelsus stands forth as a figure of considerable his-

torical importance; by the limitations of his character it
is wholly improbable that he attained the end of mysticism, but to divine it in virtue of his great intellectual
lucidity was however permitted him, and he was conscious in no ordinary manner of the arcane possibilities
which exist in the soul of man. In him the physical
and spiritual mystics may be said to have met and joined
hands; for the alchemists were truly mystics; they
sought to ameliorate an individual substance by its
application to a universal substance, and this, in relation
to another subject, was equally the end of the spiritual
adepts. In the illuminated philosopher of Hohenheim,
the dual aspiration may not have attained its height, but
it attained its union, and Paracelsus is useful in the history of philosophy not for what he personally achieved
but for the juncture which he represents, and which
materially aids in the realisation of the integral nature
of Hermetic work in all its fields of elaboration. He is
the sign-post which indicates the locality of the focus of
Christian mysticism. That is undoubtedly Germany,
which stands philosophically supreme among all the
nations of Europe, and is the source of light and leading
for all forms of speculative thought, however high or low.
It is not there, needless to say, that we are to seek the
fundamental elements of that aspirational Science of the
Life Within which, during all its centuries, has spiritual-
ised the church of Christ. It has been truly said that
the appearance of mysticism in the West is coincident
with the exhaustion of Greek and Jewish civilisation.
But thence it should not be concluded that these aspirations are confined to periods of decadence, or that they
are in themselves a sign of weakness and of religious dis-
integration in any opprobrious sense. The anxieties and
desires of the soul are quickened in those periods of
sorrow when the landmarks of the spiritual life are being
effaced for a period, and out of the great fermentation
which follows the operation of a strong dissolving instrument, a new religious order is being slowly evoked. The
prevalence of mysticism during such periods is a sign of
strength and vitality; it shows the religious instinct

N

rising superior to doctrinal formalism, and while all things

> "change and wear out;
> Change and are turned about,
> Falter and fail;"

asserts very plainly and certainly its permanent vitality and strength.

The foundation of Christian mysticism is in the Neo-Platonic, or Alexandrian quest after the ecstatic intui-tion of the Ineffable and Substantial All. It is probably derived through Philo, whose God, the end in view, is defined in terms of "absolute transcendency." On the authority of the last edition of the "Encyclopædia Brit-annica," it may be stated that Neo-Platonism appeared during the first half of the third century. The influence of Philo was probably strong in the early Church. Josephus, the pliant and courtly Israelite, tinctured so strongly with the worldly elements of the Paganism with which he was surrounded, was useful historically as an ally, because he represented, well or otherwise, the his-torical actuality of the central figure of the new and more divine dispensation ; but Philo, among all the Jews, most nearly approached the philosophic side of Chris-tianity. Yet his influence was destined to be absorbed by that of the so-called Areopagite Dionysius, who, at the end of the fifth century, incorporated Platonic theo-sophy with Christian dogma, and developed his scale of the universe in consonance with the Hermetic doctrine of successive emanations. This scheme is essentially mystical, and is a methodical application of Platonic and Hermetic conceptions to the Christian realisation of heaven and the angelical intelligences which inform the superior spheres. His transcendental tradition passed over to Scotland, and influenced profoundly the extra-ordinary mind of his translator, Erigena, whose perished works are a distinct and irretrievable loss to the broader school of Christian theology in the past. The golden chain of speculation and the philosophy of transcenden-tal desire were continued by St Bernard and his contem-porary St Victor, who originated a school of thought in which the illuminated Bonaventura was a prominent disciple, his little treatise, *Itinerarium Mentis ad Deum*, being, within certain limits, a complete handbook of transcendental thought, having direct reference to Pseudo-Hermes, and destined in turn to influence the great mind of Pascal. Mediæval societies of mysticism sprang up by degrees in Germany, both for men and women, who devoted themselves to the cultivation of the interior life, and whose ascribed writings were not devoid of effect upon the powerful mind of Luther, in spite of its native grossness. Along with these Christian schools, it is, on the whole, probable, though the evidence is of an indirect character, that secret fraternities perpetuated the doctrines of Gnosticism and the illuminism of the Pagan religions for many centuries after their supposed disappearance, and thus originated the colleges of magic in conjunction with Jewish Kabbalism, which entered so largely into the practical mysticism of the period. Men like Eckart and Tauler were the product of many elements, and, in a sense, all of them lead us towards Paracelsus as a central point, though the spiritual powers of Paracelsus, whatever they may have been, seem to have been possessed as a gift, and were not traceably consequent on any distinct personal advancement in the spiritual life. It was chiefly by translations of this hierophant and of Cornelius Agrippa that mysticism was implanted in England after the searching fires of the Reformation, and their influence may be traced from the period of Thomas Vaughan * and More, his Platonic critic, till the beautiful light of Jacob Böhme absorbed it finally. The marvellous shoemaker of Görlitz, practically the last of the German mystics, not only exercised an immense influence in his own Fatherland, but also on the French sect of the Martinists, whose head was the refined and delightful character, Louis Claude de St Martin, originally the disciple of a

* Vaughan is deserving of more than a passing notice. His writings, the most remarkable of which have been recently reissued in London, reveal him as an advanced mystic, devoted to the development of the interior powers of the soul, in which he seems to have made progress of no ordinary kind. He was also a practical alchemist, and conducted experiments with his wife, whom he regarded as his spiritual counterpart.

man only second to himself in interest, and whose name
of Pasquales Martinez still exercises a spell of glamour.
Perhaps it escaped Madame Guion, who belonged to another school, but it bade fair to revolutionize England in
the hands of William Law and writers like Jane Lead.
This is possibly an extreme statement, but it is not devoid
of warrant.

In our own day the philosophy of Emerson and
Carlyle was a kind of modified mysticism, secularised
for the first time; while actually and at this moment,
along with Spiritualism and Theosophy, there has
occurred that second spring of transcendental aspiration
which has at once been the source and the warrant of
this book, and in which with all humility we desire to be
included as discriminating but earnest followers.

We cannot sufficiently warn our readers that this is a
bald and meagre sketch, but it is sufficient to indicate that
there has been a tradition of the interior life perpetuated
through all the ages of Christendom. By it there is
proclaimed the possibility of passing into a state which
transcends normal consciousness and constitutes a partial
union with a higher principle of being than that with
which we are normally acquainted. This union was
approached in the ecstasies of the Catholic saints, but it
is not confined to the disciples of any special creed or
dogma. Those who are in search of their souls must
devote themselves to the study of the men called
mystics. The most that can be offered by the phenomena, however wonderful, of magic, and of spiritualism
in its most exalted forms, is a guarantee in fact that
this search, properly conducted, is no insensate quest.
They afford a fundamental source of conviction to
warrant the prosecution of that grand experiment with
our own selves which the mystics claim to have conducted to a successful issue. In their large and suggestive literature will be found the way and the life which
are calculated to reach that end, but the student must remember the Hermetic warning to reject all that is superfluous, and the aspirational flights of the mystics, and, as
we are tempted to add, their attainments, were weighted
and circumscribed by all that was unworthy of Divinity,

of-all that fell short of God, in their exoteric beliefs. The "free perspicuity of thought in universal consciousness" is beyond all the regions of defined doctrine; it is the inmost sanctuary of that true religion of the spirit which is behind all systems of religion, and it is there alone in the full sense of the term that the reader can find his soul.

An exhaustive account of the theurgic doctrine of Alexandria will be found in a "History of the Neo-Platonic Philosophy," by Vacherot, published in three volumes at Paris in the year 1850; Dr. Franz Hartmann's analysis of the writings of Paracelsus will be valuable to the elementary student; the same author has just issued a compendious digest of the works of Jacob Böhme; a mine of theosophic wealth will be found in the correspondence of Saint-Martin; and a complete exposition of Mystical Philosophy from the modern standpoint has been undertaken by Baron Carl Duprel, and has been admirably rendered into English by Mr. C. C. Massey.

THE ROSICRUCIANS.

THE subject of the Rosicrucian Fraternity has long been of interest from the impenetrable mystery which has surrounded it, but that mystery is not its only interest. No student of occultism can afford to ignore the Rosicrucian claims, which are part and parcel of the great and universal claim of the transcendental sciences. While the facts which are alone ascertainable concerning this arcane Fraternity have done much to dispel the romantic associations which have been connected with the name Rosicrucian, that name, and not altogether unaccountably, still exercises a certain spell upon persons of imaginative temperament, and continues to accomplish the transfiguration of facts, which in themselves are prosaic. While the name Rosicrucian originated among mystics at a definite historical period, and has a defined limit of application, its original significance is eliminated, it is treated as the equivalent of Magus, of Man of Wisdom, and other general terms, and is considered as an appropriate designation for the true mystic, whether he is affiliated or not to the Brotherhood which invented the name. Made use of in this manner as a fanciful or ornamental appellation, or as a titular dignity which is merely melodious and pretty, it is certainly unmeaning and childish, but it is dear to some modern mystics, who more than the rest of humanity are dominated by the pleasing tyranny of verbal tinsel.

Now, at the outset of a historical inquiry, however brief and imperfect, into the origin of Rosicrucianism, it is eminently needful to put aside from remembrance all preconceived theories, the glamorous accretions of romantic fabulists, and the fables of extravagant historians, and to consider the Rosicrucian problem, as all historical problems ought to be considered, in the light of facts alone. It is needless to observe that, working upon this principle, the nomenclature which distinguishes the Society, should not be applied indiscriminately outside the pale of the Society.

Was there really and truly at any period of the past a genuine Rosicrucian Fraternity? If so, what is its history, what are the powers it possessed, and what has become of it? When we hear of Rosicrucian associations at the present day, are we to consider them affiliated with the mysterious order of the past, or are they simply unimportant gatherings of a semi-antiquarian character, and as much in the dark as ourselves about the arcane history and unavowed objects of that Brotherhood whose name they have assumed? These are the palmary questions which concern the Rosicrucian mystery.

Now, whether the laudable and honourable Fraternity of R. C. had a real or an imaginary existence, the derivation of its name is a point of considerable importance, and throws some light on the uncertainty which involves the subject. It is not derived from the name of the supposed founder, Christian Rosenkreuze, because the given history of the founder is that of a fabulous person, and is therefore worthless from the philological standpoint. It is, we think, not derived from the Latin words *Ros*, dew, and *Crux*, cross, although this explanation was adopted by the historian Mosheim, and has been accredited by his great reputation. It was founded on the assumption that the originators of Rosicrucianism, in common with numerous alchemists, considered the dew of the philosophers to be the most powerful dissolvent of gold, while the cross was, in chemical symbolism, equivalent to *light*—another important factor in the performance of the *Magnum Opus* —because the figure of a + was supposed to exhibit at the same time the three letters of which the word *Lux*, or light, is compounded. We believe that the name Rosicrucian is derived from *Rosa*, a Rose, and *Crux*, Cross. In accordance with this opinion, the general symbol of the supposed Order was a Rose crucified in the centre of a Cross, generally of gold or of ebony. But there is a variation of this emblem which has long been practically unknown. Yet if ever Rosicrucians existed it was their true and arcane badge. This was a red cross-marked heart in the centre of an open Rose, which appears more than once in an old Rosicrucian book of the last century. It has no connection with the sublime symbolism of the Oriental world; Egypt, Thebes, Eleusinia, and the sanctuaries of antique initiation are innocent of its import. It is a development of the monogram of the monk, Martin Luther, which was a cross-crowned heart rising from the centre of an open Rose. We think that this is a point of importance, and the connecting link in a long chain of evidence which has been formed by our independent researches.

Separately taken, the Rose and the Cross are hierograms of the highest antiquity. Their union is modern— that is, it is subsequent to the Renaissance and the Reformation. So far as history is concerned, the name Rosicrucian was unknown previously to the year 1598. The history of Rosicrucianism proper begins in Germany, where, in the city of Cassel, in the year 1614, the world of alchemists, Paracelsians, Theosophists, and professors of magic and mysticism, was startled by the publication of a pamphlet of unpretending appearance but colossal importance, which bore for its title, "The Fame of the Fraternity of the Meritorious Order of the Rosy Cross, addressed to the learned in General and the Governors of Europe." It embodied the universal proclamation of certain anonymous men, endued with great wisdom and raised up by God for the renewal and perfection of all arts for the instruction of mankind in his own worth and nobility, and for the revelation of the true and occult nature of the Microcosmos. It informed the rude world of quarrelsome literati that by combining their forces they might establish a synthesis of science, the true *Librum Naturæ*, the Perfect Method of all the arts. But they were fostering squabbles and divisions, were loth to leave the old courses, and clung blindly to the traditions of Aristotle and Galen, and the antiquated authorities of the elder world. Yet never since the beginning of Christendom had the wise and all-merciful God so poured out upon mankind the sublime knowledge of his Son, Jesus Christ, and of the sacred arcana of Nature. A reformation had taken place in religion, the sanctuaries of the Church had been cleansed; there was a grand and a radical reformation preparing in science and philosophy. "Europe is with child," cried the Fama. "It will bring forth a strong child, who will stand in need of a great baptismal gift." They, the high-illuminated Brotherhood, throned on the pinnacles of initiation by a godly and high-illuminated father, were the pioneers of this glorious revolution. Heirs of the ages of occultism, children of light and benediction, initiated into the mysteries of the Grand Orient, they were exalted in the midst of the obscurity, a miraculous and magian star, to light and lead the age.

And this was their lineage and history.

The chief and original of their Fraternity was an illustrious and immortal Teuton, anointed with the most choice chrism of the supreme, magical hierophant, who was at that day a beatified participator in the uncreated light of God, and in the everlasting triumph of their King, Christ. In the fifth year of his age, C. R. C., offspring of the kisses of angels, and beautified by the benediction of the stars, was placed in a cloister where he learned Greek and Latin, and at the age of fifteen was associated with one, Brother P. A. L., who was minded to travel to the Holy Land. Now, this brother died at Cyprus, but the seraphic boy, fired with heroic resolves and protected by angelical hierarchies, pressed on to Damascus, meaning to proceed to Jerusalem. At Damascus, he had intelligence of an illuminated circle of theosophists, who abode in an unknown city of Arabia, called Damcar, of the wonders which they wrought therein, and of the mysteries of Nature which were discovered to them. The vision of the holy sepulchre faded from the boy's mind; he burned with the laudable ambition to become acquainted with these marvellous men, and he bargained with certain Arabians that they should carry him for a sum of money to Damcar. He reached that unknown city when he was sixteen years of age, and there he was cordially welcomed by the wise men, who did not receive him as a stranger but as one whom they had long been expecting. They welcomed him, called him by his name, revealed to him several secrets of his past life, and otherwise astonished him by their knowledge in things divinatory.

He was a pure, virginal boy; they took him at once into their confidence, and instructed him duly and daily in the mysteries of occult mathematics and of occult physics. He easily attained proficiency in the Arabic tongue, and accomplished the translation of the divine book M into good Latin. At the end of three years he departed from Damcar, shipped himself over *Sinus Arabicus* into Egypt, and thence sailed into Fez, whither his magical instructors had directed him. There he performed evocations of the elementary spirits under the tuition of new masters, and became familiar with the secrets of the Invisible World. He abode for two years in the city of Fez, and accomplished the period of his initiation, when, enriched by the possession of many costly secrets, he proceeded to Spain to confer with its best literati, and convince them of the errors of their arts. He recounted the result of his travels, and prescribed them a series of axioms for the foundation of a universal natural science. But the enthusiasm of the young initiate was simply a laughing matter to the fossilized scholars of Spain. Had not the devil himself instructed them in the principles and practices of the Black Art at the renowned university of Salamanca? "Whoso loveth unquietness, let him be reformed," said they. He retired in just indignation, but the same treatment awaited him among several nations. The true and infallible Axiomata, out of all faculties, sciences, and arts, the "concentrated centre of Nature," were generally disregarded, and he returned disappointed to Germany, where he ruminated in solitude and seclusion on his travels and his universal philosophy. The latter was reduced into writing, and he also constructed several fine instruments by the power of natural magic.

After five years, his projected reformation returned very strongly to his mind. Was he not in possession of the great art of transmutation? Had not the method of prolonging life rewarded the zeal of his studies? And must these many-sided marvels be lost to the worthy because the world at large was unfitted to receive or understand them? No; a society should be established to secretly instruct the elect in the deep things of Nature, and in the resources of Art, her handmaid. "After this manner," says the *Fama*, "began the Fraternity R. C.— first by four persons only," who invented a magical language, a cipher writing equally magical, and a large dictionary replete with sublime wisdom. They caused a House of the Holy Ghost to be erected, healed the sick, initiated further members, and then under orders from the founder, C. R. C., departed as missionaries into several countries to disseminate their wisdom in secret. Many years passed away, and at length their loving Father C. R. C., having finished his labours and his pilgrimage, gave up in the odour of sanctity his initiated spirit to God. The secret of his sepulchre was concealed for the space of one hundred and twenty years; the earliest members of the Fraternity died; it is doubtful whether those who succeeded had attained as much wisdom, but when the fulness of time was come, a great and profitable discovery was made by the adepts of the third generation. This was the mystic tombstone of their illustrious founder, C. R. C., the lost treasure of the Society, the receptacle of the most hidden mysteries. It was unearthed in a casual manner during the reparation of an arcane abode of the Rosicrucians, and was, in fact, a septagonal vault, illuminated by the concealed Sun of the Magi, and overwritten with mystic characters. The corpse of their "careful and wise Father" was found perfectly preserved, along with *minutum mundum*, and a select variety of exceedingly high-class marvels, which operated so strongly on the enthusiasm of the existing members that they decided to share the unexpected increase in their possessions, their powers, and their knowledge among all worthy persons who might apply to them for initiation.

In accordance with this determination, after prophesying the dawn of aurora—a divine light in the intellectual sky—the *Fama Fraternitatis* concluded by inviting a select number of suitable and like-minded persons to join their Fraternity. The writers, however, declined, in the first instance, to supply their names and addresses; they were sounding the temper of the time. Those who desired to communicate could do so by the publication of printed letters which would not escape the notice of the Brethren. For the rest, having stated their absolute faith in the reformed Church of Jesus Christ, they denounced, in a solemn and categorical manner, the innumerable impostures of pseudo-alchemists, claiming the possession of a thousand secrets superior to the art of the goldmaker. They also warned the wicked, the false-hearted, and those who were covetous of worldly riches, that they would never discover the Fraternity, and that their House of the Holy Spirit, though it had been beheld by a hundred thousand persons, should ever be concealed from the world.

Such was the first proclamation of the Rosicrucian Society, and it is no matter for surprise that in the high-holiday of alchemy, astrology, and magic, it created an unexampled excitement. Letters without end were printed in every part of Germany by persons who sought initiation. Pamphlets were published by the score, criticising, attacking, or defending the Society and its manifesto. The fabulous history of C. R. C. abounded with palpable discrepancies; there was no such a city as Damcar; there was no House of the Holy Ghost in existence; a building which had been seen by a hundred thousand persons could not be concealed from the world; a boy of fifteen could scarcely have astonished the Turks by his great skill in medicine; and the very existence of a boy mystic must have appeared somewhat phenomenal even to that age. Yet the story was very generally accredited. Twelve months passed away, and then, in the same unobtrusive pamphlet form, and in the same anonymous manner, there appeared in 1615 the "Confession of the Rosicrucian Fraternity, addressed to the Learned in Europe." It still insisted on the necessity of a reformation in philosophy, still offered initiation by gradual

stages to meritorious applicants ; but, for the rest, its
energies were expended in scurrilous abuse of the
Pope. It charged him with blasphemy, publicly exe-
crated him, and looked forward with intense eagerness
to the time when his " asinine braying " should be put an
end to by the singular process of tearing him in pieces
with nails.

Fresh excitement, renewed confusion, further con-
troversy followed ; and again twelve months passed
away. In the year 1616 the " Chymical Nuptials of
Christian Rosencreutz " made known for the first time
the full name of the supposed founder of the Order.
This is a wonderful allegorical romance, which relates in
an autobiographical form how an artist, a prepared
student, was present in the year 1459 at the accomplishment of the *Magnum Opus*. The *Fama Fraternitatis*
embodied the history of a divine boy who obtained
initiation in his 'teens. The " Chymical Marriage "
recounts the initiation of an old man who had devoted
the whole of his life to a search after the Grand Secret.
The history of C. R. C. is not, therefore, the history of
Christian Rosencreutz.

After the publication of this prolix but meritorious
romance, a new element was introduced into the con-
troversy. People had sought initiation, and had failed.
Their feelings were naturally hurt, and they adopted a
hostile tone. Alchemists and theosophists compared
notes ; if they had failed, who deserved to be successful ? Had anyone succeeded ? No ; the Society was
cheating them. Such was the general decision ; the
tide turned, the craze ceased, and by 1620 the subject,
threshed to death, relapsed into its original obscurity
for a considerable period of years.

The authorship and origin of the Rosicrucian manifestoes have occupied the attention of numerous erudite
investigators. It is impossible in the space of this
brief essay to do justice to the theories which have been
propounded. After an adequate consideration of the
evidence, we are forced to conclude that none of their
views are tenable, while that one in particular which has
been most extensively received is open to the most

serious, and indeed to innumerable objections. We refer to the theory which accredits the theologian Andreæ with the production of the Rosicrucian manifestoes as a sort of laborious jest.

We have traced briefly the origin of Rosicrucianism so far as its exoteric history is concerned. On the one hand, the narrative contained in *Fama Fraternitatis* is concerned with a mythical person; on the other, all the manifestoes bear the indisputable marks of a terribly earnest purpose—that purpose being a reformation in the principles of philosophy, and in the methods of scientific research. It is therefore preposterous to consider them a planned hoax. On the contrary, it is reasonable to suppose that they were the work of a man, or of men, who hoped to obtain fellow-workers by their publication in a cause which was near to their hearts. It is not incredible that they emanated from a secret sect of theosophists: the existence of such an association was almost inevitable during that age of alchemy So, in answer to the first question—Was there ever at any period a genuine Rosicrucian Society?—it may be affirmed that there probably was. There is fair presumptive evidence to show that some corporate body of the kind did exist, and may have published the manifestoes called Rosicrucian. But the documents which are the basis of this belief give evidence also that the association did not originate as it pretended, while it is clear from its subsequent history that it was devoid of the powers which it claimed. Its prophecies have not been fulfilled; its opinions have not been substantiated; its anti-papal hysteria has passed into utter contempt, and it has never in any way contributed to the reformation or improvement of philosophy. So far as we can tell, it became an alchemical Order; whether it succeeded in performing the transmutation of metals, there is no evidence to decide.

The true origin of the Rosicrucian Fraternity has been food for incessant conjecture. Romance, which accredited its adepts with all the superhuman attributes which have ever been imagined by alchemist, Kabbalist, and retailer of magical traditions, has been at work on this problem, and has variously interpreted the mystery. Persons of excessive credulity and addicted to the largest views, have represented it as an Order of preternatural antiquity, and its principles as the origin of every theological system. They are seen in the solar mythologies and in phallic worship; their symbolism has permeated East and West alike; it is in Hindustan to-day as it was in Egypt, Greece, and Scandinavia at various epochs of the past. There is not a vestige of true evidence for all this romantic extravagance, but it has gained some believers because it is big, wonderful, and incredible.

The opinions, religious, scientific, and philosophical, which are to be found in Rosicrucian manifestoes, are the foundation of the most acceptable hypothesis concerning them. These opinions are essentially modern. In things which are magico-scientific, they were the followers of Paracelsus. This statement is founded, not on the simple fact that, in common with that mediæval hierophant, they believed in alchemy, astrology, and occult forces in Nature, but on the identity of their alchemical, astrological, and occult theorems with those which are propounded by Paracelsus, who in such matters was essentially an innovator. In things religious, they were equally modern. They were theosophical disciples of the great Lutheran reformer; their chief symbol, and, indirectly, their name, being borrowed, as we believe, from his own allegorical seal.

The actual date of their origin is to be sought in the grand old town of Nuremburg, which in 1598 was the abode of a singular mystic and alchemist named Simon Studion. This individual, whose personality is enveloped in mystery, established a *Militia Crucifera Evangelica,* which held periodical meetings in Nuremburg. Its proceedings are reported in an unprinted work of Studion's; and it can be shown that, in opinions and objects, it was substantially identical with the subsequent Rosicrucian Society. "Both associations were ultra-Protestant, both believed in the inner sense and mystical interpretation of Scripture, both expected the end of the age and the second coming of Christ, both abhorred the Pope, both called him Antichrist, both coupled him with the detested name of Mahomet, both studied the secret characters of nature, both appealed to the appearance of new stars in the sky as portentous of future events." Finally, the founder of the *Militia Crucifera Evangelica* was an avowed alchemist, and he was the first who elaborated the symbolism of the Rose-Cross. Evidently, the Rosicrucian Society of 1614 was a transfiguration or development of the obscure sect established by Simon Studion.

This view receives unexpected confirmation in a work of the eighteenth century. After a silence of nearly a hundred years, the Rosicrucians reappeared in Germany. In 1710, a writer calling himself Sincerus Renatus, but whose true name was Sigmund Richter, published a "Perfect and True Preparation of the Philosophical Stone, according to the Secret Methods of the Brotherhoods of the Golden and Rosy Cross." To this treatise, which, in itself, is excessively curious, there were annexed the "Rules of the Rosicrucian Fraternity for the Initiation of New Members." These rules, which, in effect, are the laws of the Order, not only are equivalent to a proof of the society's existence at the period in question, but they establish the important fact that it still held its meetings at Nuremberg, where the *Militia Crucifera Evangelica* was originally established by Studion.

In 1785, the publication of the "Secret Symbols of the Rosicrucians of the Sixteenth and Seventeenth Centuries" took place at Altona, showing that the mysterious brotherhood was still active. This was their last manifesto; it established the true nature of the Rose-Cross symbolism, and fitly closed the memorials of the Fraternity.

Several important points have now been ascertained. The existence of a secret society in or before the year 1614 has been shown to be necessary, in order to explain the successive publication of the numerous Rosicrucian manifestoes; it has been traced to a rational origin; the value of its pretensions has been appreciated, and

Q

its literary history sketched. What became of it must now be ascertained. So early as the year 1618, Henricus Neuhusius testified in a Latin pamphlet, which is generally unknown, that the "high Rosicrucian adepts" migrated to India; and it is asserted at this day that they inhabit the table-lands of Thibet. Their supposed Oriental pilgrimage may be traced as far eastward as the Island of Mauritius. The recent dispersion of a valuable private library has brought to light the existence of a very curious and seemingly genuine manuscript, which relates how the Comte de Chazal, having accomplished the performance called the *magnum opus*, or great work, proceeded to initiate Dr Sigismund Bacstrom into the mysteries of the Rose Cross Order, exacting many extraordinary conditions and many solemn promises. This wonderful proceeding took place on September 12th, 1794, in the Isle of Mauritius, District of Pampelavuso. It is the last known act of any member of the society, real or supposed. There remains to be stated, on the authority of personal researches, that the modern Rosicrucian Fraternities which are not infrequently heard of, both in England and America—such as the Rosicrucian Society of England, which has branches in several of our largest towns, and a Metropolitan London College, the Rosicrucian Society of Boston, &c.—have no connection other than the names which they have adopted with the old and original association, and they are devoid of mystical tradition. For all that is known to the contrary, the genuine Order of Rosicrucians may still exist, but its brethren keep well the secret of their initiation.

It is only just to add, that the late Mr Hargrave Jennings who for many years had endeavoured unsuccessfully to revive the Rosicrucian philosophy of Robert Fludd, the Kentish mystic, has obtained considerable credence for an extravagant hypothesis concerning the origin of the society, which identifies them with the builders of Stonehenge and Carnac, and discerns in their philosophy the historical basis of all the religions of the world. It has obtained a considerable following among uncritical persons; but his opinions, whether considered in themselves or in the manner of their presentation, are wholly beside any serious consideration, and they have been sufficiently dealt with in a history of the Rose Cross Fraternity and its traceable origin, which was published in the autumn of 1887. To that work we must venture to refer our readers, as the only source of unperverted historical information which exists in the English language.

THE FREEMASONS.

THE existing connection of Masonry with the science of the mystics is confined now to its emblems, but the fraternity originated in magic, and among alchemists and magicians. Here it is necessary to distinguish. There are two branches of Masonry as there are two of alchemy. There is the ancient Craft Masonry which is unconnected with occultism, and there is the more modern symbolic form which absorbed the operative degrees, and it is that which originated in mysticism. The present constitution of the brotherhood as an association for the diffusion of benevolence, of the principles of humanity, and the development of moral perfection, offers naturally a suitable field for the labours of the modern mystic. The foundation of all transcendental philosophy is the doctrine of interior regeneration, and its end is the Perfect Man. This also is the foundation, and such the end, of Masonry. In considering the institution, we must have regard to its true principles. Undeniably these have been obscured in the process of time; it has been corrupted by worldly wealth and magnificence; it has turned away its eyes from its objects; the transcendental eucharist has been abandoned for the banquet, and the pomp of power has out-glittered the spiritual splendour of the great reconstructive work; but the principles are there, and let us hope that within the ranks of the brotherhood, but without if not within, it will be possible to inform them with new life.

The present paper will be necessarily of a brief character, and is intended merely to indicate the line of thought which the student would do well to follow in his researches into the mysteries of the symbolic architects. Here, as occasionally in other cases, where

the results of long reading are unavoidably compressed
into the smallest possible space, we must entreat the
good will of the student, and trust that he will forbear to demand in a summary the explicit reasons and
detailed authorities for the statements we are about to
make. At the same time, we ask only a tentative faith.
In a forthcoming "Esoteric History of Freemasonry," he
will find the entire subject exposed, with the necessary
proofs, documents, and available sources of knowledge, or
if specially interested in the Masonic problem, he may
profitably undertake an independent course of research.

The first statement that it is necessary to make embodies a word of warning; we are addressing in this work
a circle of readers who, we suppose, are in search of a
positive knowledge concerning the world beyond. We
suppose them to be dissatisfied with what is called supernatural faith as an evidence of things not seen. We
suppose them to have turned to mysticism as to a possible instrument of communication with the things transcending sense, or as a means of providing that instrument. As such, we have warned them continually against
stultifying their noble ambition by practices of superstition or by accepting principles of credulity. To the
best of our ability we have shown them where it is possible that they may find the light, and we have shown also
the by-paths which no man can traverse with profit.
Now, it is needful that we should add another word of
counsel. Masonry is second to Rosicrucianism alone in
the remote and misty magnificence of vast claims, of
weird associations, of symbolic grandeur, and historic
mystery. Its origin is supposed to be merged in the
night of time; it is referred to Solomon, and still in the
hearts of the brotherhood is edified the parabolic temple;
it is referred to the Eleusinian mysteries, and mystic
words and inviolable secrets are spoken daily in the innumerable lodges of the Order; it is referred again to
the Rosicrucians, and Masonry still embodies, together
with its moral precepts, a tradition of alchemy and
magic which is expounded in the books of its old
initiates.

From a century of contradictory sources it borrows

a many-splendured aureole of romance and of esoteric fable, which is eminently liable to attract the soul-student at the threshold of mystic research, and to tempt him to seek in the penetralia of this unique institution a certain guiding light, till the day dawn and the day-star arise from on high upon his mind. We must counsel him to overcome this gravitation of his desires towards Masonry. There is no light there; there is no secret of the soul enshrined in the recesses of its suggestive cere- monial; whatever it may have been in the past, at the present day it neither is, nor claims to be, more than "a beautiful system of morality veiled 'in allegories· and illustrated by symbols." It is true that the alle- gories and the symbols admit of a profound inter- pretation, but of its nature Masons, as a body, have no conception. If anyone desire to be affiliated with the Fraternity, so as to participate in the good work of a benevolent society, to share in the privileges of an influ- ential body, or because they are attracted by "the boast of heraldry" and the "pomp of power," let them do so by all means; but not in the search after mystic truth, not in the hope of discovering the secrets of the regeneration and reconstruction of humanity; for though ostensibly these are the objects of association, it is clear that since the advent of symbolic Masonry, it has accom- plished nothing of the kind, and no one is seriously con- cerned with the realisation of such an idea. The exist- ing relation of the mystic to Masonry should be that of an apostle towards a field which is suitable for his labours, and not of an earnest seeker towards a source of light. Otherwise, to the student it is simply time squandered to master the ritual and the mysteries of Freemasonry, or to concern himself in any way with the bogus hypotheses which do duty in many cases for a sketch of its early history. It is interesting only by reason of those aims which are so largely forgotten, though they are still written about, and by reason of the original connection which it possessed with magic and alchemy—a reiterated statement which brings us back to a former point.

The ascertainable origin of symbolic Masonry is in

ancient Craft Masonry, and of the latter it may at once be affirmed that we have no means of tracing it to its genesis. It is asserted by Paton to have subsisted from the first ages of human history. This, of course, is a statement which transcends verification, and essentially is of the sphere of the faith masonic, which students acquainted with the gigantic literature of the Fraternity will acknowledge to be large in its demands upon members. Mr Paton adduces, and, of course, is able to adduce no arguments in favour of his position, but some have been occasionally attempted by anterior writers committed to similar views, and they are uniformly confined to such sophistic generalisations as follow. "Architecture could only have been preceded by Agriculture, so that in this science the first efforts of human skill must have been tried, and man's first successes achieved over Nature. The first architects therefore would be philosophers; the information acquired individually would be imparted to others of the same profession, and an association would naturally be formed for the communication of knowledge amongst its members, and their improvement. Initiation ceremonies would be adopted to excite in outsiders a respect for the profession, and such a society did exist in Egypt, and there only we discover the first traces of Freemasonry."

When the cogency of this kind of reasoning is once admitted, it is only a further step to assert that the origin of Masonry is not merely to be referred to the first ages of human history, but that it is identical with the first man, who in all probability was an architect after a primitive fashion, and whose rudimentary experience was communicated to his posterity. Needless to say the claim has been made by a number of ingenuous authors, and as there was no assignable reason why it should stop with Adam, it has transcended the sublunary world, and as the universal Creator may in a sense be regarded as the Architect of the Universe, he has also been strenuously affirmed to be the first Freemason, and in the minds of romantic historians the Order is most logically regarded as invested with a divine character.

Happily such reasoning has passed away with the childhood of Masonic literature. Later and more sober historians are content to refer it to Solomon and the architects whose consummate genius elaborated the eastern splendours of the first Temple; to the mysteries of Eleusis and Bacchus; to the mystic sect of the Jewish Essenes; to the Christian Gnostics; to the secret assemblies of pagans who cultivated the proscribed worships of Greece and Rome after the death of the Emperor Julian, and very possibly perpetuated their existence through the whole of the dark ages; to the orders of chivalry, and especially to that of the Templars; to the secret tribunal of Free Judges; to the mediæval Kabbalists; and to many other sources which, because they are unaccountable themselves, are thought adequate to explain the origin of an association which is supposed to have existed in all ages and in all nations, yet is practically without a history.

It is impossible in a brief space to do justice to these opinions, which are all very curious, very interesting, and an essential part of the romance of history. But, as far as possible in the words of masonic writers, we shall cite what has been advanced in support of the most important of these theories.

The Rev. George Oliver claims to have most carefully and impartially weighed an enormous mass of evidence, collected from all quarters of the historical horizon, on the question of the alleged connection which subsists between Masonry and the Ancient Mysteries. He is personally of opinion that the latter were simply an idolatrous corruption of the sacred, primeval principles embodied in the great fraternal order, and that Masonry originated initiation. "The rites of that science which is now received under the appellation of Freemasonry were exercised in the antediluvian world, revived by Noah after the Flood, practised by mankind at the building of Babel . . . , and at the dispersion spread into every settlement . . . , and modelled into a form, the great outlines of which are distinctly to be traced in the mysteries of every heathen nation, exhibiting the shattered remains of one true system whence they were derived." But the analogies—real or supposed—are independent of personal opinions, and it is with those alone that we are concerned.

The researches of various writers seem to have established the fact that all ancient mysteries of which we have any trace, whether in Egypt, India, Greece, or Rome, were radically identical, though formally different. Those of Egypt, says Oliver, contained all the secrets of their religion and politics, and inspired dread and terror throughout the world. By the uninitiated they were regarded as vehicles of knowledge more than human, and their dispensers were reputed to possess some high and peculiar attributes of divinity. When Grecian philosophy began to prevail, the mysteries were applied by wise men to a particular investigation of the nature and attributes of the Deity. After Pythagoras had remodelled them, and different sects of philosophers began to entertain new and irreconcilable opinions on the subject of research, the same speculations were continued with untiring avidity. They had very indistinct notions of the true God, and entertaining gross and sensual ideas of his nature, it is no wonder that vice became deified, and that the commission of every unnatural lust was not only permitted but even made a test of reverence to the deity. Purity fled from these institutions as they retrograded from the true worship of God. All, however, preserved a disguised tradition of the creation and fall of man, as well as of the universal deluge; their most significant emblems were the theological ladder, the triple support of the Universal Lodge —called by Masons Wisdom, Strength, and Beauty; the Point within a Circle, and many other undoubted emblems of Masonry. They used the same form of government which is now common to the whole Fraternity, the same system of secrecy, allegory, and symbolic instruction, all tending to the same point—the practice of moral virtue. No one was admitted without previous probation and initiation; candidates were bound by solemn oaths, united by invisible ties, taught by symbols, distinguished by signs and tokens, and impelled by a conscientious adherence to the rules of their Order.

They professed to practise the most rigid morality, justice towards men, and piety towards the gods.

Those who connect the first Temple of the Jews with Masonic architects do not lose sight of the Mysteries, though they consider them under another aspect. They affirm on historical grounds that the people of Attica went in quest of superior settlements a thousand years before Christ, and settled in Asia Minor, and the provinces they acquired were called Ionia. For a short time these Asiatic colonies surpassed the mother country in prosperity and science. Sculpture in marble and the Doric and Ionic orders of architecture were the creations of their skill and experience. They returned to instruct the mother country, and the world is indebted to the Dionysian artificers for the noblest of the classical styles. The Dionysiæ were an association of scientific men who possessed the exclusive privilege of erecting temples, theatres, and other public buildings in Asia Minor. They existed under the same appellation in Syria, Persia, and India. They supplied Ionia and the surrounding countries as far as the Hellespont with theatrical apparatus by contract, and erected the magnificent temple at Icos to Bacchus, the founder of their Order. The members of this association, which was intimately connected with the Dionysian mysteries, were distinguished from the uninitiated by the science which they possessed, and by appropriate words and signs devised for purposes of recognition. Like Freemasons, they were divided into lodges, which were distinguished by different appellations. They occasionally held convivial meetings in houses erected and consecrated for this purpose, and each separate association was under the direction of a master and president, or wardens. They held a general meeting once a year, which was solemnized with great pomp and festivity, and at which the brethren partook of a splendid entertainment provided by the master, after sacrifices had been offered to the gods. They used particular utensils in their ceremonial observances, some of which are exactly similar to those which are still employed by the Fraternity of Freemasons, and the more opulent artists were bound to provide for the necessities of poorer brethren. The very monuments which were reared by these Masons to the memory of their masters and wardens remain to the present day in the Turkish burying grounds at Siverhisson and Eraki. The inscriptions they bear give expression in strong terms to the gratitude of the Fraternity for the distinguished exertions of their departed superiors in behalf of the Order, for their generosity and benevolence to individual members, and for their private virtues, as well as for their conduct in public. If it be possible to prove the identity of any two societies, says Mr Cross, an earnest American Mason, from the coincidence of their external forms, we are authorized to conclude that the Fraternity of Ionian architects and the Fraternity of Freemasons are exactly the same.

Now, it is maintained by the same writer that the Dionysiæ existed in Judea, while, on the authority of Josephus, the architectural style which they created was used at the erection of the Temple. "The vicinity of Jerusalem to Egypt, the connection of Solomon with the royal family of that land, the progress of the Egyptians in architectural science, their attachment to mysteries and hieroglyphical symbols, and their probable employment by the King of Israel, are together a considerable argument for the Syrian plantation of masonry in ancient times."

It will be seen that the writers whom we have cited are by no means content with referring the origin of Masonry to either the Mysteries or Solomon. Depths beyond depths, heights above heights, vistas behind vistas, were discerned by their capacious intelligence till the prospect was lost in the nebulous splendours of a primeval revelation, indefinite, yet dimly sensed. These reasoners are on the whole more acute than the circumscribed visionaries who are content to refer Freemasonry to one mythico-historical source, and as the analogical value is fairly well balanced in either case, they are equally pertinent for citation. Those who in the mystic sects of Judea at the dawn of the Christian age are delighted to trace the supposed presence of the typical trowel and compass, and especially to identify Masons with Essenian mystics, find it possible to arrange their hypothesis in harmony with both of the preceding views. Once it is allowed that the Dionysiæ abode in Judea, and edified the Temple projected by the wisest of men, it is desirable to know what became of them in subsequent ages, and fortunately it can be shown, to the complete satisfaction of the theorists, that there did exist an association of men in Palestine who had striking similarities to the Freemasons, and that they were called the Essenes. When a candidate was proposed for admission to this society, the strictest scrutiny was made into his character. Had his life been hitherto exemplary, did he seem capable of curbing his passions and regulating his conduct according to the austere maxims of the Order, he was presented, at the expiration of his novitiate, with a white garment as the emblem of the regularity of his conduct and the purity of his heart. A solemn oath was then administered to him, that he would never divulge the mysteries of his Order, that he would make no innovations on its doctrine, and that he would continue in that honourable course of piety upon which he had already entered. Like Freemasons, the Essenes instructed their young members in the knowledge which they derived from their ancestors; they admitted no women into their Society; they had special methods of recognition, strongly resembling Masonic devices; they had colleges of retirement, where they resorted to practise their rites, and settle the affairs of the society. After the performance of these duties they assembled in a large hall, where an entertainment was provided by the President or Master of the Cottage, who allotted a certain quantity of provisions to every individual. All distinctions of rank were abolished, and if preference was ever given it was to piety, liberality, and virtue. Treasurers were appointed in every town to supply the wants of indigent strangers. The Essenes pretended to higher degrees of piety and knowledge than the uninitiated vulgar, and albeit in this respect their pretensions were great, they were never questioned by their enemies. Though austerity of manner was one of the chief characteristics of the initiated Essenians, they frequently assembled in convivial parties. "These remarkable coincidences between the chief features of the Masonic and Essenian Fraternities, can be accounted for only by referring them to the same origin."

If we pass to a later period, one of the most interesting hypotheses is that which endeavours to establish a connection between Masonry and Chivalry. It asserts that the mysteries of the Fraternity were preserved and transmitted by the Orders of knighthood, and especially by the Knights Templars. Both, it is argued, were ceremonial institutions, both were symbolical, the objects were in each case identical, promotion took place by degrees, and different Orders were in both cases distinguished by different appellations. In regard to the Templars, it is advanced that almost all the secret associations of the ancients either originated or flourished in or about Syria. "It was here that the Dionysian artists and the Essenes arose. From this country also came several members of that trading association of masons which appeared in Europe during the dark ages, and we are assured that notwithstanding the unfavourable condition of that province, there exists at this day on Mount Libanus one of these Syriac fraternities.* As the Order of the Templars, therefore, was originally formed in Syria, and existed there for a considerable time, it would be no improbable supposition that they received their knowledge from the lodges in that quarter. But we are fortunately in this case not left to conjecture, for we are expressly informed by a foreign author, who was well † acquainted with the customs and history of Syria, that the Knights Templars were actually members of the Syriac Fraternities."

On the other hand, Éliphas Lévi supposes that this, the most mysterious of the Orders of chivalry, was a branch of Johannite mystics who were bent on rebuilding the Temple, and that, at the suppression of the society, Jacques de Molay, the last grand master, founded, on the night before his execution, the first three lodges of Masonry to perpetuate, under another name and in a

* "Anthologia Hibernica," 1794, pp. 279-86.
† Alder—*De Drusis Montis Libani*, Roma, 1786.

still more disguised form, the secrets and designs of the Templars.

The diversity of all these views is a sufficient index of the uncertainty which involves their subject, and it justifies the statement already made that the genesis of Craft Masonry is historically untraceable, a fact which, however, in itself is not an undeniable proof of immense antiquity. The "Encyclopædia Britannica" accounts for the correspondences with the great secret institutions of the far past by the doctrine of psychical identity, "one of the most important results of anthropological science." It considers the mediæval building corporations to be the true historical precursors of Freemasonry, a view which has simplicity to recommend it, which does violence to no probability, while it fairly covers the facts. These corporations were originally grouped around the monasteries, and in the twelfth century the authority last cited affirms that "there are distinct traces of a general association acknowledging one set of craft laws, one set of secret signs and ceremonies, and, to a certain extent, one central authority at Strasbourg. Albertus Magnus is supposed to have introduced many of the Jewish and Arabian symbols which were appropriated by the craft," while the initiation ceremonial is said to have been copied from a Benedictine consecration. The architectural erudition and lodge-organization were imported from Germany into England, where the authentic documents of operative Masonry extend back to the year 926 A.D. About two centuries later, the principles of the craft were imported into Scotland, and there they are said to have been continued long after they had become extinct in continental kingdoms. "In this manner, Scotland became the centre from which these principles again issued to illuminate not only the nations on the continent, but every civilised portion of the world."

It is impossible here to attempt even a brief sketch of the progress of Craft Masonry in Great Britain. It is sufficient to state that in spite of its secret organization, its use of symbols, and its patronage by the great, who were occasionally invested with high ornamental dignities, it was exclusively of a practical nature, and its secrets were trade secrets. The first signs of its transformation are found towards the close of the seventeenth century, when the celebrated alchemist Elias Ashmole was, for some unexplained reason, accepted as an ordinary member of the great trade guild. Under his influence, and also, it is said, under that of Lord Wortley Montagu, it rapidly developed into a purely symbolic institution, the operative craft disappeared, and its ostensible objects became purely of a moral and intellectual kind. Under this aspect it spread rapidly, and about a century later took root in France, where it diffused a great light, and attracted universal attention at a period of social upheaval and restless research after every species of novelty.

It is there and in Germany that symbolical Freemasonry became largely and almost inseparably identified with magic, alchemy, and the rest of the secret sciences. It is there that its ranks were recruited from the members of the mystic sects of the Martinists; it is there that the so-called adept Cagliostro established his Egyptian grades and revived the wisdom of the Magi; it is there that Baron Tschoudy instructed masonic apprentices in the arcane doctrine of practical alchemy; it is there that the Masonic grade of Rose-Cross was developed from the typology of the Rosicrucians; it is there that the mysterious Misraim Rite was imported from the coast of the Adriatic, bearing Chaldaic statutes, distributing symbolic and mystic degrees, conferring alchemical titles, and possessing veiled masters; it is there that the masonic children of the Primeval Light pretended to accomplish the work of human reconstruction; it is there that the mysterious Count de St Germain "scoured the Masonic Lodges, commercing in immortality, and recounting his experiences in previous centuries;" it is there that the charitable and interesting *Loge de la Bienfaisance* shone at Lyons with a pure light of advanced mysticism; it is there that the doctrine of the Fraternity was adorned by the magnetic discoveries of the Austrian doctor Anton Mesmer; it is there, and in Berlin, that the allegories of the Order were interpreted in a transcendental sense. It was under the shadow of Masonic protection that "Rosicrucians and theosophists performed innumerable prodigies," that Schöpfer evoked the dead, and a Swedenborgian propaganda began. During the whole of the eighteenth century, the European history of magic and Hermeticism is coincident with that of Freemasonry, facts which sufficiently substantiate the statement which opened this article, that symbolic Masonry originated in mysticism, and was to a large extent promulgated by magicians and alchemists.

No history of Freemasonry in its connection with Mysticism has been yet attempted, and as Freemasonry, independently of Mysticism, is without direct interest to the occult student, we shall omit the bibliographical paragraph with which most of our articles have concluded, and shall refer him to the forthcoming work— "The Esoteric History of Freemasonry"—of which we have made mention above—as a methodical account of the Order in its connection with transcendental science.

PART IV.

———o———

MESMERISM.

THE student who has followed us thus far in our account of the methods and processes of the mystics, will be aware that the wonders of old magic were accomplished in most cases by a certain suspension of the senses, and by a powerful artificial exaltation of the interior faculties. An elaborate, if uncouth, ceremonial surrounded the operator for the time being with a species of new environment. Prayers, fasts, ablutions, watchings, and weird incantations, combined for the elevation of his intellectual nature into another plane of existence. The process at times may have missed its proper end, and the Magus may have been plunged into a chaos of hallucination. At others he emerged with cleansed and clarified perceptions into a higher "magnetic" atmosphere, and created for himself a brief correspondence with the transcendent intelligences in superior forms of subsistence. Clairvoyant, clair-audient, clairsentient, he invoked spirits, and they made answer to his will because he was "within their plane." Now, this extranatural condition, produced by the formulæ of practical magic, was also attained, and apparently in an advanced degree, by the contemplation and absorption of the purely interior mystics, who in solitude and isolation entered into the thought-world, and inquired within themselves for that instrument of correspondence which was to unite their better nature with the higher law and higher intelligence of the universe. In the monasteries of the Latin church, the saintly men of Christendom appear to have achieved the highest altitudes of the spirit which are possible to embodied man, by the process of introspection. This process, however, is particular to no age and to no religion. It was practised in the extreme Orient many centuries before the first words of the Christian Evangel resounded through barbaric Europe; and it is undoubtedly a higher branch of that singular condition, which after so much unbelief and misconception has at length been recognised by modern science under the name of hypnotism. The hypnotic state is, however, but one out of many series of phenomena which have long been familiar to professors and students of that unexplored region of pathology which has been termed mesmerism and animal magnetism.

Magic is older than history; it is older than the Records of the Past; it is older than the Book of the Dead, and the hieroglyphic literature of primeval Egypt; and whether in Egypt or Chaldea, or in those highlands beyond the Himalayas which are the supposed cradle of the Aryan race, wherever magic flourished, it has ever been intimately associated with rites and observances calculated to produce in the operator either one or more of the magnetic states. Mesmerism, therefore, to make use of the older term, and of one which commemorates an illustrious, if not wholly high-minded discoverer, was known to the ancients, while the trances and ecstasies, which are included among its most frequent phenomena, are coincident with the entire history of mystical religious experience, and constitute, in fact, that state of interior repose which, according to the Platonic philosophy, is the source of inspired visions, and wherein "the light of eternity . . ., the light revealed to Zoroaster, and all the sages of the East," is manifested to the mind's eye. It will also be obvious, even to the least thoughtful reader, that the trance artificially induced by the ceremonies of magic, by the vigils of the saints, by the contemplation of the quietists, by the passes of the disciples of Mesmer, and by the hypnotic disc of the modern pathologists of France, is essentially connected with the natural trance of cataleptic patients. Now, the history of cataleptic affections has an antiquity which is so generally accepted, as to be practically beyond dispute.

The power of the hand, the power of the word, and the power of the human eye, take rank among the most conspicuous subjects of ancient symbolism. In a remarkable representation of a mummy case, preserved in the priceless folios of the illustrious Abbé Montfaucon, we find "a bed or table, on which lies a sick man, before whom stands a person clothed in a brown garment, with his eyes open. His countenance is turned upon the patient; his left hand is placed upon the breast, while the right is held over the head of the sick man, quite in the position of a magnetizer." A French writer, in the "Annals of Animal Magnetism," appears to have been the first to draw attention to the mesmeric signifi-cance of this picture, and he makes mention of other mummies, "where standing figures touch the feet, the head, the sides, or the thighs" of recumbent sufferers. Elihu Rich, in a short cyclopædic account of magnetic heal ing, has assured us that these scenes do not stand alone. "Figures occur on the amulets or charms known as 'Abraxei,' all more or less manifesting an acquaintance with magnetism. The priest with the dog's head, or mask of Anubis, occurs repeatedly, with his hands vari-ously placed on the supposed patient. Some of these figures are given by Montfaucon. In one of them, the masked figure places one hand on the feet, the other upon the head of the patient; in a second, one hand is laid upon the stomach, the other upon the head; in a third, the hands are upon the loins; in a fourth, the hands are placed upon the thighs, and the eyes of the operator are fixed upon the patient's countenance." These are facts which might be multiplied almost in-definitely could reference be extended to the medical marvels of the temple of Serapis at Memphis, where cures are alleged to have been performed by the hierophants in part by the imposition of hands, and in part by the creation of an artificial lethargy in the patient; or again, to the thaumaturgic ritual of initiation made use of by the Greek mystics at Thebes, Lemnos, and Samothrace.

The traditional secrets of magic which Greece acquired from Egypt and other regions of remote antiquity, and which she imparted in turn to the Latins, were combined with the Babylonian and Assyrian magic of the Jews, and were somehow preserved to the Christian centuries, and inherited by Western mystics. The saints of the Catholic church required no traditional secrets to initiate them into the transcendental possibilities of ecstasy, for they pursued independently, and, as it were, by a natural instinct, the path of hypnotic sense-suspension, and acquired a forced correspondence with the spiritual world by a life-isolation from all but inevitable connection with earthly things. But the healing branch of that science, which at its highest is supposed to have made souls whole by connecting them with the source of the soul's health, and at its lowest is supposed to have cured the diseases of man's flesh, reappeared after a slumber of centuries, or is, at least, for the first time, openly referred to by Paracelsus in the sixteenth century; and, so far as we can trace, it was he also who from the analogies of the natural magnet, would first appear to have endowed it with the dignities of a magnetic hypothesis.

"This remarkable thinker maintained," says a recent French work which is of high medical authority, "that the human body was endowed with a double magnetism; that one part attracted to itself the planets, and was nourished by them, whence came wisdom, thought, and the senses; that the other portion attracted to itself the elements, and disintegrated them, whence came flesh and blood; that the attractive and hidden virtue of man resembles that of amber and of the magnet; that by this virtue the magnetic virtue of healthy persons attracts the enfeebled magnetism of those who are sick. After Paracelsus, many learned men of the sixteenth and seventeenth centuries — Grocenius, Burgrave, Helmont, Robert Fludd, Kircher, and Maxwell—believed that in the magnet they could recognise the properties of that universal principle by which minds addicted to generalisation thought that all natural phenomena might be explained," and the external mineral loadstone was combined with the interior Paracelsian *magnes* for the alleviation of all disorders.

It has been generally concluded that Mesmer made profit out of the magnetic speculations and experiments of his predecessors, and indeed in his capacity as physician he could scarcely have ignored what was once so important a branch of empirical healing. Moreover, his explanatory theorems are proof positive that he was very largely indebted to the theosophical physics of the past. If it be evident, however, from the monuments of remote antiquity that the most enlightened nations of the elder world healed by the imposition of hands, by the willed transmission of "vitality," and by the passes called magnetic, it is still more certain that the professors of the all-curing loadstone, and the healing qualities of the hand and eye, were completely unacquainted with this fact, and though the literature of mesmerism is exceedingly comprehensive and large, it does not inform us by what process of observation or reasoning the physician of Geneva was led up to the secret of the old sanctuaries—more accurately, the information which it gives is insufficient to account for the felicitous guess which recovered a lost science for the benefit of the modern world.

Mesmer, a German by birth, was born in the year 1734, and he took his degree as a doctor of medicine at Vienna in 1766. He immediately preceded the Revolution, and he just out-lived Waterloo. His doctrine was diffused at a time when the pure mysticism of the Christian centuries seemed destined to perish with the recluse philosopher Saint-Martin, and, speaking from the historical standpoint, his discovery was the one thing which saved mysticism from complete oblivion.

The connection between mysticism and mesmerism will seem naturally remote to the ordinary pathological student, but experiments in dual consciousness, in the possibilities of suggestion, in the transference of thought, and in the production of a profound artificial sleep, appear after a careful study to be only the outer fringe of an ancient secret knowledge by which the sanctuary of the inmost man might be unlocked, and whereby the interior mystic might enter into the realities which transcend the superficial truths of the phenomenal world. We speak tentatively and hypothetically, but we base our statement upon investigations other than our own, and upon authorities in occult science who are greater than ourselves. It is open to any one who has the necessary qualifications of aspiration, patience, and energy to learn by his individual experience that mystic practice is not hallucination, and that it is not fraud. He need not go further, though it is true that he must step with care, than the modern phenomena of Spiritualism, to find out that there is an intelligent world transcending sense ; and on the faith of the evidence of all the mystics, we must set down that it is possible to enter that world, and that the door of that entrance is mesmerism, by which we must be understood to refer to the thing—whatever it may be—and not to the multitudes of false conceptions which attach to the name. We are writing a hand-book for inquirers, it is once again necessary to observe, and' if any one wishes to become acquainted with the quality of this evidence, he must be referred to the fountain-head, to the unwritten history of mysticism, as it exists in the lives of the mystics, and he will there find after what manner the ecstatics of all the Christian centuries performed the interior *Itinerarium Mentis ad Deum*, and attained the beatific absorption of Nirvana in Christ. Then he must compare what he has learned with the facts of pathological history in natural and artificial catalepsy, and if he can discriminate between disease which has its seat in organic weakness and disruption of mind and body, between the plunging of an unprepared nature into a condition which is outside nature, and between the sanctified introspection of a pure mind, a purged will, and an exalted aspiration and purpose, he will be in a position to understand what is essentially identical and what is incidentally diverse in the mystic and magnetic trance. His practical acquaintance with psychology and hypnotism may then be applied to an appreciation of the claims of the mystics in respect of their ecstatic absorption, when, if he should bear in mind the reiterated statement which has been the keynote of this book, he will conclude that these things are not of faith, that is to say, that any one who is vitally concerned in them should not stop short at the evidence and be content to believe. The mystics will tell him that it is open to him also to participate in the *bona Dei in terra viventium*, but that if he will share their privileges, he must also live their life.

We are conscious that we have been unwillingly speaking in terms somewhat enigmatical, and it will be well, therefore, if, avoiding all involved details, we can afford to the student a few lines of plain information on the end that was sought by the mystics through their profound process of introspection, and transcendental self-hypnotising for the suspension of sense-correspondences, and the manifestation of the interior light and life. There was neither secret nor mystery about it ; it was always openly referred to, precisely defined and described. At the same time, the methods necessarily were of an arcane or, at least, recondite character, because they were concerned with the mystery of spiritual growth, and that great psycho-alchemical reconstruction which has been emphasized in one term of many heights and wonders—the New Birth, or Regeneration. Here is what we read in a popular hand-book of mysticism, which circulated widely in France in the middle of this century :—

"The union of God with the soul is the principle of all mystic life. But this union, the fulness and final consummation of which cannot be experienced till death has been passed through and eternity has been achieved, can be accomplished on this earth in a more or less perfect manner, and the literature of entire mysticism has no other end than to unveil to us, by a full and profound analysis of the different stages of evolution in the spirit of man, the diverse successive degrees of this divine union. Seven distinct stages of the soul's ascent towards God have been recognised by mystics, and they constitute what has been emblematically called the castle of the interior man. They represent the seven absolute processes of psychic transfiguration. The first link in this arcane sequence is called the state of prayer, which, from the pneumatic standpoint, is the concentration of the intellectual energies upon God as the object of thought, which is commonly assisted by the ceremonial appeal made by religion to the senses. It has, however, a higher aspect, comprised in the second evolutionary process, and called the state of mental prayer. Here the illusory phenomena of the visible world, are regarded as informed with an inner pneumatic significance, to divine which is a chief end of mysticism. In order to make progress therein, and so attain the third stage, it is necessary that the aspirant, shaping all practical life in conformity with his theory, should perform no outward act except with a view to its inward meaning, all things which are of time and earth and man being simply figures and symbols of earth and heaven and God. The postulant, as he advances, will perceive that the inmost thoughts of his own conscious being are only a limited and individual speculation of the speech or word of God, concealed even in its apparent revelation, and itself a veil of that divine truth which must be removed for the contemplation of the truth absolute which is behind it. When he has reached this point the mystic will have entered on the third stage of his illumination. This is the most difficult of all. It is termed by mystics the obscure night, and here it is necessary that the aspirant should become stark naked, should empty himself completely, should be stripped of all his faculties, renouncing all his own predilections, his own thoughts, his own will—in a word, his whole self. Aridity, weariness, temptation, desolation, darkness, are characteristic of this epoch, and they have been experienced by all who have ever made any progress in the mysteries of mystical love. The fourth condition is denominated the prayer of quietism. Complete immolation of self and unreserved surrender into the hands of God, have repose as their first result. Such quietism, however, is not to be confounded with insensibility, for it leads to the sole real activity, to that which has God for its impulse. The fifth degree in the successive spiritualization of the human soul is called the state of union, in which the will of man and the will of God become substantially identified. This is the mystical irrigation which fertilizes the garden of the soul. During this portion of his development, the individual, imbued with a sovereign disdain for all things visible, as well as for himself, accomplishes in peace, serenity, and joy of spirit, the will of God, as it is made known to him by the Word of God supernaturally speaking within him. On the extreme further limit of this condition, the mystic enters the sixth state, which is that of ecstatic prayer, which is the soul's transport above and outside itself. It constitutes a union with divinity by the instrument of positive love, which is a state of sanctification, beatitude, and ineffable torrents of delight flowing over the whole being. It is beyond description, it transcends illustration, and its felicity is not to be conceived. Love, which is a potency of the soul, or of that anima which vivifies our bodies, has passed into the spirit of the soul, into its superior, divine, and universal form, and this process completed comprises the seventh and final stage of pneumatic development, which is that of ravishment. Renouncing all that is corporeal about it, the soul becomes a pure spirit, capable of being united, in a wholly celestial manner to the Uncreated Spirit, whom it beholds, loves, serves, and adores above and beyond all created forms. And this is the mystic marriage, the perfect union, the entrance of God and Heaven into the interior man."

The history of Christian supernaturalism informs us that in these seven stages of transcendental adoration the body of the mystic was seen to rise from the ground, and to poise itself mysteriously in space. Ravished by interior visions, he became insensible to all that was passing around him, and at the same time his physical senses, which had suspended correspondence for the moment with normal exterior environment, were ministered to in a manner which we should term magical ; he saw, heard, felt, tasted, but on another plane of being ; and occasionally his indescribable ecstasy was manifested in the apparition of lights and halos about him, and in the diffusion of an unearthly fragrance. If all these phenomena are to be accepted as literally true, they surpass in degree what has been achieved by psychological experiment at the present day, but in respect of their kind and class they are the phenomena of ecstatic hypnotism.

We have sufficiently indicated the historical foundation for the antiquity of those classes of transcendenta phenomena which are generically embraced by mesmerism, and we have exceeded the limits of our purpose to establish a connection between them and the highest altitudes of mystic end and action. If it be impossible to do justice to the latter subject in an elementary treatise, it is equally beyond our scope to supply the student with an account of the various methods by which the hypnotic and mesmeric conditions can be induced in suitable subjects. It has been throughout our endeavour to make this handbook as practical as its design would permit, and in the ceremonies and ritual of occult science we have given information at first hand from the most rare and authentic sources. In the present instance, however, we are dealing with a matter which is almost of popular knowledge, which possesses a vast literature in almost every form and language, while its methods and processes may be learnt from any one of the innumerable pamphlet guides which may be obtained at a nominal cost. What is superfluous from its general diffusion may be therefore reasonably spared. On the other hand, in the elaborate courses of experiment which have been undertaken by investigators who have become authorities through experience, there is obviously more than can be comprised in a preliminary sketch. It only remains for us to tabulate the several classes of phenomena which occur in the various phases of mesmerism, and to refer the student who desires to extend his knowledge beyond the scope of this paper to the authorities which he will require to consult.

Both mesmerism and hypnotism, in so far as they can be distinguished one from another, may be divided broadly into two sections, of which the first and most important has reference to therapeutics, and is, in fact, the development of the so-called magnetic condition for the cure of diseases in the subject, for the performance of painless operations, and for the diagnosis of medical cases, when the stage of clairvoyance is reached. In a sufficiently susceptible subject, the passes and will of the mesmerist induce a condition of profound trance, which, before the discovery of anæsthetics, was made use of by Dr Elliotson in India, with precisely the same success as anæsthetics, for the amputation of limbs, and the removal of cancers; which were suffered by the patient unconsciously, and in the absence of any of those subsequent ill effects which not infrequently attend upon chloroform and stupefying gases.

The curative effects of mesmerism are not less astonishing than its power in the suspension of consciousness during agonising operations, nor do they by any means invariably depend upon the entrancement of the subject. Passes made over affected portions of the body, sometimes the simple imposition of hands, at others that process which is now termed Massage, being a department of medical rubbing, and fundamentally a mesmeric treatment, have produced wonders in healing, which rest upon unimpeachable evidence, and their citation would fill volumes. It would be scarcely exaggeration to say that almost every species of disease, other than hereditary, has been successfully eradicated by the methods which transcendental therapeutics have inherited from Anton Mesmer and from the psychologists who succeeded him. Painless parturition, the cure of paralysis, the restoration of sight and hearing, are included in the long list. Yet the nature of the agent which is at work in these remarkable physiological reconstructions is entirely unknown. The hypothesis of an imponderable magnetic fluid projected by the will of the mesmerist is now very generally rejected; the influence of the imagination is insufficient to cover the facts. The transmission of a vital fluid would seem to have a side of truth, for the operations of curative mesmerism exhaust the vitality of the mesmerist, but this again is insufficient, for the cures of some healers have been performed on a scale which is so colossal as to be out of all proportion with the extent of their vitality. The insufficiency of existing explanations has led many to have recourse to a purely spiritual theory, which, whatever its value, is naturally distrusted by most scientific investigators.

An acquaintance with the methodical forms of mesmerism is by no means indispensable to the healer, and, as a rule, the most extraordinary cures have been effected without any devised process. In the present century the Prince of Hohenlohe and the Zouave Jacob performed cures which in nature and number might well be termed miraculous. In the last century we have the authority of Prince Bartenstein, who witnessed on one occasion the complete restoration of four hundred blind, deaf, dumb, and paralytic people. The simple *attouche-ment* which in the case of a royal hand was once considered sufficiently potent to cure the most ineradicable of diseases, "the king's evil," appears to have been the one formula which was adopted by both these phenomenal persons, while the mere presence of Jean Baptiste Viannay, the saintly Curé D'Ars, in the public ministrations of the altar or in the private *séance* of the confessional, is said to have been all that was needed to effect conquests over a variety of complaints, commonly termed incurable.

Therapeutic phenomena taking place in the presence of the holy are another phase of the grand mesmeric mystery which is as ancient as sense-suspensions, trance, and hypnotic vision. Miraculous healing, indeed, has ever been considered a prerogative of saints, and a test of divine mission. At this day it is still credited, and still practised, and still applied to by numbers, who would scorn to debase it by association with the name of Mesmer, and who, disregarding fundamental identities, would deny that it had any connection with "animal magnetism," with the transmission of vitality, or the existence of an odic force. By these it is commonly classed among the miraculous effects of prayer, and Faith-Healing, in one or other of its phases, is notoriously a fact of the times. It is practised in many ways; it is associated with many types of religious opinion; by some of its apostles it is connected with certain dogmas, a belief in which is held to be indispensable; others would identify it with no creed and no doctrine; for them it is an universal influence of the universal Spirit of God. In many cases the belief in this abnormal power, and personal experience of its working, have created currents of enthusiasm which have exceeded reasonable bounds, discrediting testimony which might otherwise have been more generally accepted, and bringing disrepute upon movements which in their aspirations were just and good.

There is one form of psychic cure which is carefully distinguished by its professors from the medley of marvels which pass all confused under the name of Faith-Healing. It is termed Christian Science Healing, and it claims to have reduced the subject into the shape of a methodised spiritual gnosis. Its disciples will charge us with confusion for referring to it in a paper on Mesmerism, but we are treating in a broad and comprehensive manner of matters which in their deep centre are either one, or, at least, are radically joined, and defects of terminology are a common disability to which forbearance should be extended in what is still the infancy of psychological research. Among many systems and claimants, we recognise in the principles and disciples of this so-called Christian science, the most profound elements which have entered into the higher mysticism of all the ages, and, whatever the results which have been achieved, and we have heard personal testimony from cultured and thoughtful persons which is of real weight and value, we recognise that Christian Science Healing is to all appearance on the path of the mystics; it is on the path of Vaughan, Böhme, Saint Martin, and the best of the Quietists; and it is our duty in this section to refer the student to its literature for the purest quality of light in the recondite problems of that spiritual reconstruction of physical man which is said to be performed under the arcane potencies of prayer and faith, whether it be identified by name, or not, with what is called Faith-Healing.*

* Particular attention is invited to the *Christian Science Healing* of Miss Frances Lord. It is regarded by a certain section of modern mystical criticism as, in some sense, a clue to the old mystery of the Elixir of Life. On the outer plane there is, however, a correspondence between medicine, diet, and the conduct of physical life.

We have said that the cures which are attributed to mesmerism and its collaterals are not to be explained by the power of imagination, whatever the stimulus which may be applied to it. The statement was not made in the interests of any hypothesis, but simply in view of the evidence. Imagination, at the same time, is a great curative agent, and accordingly it has been the fashion for over half a century to explain all the phenomena of mesmeric therapeutics by that alone, or by that in conjunction with a theory of planned imposture when the explanation would be obviously misapplied. Both methods are now practically abandoned. Men of science have discovered, that in addition to the phenomena of healings, there are other branches of mesmeric experiment which it would wholly fail to cover, and under the name of hypnotism the whole subject is receiving gradual investigation. Scientific processes are like the mills of the gods, they grind slowly, but in the end they grind exceedingly small, and the generation of the moment very usually does good work by exploding the hypotheses, if not the methods, of its predecessor. This very hypothesis of the imagination in its relation to curative mesmerism is beginning to be reduced to its due proportions, and the power of the agent in question is now being confined to those diseases which are said to have been caused by imagination, the existence of real diseases which have originated in this manner being proved by the fact that imaginary or fictitious complaints can have no existence, and, positively speaking, by the collateral fact that complaints which have sometimes taken genuine hold of a patient, have demonstrably begun in his fancy acting on a nervous and abnormally susceptible temperament.

The second of the two sections with which the phenomena of mesmerism and hypnotism may be broadly divided, includes all experiments which are not of a therapeutic character. Their variety. is enormous, and their psychological significance as investigations into the undeveloped potencies of mind is so great that it is difficult to attempt its expression without using terms which would seem to be sensational. We are speaking of experiments which reveal to us the existence, deep down in our being, of faculties which may be called unknown, of other senses than those which we normally use, and of apparently foreign personalities behind our legitimate manifested personality, which ever we have considered as our most inalienable part, and as that which constitutes our *selves*.

The phenomena included in this section admit of further subdivision. There are those which are connected with simple muscular affections which are the first results of the trance condition, in whatsoever manner produced. What is generally observed at the beginning is, in the words of a recent writer, a remarkable quivering of the eyelids, a " contraction and then a dilation of the pupil of the eye," followed by a gradual closing of the eyelids and " by all the outward appearances of deep slumber. The arms fall listlessly by the side, the limbs are relaxed, and to anyone not in the secret the subject would appear to be sleeping heavily after some great and fatiguing exertion." The nervous centres which control the action of the muscles are at the same time stimulated into an abnormal excitability. " Even a gentle stroking of the skin is enough to produce the contraction of the muscles underlying ; a continued irritating of the same spot will cause the contraction to extend to the neighbouring and distant groups of muscles. . . . By employing the appropriate stimuli we are enabled to produce the continued contraction of any set of muscles we may select, and even to induce rigidity of the whole body." This rigidity constitutes a second stage in physical entrancement. The senses are imperfectly suspended in ordinary normal slumber. In the hypnotic or mesmeric state, the subject is unmoved by the strongest light directed straight upon his eyes, or by a stunning report at his ear, and he passes into a condition which closely resembles that of catalepsy. Experiments connected with the artificial suspension of the senses in the hypnotic, indifferently with the mesmeric, states, are of a very interesting character, but they are exclusively of an elementary kind. " In our

waking moments we enter into relation with the outer
world by means of the external senses; and the organic
functions of the body are controlled by nerve centres,
which are to a large extent subject to the higher
faculties of sense.   In this state our senses reveal to us
the other world as it is, and direct the functions of the
body appropriately to the nature of the external agents
by which they are impressed.   But in the hypnotic
slumber the functions of external and inner sense are
perplexingly disordered.   The hypnotised subject does
not see what is before his eyes, or hear the sound in his
ears; he sees and hears only the sights and sounds suggested to him by the magnetiser.   And the lower functions, such as nutrition, which are dependent upon the
perceptions of sense, are affected in like measure.   This
power of controlling the sense perceptions enables the
operator to make the patient blind or deaf to the present sights and sounds, and to make him see and hear—
and so of the other senses—what has no present existence outside the suggestions of the magnetiser. . . .
This kind of hallucination has been called *positive*, to
distinguish it from the former, to which the name
negative has been assigned."

What is suggested to the entranced sight of the subject must not, however, be identified with the normal
figments of imagination.   What is imposture on the part
of the operator is a vivid actuality to the patient.   The
entranced senses are, moreover, the slaves of the hypno-
tist; what his methods have deadened, they can also
quicken; he can arouse them into abnormal activity,
and, if he so wills it, his own arbitrary motions may be
imitated automatically by the subject with eyes gripped
close in the vice of catalepsy.

The control of the external senses must obviously
affect the intellectual faculties and the scope of will.   In
a lesser or greater degree, as the power of the operator
and the susceptibilities of the subject may vary in different persons, both are under the direct influence of the
mesmerist.   It is said that under circumstances which,
however, are seldom met with, the interior personality
of the subject may pass away from the influence of the

operator, but as a rule he controls for the time being the whole individuality of his patient. As a rule also the intellectual faculties are exceedingly quickened; a dull person becomes an acute reasoner; he will give answers upon subjects with which in his normal state he is practically unacquainted; he may occasionally be addressed in a language which he notoriously does not understand, but he will reply pertinently, his mind seeming to be for the time identified with the understanding of the mesmerist. It is said that he will himself speak in what, to him, are unknown tongues, but evidence in this direction should be received with extreme caution. The memory is also quickened to a surprising extent; there are instances of ignorant servant girls automatically repeating in the magnetic condition, with absolute accuracy, long passages from the Greek poets which they have heard recited by their masters at a period considerably previous. The creative faculties are also frequently developed, some manifesting a remarkable lyrical gift, and improvising lengthy poems with conspicuous fluency; while others exhibit an astonishing and hitherto unknown aptitude for musical composition or painting.

The suspension of will which accompanies the hypnotic state, placing the subject, in mind, morals, and body, at the complete disposal of the operator, also controls the individuality, which can be effaced and transformed according to the necessities of any experiment. "Tell the sleeping individual he is a child, and he will begin to play at the games of children; that he is a girl, and he will begin to sew; that he is a priest, and he will begin some sacerdotal function; that he is an old man, and he will call for a stick to support his steps; that he is a general, and he will draw himself up, give the word of command, &c.; that he is a dog, and he will crawl on all fours and bark." These, are, however, but elementary and surface phenomena. In some cases a new and underlying personality will spontaneously manifest, and if the hypnotic condition be prolonged, several of an opposite kind, and all more or less foreign to the patient's normal nature, will appear in periodical succession; an educated and virtuous person may develop a low and vicious character, while a low type of humanity will exhibit in the profundities of his being a higher form of consciousness. We are thus brought face to face with some of the most inscrutable problems in the esoteric nature of man.

Where new personalities are not developed, we have frequently new senses or new forms of perception; the chief of these are clairvoyance, clairaudience, and the phenomena which constitute psychometry. CLAIRVOY-ANCE is the development of the faculty of interior sight. It was discovered to the modern world by the Marquis de Puségur, a disciple and friend of Mesmer; but vision at a distance was familiar to the old operators of those forms of divination which have been described in a previous paper. That enlargement of mind to which we have already made reference is in itself a part of clairvoyance, and, under favourable conditions, it is brought to the test by the subject shewing acquaintance with mere matters of fact, as, for instance, the private history of another person outside the sphere of his knowledge. In other cases he perceives what is taking place at a distance, can read in a closed book, in a locked slate, or in a sealed letter. There is also a therapeutic variety in which the seer perceives the interior condition of a sick person, and of himself occasionally, and indicates the nature of the required remedy. The third degree is closely connected with the phenomena of modern spiritualism, and in some cases perhaps not less intimately with those of hallucination and illusion. In those cases, which may be reasonably included in the first of these categories, the interior being of the seer seems elevated into another form of subsistence, and he enters into correspondence with the spirits of the departed, and with other hierarchies of extramundane intelligence. CLAIR-AUDIENCE in the hypnotic and mesmeric states is of uncommon occurrence, and this also more properly belongs to spiritualism. It is that state in which Swedenborg, Böhme, and the mystics of all the ages have conversed with voices from the unseen, while absorbed in any one of the known species of entrancement. It takes a

more readily intelligible form when the spirit of the
subject is supposed to travel into distant earthly scenes,
where it hears the conversation as well as perceives the
actions of other human beings.

PSYCHOMETRY is comparatively a new departure in
psychic science. Here the clairvoyant is placed in correspondence physically with any object whatsoever, and
beholds in the interior condition the chief points in its
history. A lock of hair will reveal the entire personality
of the man from whose head it has been taken; a ring,
a fragment cut from a garment, a letter, &c., will produce identical results—whatever has been connected intimately with a human being presents that being to the
mind's eye of the seer. It is also asserted that the
natural history of a metal or mineral will be unfolded by
its mere pressure against the forehead of the hypnotic
subject; some important and apparently *bona-fide* books
have given details of numberless experiments in psycho-
metric mineralogy and geology.

The highest and rarest states of mesmerism are those
of the prophetic frenzy and of pure lucidity, but these
phases are at present outside the experience of professional men of science, and they encroach upon a region
of mysticism which transcends elementary limits.

Much, and with reason, has been written on the
dangers of hypnotic experiments and on the power which
it confides to persons who may conceivably abuse it.
Body and mind, will and imagination, consciousness and
personal identity, should not be lightly surrendered to
any custodian. Nevertheless, where an operator is possessed of all proper qualifications, we find that the
entranced subject, in the majority of cases, passes into
a higher condition of moral development. It is undoubtedly possible by the process of hypnotic experiment
to impress upon a patient the design of committing a
murder, and when he has to all appearance returned into
his normal life and senses, that impression will remain,
and he will commit that murder in exact accordance
with the directions laid down by the mesmerist. On the
other hand, it is equally possible to create an aversion in
a subject which will divert him from a habit of vice; it

is possible to awaken positive virtues which were previously wanting; and, not improbably, though adequate experiment is wanting in this direction, it is possible to originate in the trance a quickening of the intellectual faculties which shall be permanent in the ordinary state. Mesmerism and hypnotism have been termed the stone of the philosophers in action, and certainly they bring us to the knowledge of a spiritual agent which is potent both in the dissolution and reconstruction of the interior man. As such it is to be reckoned among the essential instruments of mysticism, and the careful, reverent, earnest development of its possibilities may be considered by the mystic student as indispensable to all progress in the experimental knowledge of the soul.

The literature of Mesmerism is so enormous that it is difficult to recommend any individual writers. Deleuze and Dupotet were great authorities in France, as were Elliotson and Gregory in England. Esdaile is valuable for his account of surgical operations performed during the trance state. Sandby is an instructive writer on the general subject; and there is interesting matter in some letters of Harriet Martineau. The work of Binet and his collaborator ranks high among modern books.

MODERN SPIRITUALISM.

WE have seen that the traditions of mediæval magic in the West were to some extent perpetuated in the doctrines and practices of mesmerism. The occult force which was first made known to the modern world by the physician of Geneva constituted at least a kind of connecting link between the phenomena of the old theurgic art which was familiar to the Christian masters of mysticism, and the long sequence of marvels with which every one at the present day has become more or less acquainted, under the conventional name of spiritualism. The pronaos of the spiritual temple has been said to be animal magnetism, and at a period which was prior to the date of the Rochester knockings, the German historians of magic were accustomed to interpret the thaumaturgic mysteries of the past by the light of the science of Mesmer. Insufficient as it was, this explanation had a certain base in fact, and it may be safely affirmed that both magic and modern spiritualism have had many phenomena in common with animal magnetism. Things which are thus interlinked cannot be fundamentally dissimilar; in all ages and nations the science of the soul must be reasonably supposed to consist in the development and application of the same arcane forces; between ancient and modern psychological phenomena there may be difference of mode and degree, but their manifestation must undoubtedly take place by virtue of the same laws.

In the several sections of this book we have already made reference repeatedly to the present condition of psychic science, to the facts with which it is connected, and to the investigations involved therein. We have said that the paths which we are now essaying to travel, were travelled by the old mystics, and by such landmarks of progress as we can discover in their mysterious writings, we seem entitled to conclude that they had advanced beyond ourselves. Spontaneous occurrences, such as Apparitions, Hauntings, Obsessions, and other phenomena which are not to be explained by the application of the known laws of Nature, have been common to all countries and to all times, and in the great majority of cases they involve, if genuine, the supposition of intelligence acting to some extent outside the visible world. The practical magic of the past was a series of methods and processes by which men endeavoured to enter into a conscious communication with the powers which produced these wonders, and to become acquainted, for whatever object, with the mysteries of the invisible. Modern spiritualism is simply another series of methods and processes, necessarily analogous in character, whereby men in the nineteenth century are seeking to accomplish precisely the same end. All that we have ascertained in the present by our independent psychological researches seems to substantiate the claims of the old magicians and mystics up to the point which our researches have reached, but this statement, of course, presupposes a discriminating separation of what is obviously fabulous and impossible in the history of magic. If along our own lines the mystics would appear to have transcended us, it must be because our methods are less perfect, and our perseverance is less. One of the most important divergences is indicated in the fact that the magicians pretend to have been acquainted with many hierarchies of invisible intelligences, while spiritualism is solely concerned in communication with the souls of the dead, and, in this sense, if in no other, it is, to all intents and purposes, the Necromancy of the Nineteenth Century. We have seen after what manner the Magus of past centuries adjured the apparitions of the departed, how elaborate was his ceremonial, how diffuse were his rites, how enormous was the pneumatic force which he claims to have become able to exercise, and how impressive were the results which he appears to have achieved in the process. He worked, for the most part, alone, and, indeed, isolation was essentially a part of the preparation which he was bound to undergo. No ordinary quality of perseverance, no common power of will, must have been focussed on his unearthly aim by the simple literal fulfilment of the ritual acts. Instead of the thorny and toilsome path of the adept, with its fasts and vigils, its sublimities and silences, its grotesqueries and grandeurs, Modern Spiritualism offers us a royal road to the accomplishment of the same thaumaturgic mystery —the same face to face, if not unveiled, communication with the dead of all the ages. Without fasts, without prayers, without watches, without any indispensable garnishing either outside or within the house of human life, it guarantees to us on the evidence of a great cloud of witnesses, results as phenomenally tremendous as are any that have been encompassed within the whole circle of historic witchcraft. In virtue of what law has such a simplification become possible, is a tempting subject of inquiry at the threshold of our brief study, but it is not one over which we can afford to dwell. We are concerned—as before—with alleged facts, and with the means of verifying them, not with hypotheses on the uninvestigated and perhaps inscrutable laws which may govern modes of manifestation. If the methods of the magus of old were laborious to superfluity, a cumbrous system should have interfered with the success of his work. If they were not prolix and in part unnecessary, it is difficult to see how a slipshod *modus operandi* can produce as great results. If it be fitly an operation of prayer, abstinence, and sacrifice, if it were once essentially a sacred and religious matter, to be performed with the whole heart and the whole soul, there must be danger at our doors when it has deteriorated, if not into a profane pastime, at least into a secular experiment which is stripped of its sanctity in conscious act and intention. This is a moderate and reasonable criticism which can offend no sincere conviction, and tampers with no experience, and it must be left at this point.

Modern Spiritualism, like its precursor, the mysticism of the past, asks nothing from the faith of the observer, and it is an unwarrantable blunder to establish an inclination to believe as an indispensable, or as any,

element of success in its investigation. True phenomenal spiritualism, as expounded by its reasonable
adherents, is a scientific investigation into the nature,
cause, and operation of certain forces which appear to
originate outside the normal plane of Nature, and give
evidence of human intelligence which cannot be identified with that which is resident in the observers. Like
that practical branch of mysticism which is more rigidly
denominated magic, its avowed end is the demonstration of a spiritual world about, within, and beyond the
visible horizon of things called material—a world which
is ordinarily imperceptible by the senses of embodied
man, but which, under certain circumstances, can be
openly manifested in a manner which precludes the
hypothesis of hallucination. These circumstances are
the "conditions" to which reference has already been
made, and which we have shewn to be of equal importance alike in the operations of spiritualism and old
magic. The conditions which are commonly required for
success in the experiments of modern psychology are—

I. An intention on the part of the observers to enter,
if possible, into communication with spirits ; it is this
intention which constitutes the difference between the
phenomena of Spiritualism and those of spontaneous
apparitions.

II. The presence of a certain harmony of will and
wish, and of general good feeling among a given number
of investigators who have determined to make experiments in common.

III. A favourable state of the atmosphere, which
should be free from electric and magnetic disturbance,
and should be dry and moderately warm.

IV. The formation of the circle.

V. The absence of glaring light.

VI. The presence of what is called a medium.

Speaking broadly, these are the conditions which are
laid down as generally essential. Phenomena which are
recognised by spiritualists may, however, occur in the
absence of any one of these rules, and, so far as the
conscious preparation of the observer is concerned, they
appear to have taken place on occasions when they have

none of them been fulfilled. Accounts of spontaneous manifestations from the other world in the absence of any thought, expectation, or desire on the part of the witnesses, have constituted, as already stated, a large section of supernatural history in all times and countries. So also the concordant relation between individuals comprised in the circle may be counterbalanced by other advantages ; tornado and tempest cannot always interfere when a strong force has been developed by other conditions ; hands clasped for the formation of a circle are as much a guarantee against imposture, when light is obscured or excluded, as an indispensable element of success. Under certain circumstances any class of the phenomena may be produced in open day, or in the midst of a brilliant artificial illumination, while many private circles are affirmed to have been established with the most gratifying results in the absence of any developed medium.

Experiments which are usually dependent for their success upon atmospheric conditions, upon the disposition of the observer, and upon those unknown faculties which constitute what is called mediumship, cannot be readily conducted, because it is only up to a very limited point that we are able to ensure the conditions ; the investigation of the phenomena of Spiritualism is therefore beset with uncertainties ; the communication of the two worlds is occasionally accomplished very readily and in a very complete manner ; at other times it is difficult and long in the process without any assignable reason. It is evident, therefore, that the student of mysticism, who desires to assure himself that the modern branch of magical practice can offer to the conscientious experimenter a reliable instrument of communication with supersensual planes and extramundane modes of subsistence, should endeavour by the most patient and exact observation to increase the knowledge of conditions. Those who have directed their especial attention to this branch of the subject have frequently assured us that their study is the one thing needful, the beginning and the end of all true progress in psychological knowledge. This is most emphatically a point on which we may look for assistance to the processes of the hierophants

transmitted to us in Western magical literature, and the
few who, at the present day, have reconstituted the
modus operandi of the spiritual circle along the lines of
lawful necromantic ritual, have borne testimony to the
success of the attempt.   There can also be no reasonable
doubt that researches into soul mysteries should be
exclusively undertaken by spiritual minds, and that they
should be conducted in such a manner, and with such
an end in view, as will make them an integral part of
their individual spiritual development.   It would be
unbecoming in the extreme to suggest that a large proportion of spiritualists are devoid of the interior qualities
to which we refer, but no one who is acquainted with the
movement can fail to be aware that the motives of investigation are frequently frivolous in the extreme, that it is
frequently conducted under circumstances which make
it morally unprofitable, and as a mere matter of curiosity, wonder, and amusement.   These facts are indeed
notorious, and to enlarge upon them would be a superfluous task.   It is more important to observe that the
merely scientific spirit, the simple thirst after knowledge,
the desire, lawful and commendable as it is, to extend
the field of observation, to investigate unknown forces, is
an insufficient reason for spiritual research, though what
is thus undertaken may occasionally awaken in the mind
which is devoted to science, an aspiration and a purpose
which transcends ordinary science, noble as it undoubtedly is.   A spiritual inquiry should be undertaken with
spiritual objects.   In the most exalted sense of the term,
it is legitimate only to two classes—those earnest seekers
into the interior problems of being who desire to attain
to the permanent actualities which they believe under-
lie the appearances of the external universe, who are
sufficiently absorbed by the fundamental hypotheses of
religion to be anxious for their rigorous verification,
who yearn, in the language of the mystics, to find their
souls, who are probing the bases of faith, who are in
search of an instrument of intercourse with the divine
source of life.   That is the first class, of which the
second is the fruit, being those who have passed through
this initial stage wherein the faculties of being are exer-

cised in the achievement of the grand realities, who have entered into the interior light, and on the path of spiritual evolution. Such at least is the rule which is laid down by the mystics; to such alone is promised what they term the opening of the closed eye of the unknown darkness, and the gate which gives entrance into the garden of cucumbers, and into the closed palace of the king. It is needless therefore to say that the required disposition is essentially religious. Sanctity of thought, sanctity of life, sanctity of soul and body, are the first conditions of the process, for the work is one of reconstruction, which is the significance of the word religion; the system of spiritual communication which is proposed by Spiritualism being the way of the soul's return into a conscious life in God.

Now this end which we have mentioned has been present to the minds of many persons connected with the spiritual movements of modern times, and it is identical with the ambition of the mystics, but it is far from having been generally achieved at present. The communication, on the faith of the evidence, has been indeed established; the path has been opened, but we have not as yet passed through the first avenue. In plain words, we have discovered that there is intelligence on the other side of life, that under certain circumstances it can be manifested to our own, and that it can even give evidence of itself to our physical senses, but it is the lowest scale in the hierarchy of spiritual subsistence with which we have alone communicated, or, if this be too pronounced a statement in view of our ignorance, we have evidence, notwithstanding, that the "spirits" which frequent our séances are in no sense appreciably advanced beyond ourselves. Communications which claim to come to us from high intelligences and from the superior spheres, are occasionally received, but it is seldom that they bear the impress which we have a right to expect from those altitudes, much less from the divine apex towards which the spiral paths of being are supposed to lead us.

In considering the phenomena of Spiritualism we have taken a lofty standpoint, because from our knowledge of the old mystics, and from a reasonable review of the entire subject, we are assured that no true progress can be made from any other. The great body of testimony which has been recorded by an innumerable variety of observers belonging to all classes of life and character, seems equivalent to a positive proof that the experiments of Spiritualism can be, and are, conducted in the absence of any exalted motives. They are obtained among the frivolities of the drawing-room, among the vulgarities of the public séance ; they can be produced in the presence of debauched and vicious persons. Only the nature of the manifestations and the class of the communicating intelligences corresponds to the dispositions of the investigators, and he that is himself filthy, perverse, or debased, will attract what is unclean and low on the other side of life.

As in other divisions of this volume, we have abstained from attempting a philosophical defence of Spiritualism, or of debating its *à priori* possibility ; it is equally impossible to array the evidence which exists in its favour. We are solely concerned with supplying to the student who is in search of instruction, an account of the classes of phenomena which, it is alleged, are produced, and with putting him in possession of the means by which he may verify them for himself. The conditions which are generally requisite have been already enumerated ; we have foreborne to discuss their value, for they constitute an uninvestigated region of exceptional law, and in the present state of our knowledge it is futile to attempt an explanation of the how and why of our phenomena—a disability, it may be added, which we possess in common with the professors of all branches of physical science. As in chemistry, as in the formation of crystals, we know that certain methods and processes produce certain results, but it is a matter of experience only. Our disabilities, however, are greater than those of the physicist, for he is concerned with blind forces, acting fatally, but we are the investigators of a power which under given circumstances, can at any rate assume intelligence.

Sixth in the series of conditions was the presence of a medium, and here it is necessary to summarise the little that observers have told us on the nature of what is called mediumship.   There is a want of unanimity among the old practical mystics on one important point, namely, whether it was possible for all persons to become magicians and to evoke spirits with success.   The presence of a certain occult qualification which is nowhere ex-.plained in their writings, because in all probability it was not understood, is considered indispensable by some, but it seems to have been the opinion of the majority that evocation could be achieved by all who were willing to lead the life of a magus, and to fulfil the rites of magic.   Both parties distinguished, notwithstanding, between the natural and artificial magician, between the man who was magically predestined from birth, and the man who by will and labour could effect such a transmutation in his nature as would capacitate him for a work to which he was not predestined.   As the latter person was held in superior consideration, we must understand by a predestined magician not a person who was ordained by mere automatic fate to a certain arbitrary end, but one who by his birthright was constitutionally gifted with a certain quality which was favourable to the matter.   The presence of a natural magician at the experiments of a master by art was deemed always a desirable conjunction.   Now, the natural magician appears to have been identical with the modern medium, and the term of the mystics in all respects is preferable to the slipshod designation which has been commonized past all endurance by the impostures and stupidities of the past forty years.

When a given number of persons undertake, for what purpose soever, an investigation of the phenomena of Spiritualism, they commonly go in search of the assistance of what is called a medium.   In actual significance the name is identical with the ecclesiastical term Pontifex ; he is the bridge of communication, the intermediary between the seen and the unseen worlds; it is through him that the other side of life effects manifestation to this, and if there be truth in the claims of Spiritualism, his, most assuredly, is an exalted and holy vocation, which should be prized before life itself by the possessor, which should be never prostituted, but alone exercised for the highest ends. But the Pontifex and the priest of the past too frequently abused their office, and we must not be astonished when we hear that the power of this new priesthood has gradually been converted into one of the crafts of life, that it is daily bought and sold, that it has been made subservient to the most sordid interest, that every element of consecration has been successively stripped away from it, that it has been used for abetting imposture of almost every class, and that it has become so debased in the hands of its possessors that the genuine gift can often be scarcely distinguished from the fraudulent impositions of mere mountebanks.

If we search through the large literature of Spiritualism for some account of the nature and qualities of mediumship, we find little that is satisfactory. There are many plausible theories; there is much skilful speculation, there is a quantity of untutored guessing, but there is nowhere solid knowledge. Nor is the reason far to seek. Where is the scientist who can explain to us why mustard is hot or sugar sweet? Beyond the surface of phenomena there is no penetration possible; we must be content to observe and record; to the ultimate reason of things we have no way of attainment. "What is the state of mediumship? What is the peculiarity of organisation, and how acquired?" asks one writer who himself claims to be in possession of one of its gifts. "It would be difficult to tell what it is. It is often, and usually is, possessed at birth; or may be slowly or suddenly acquired. The spirit seems to have less hold upon the body, and to be more sensitive for that reason." The explanation is poor enough; but it is useful in its evidence for one undoubted fact, that the medium is as ignorant of the nature of his strange power as is the most profound philosophical mind of the nature of its own consciousness. We must be content with the simple affirmation that there are certain persons who, by their constitution, are endowed with a force which transcends radical investigation, but by which force it seems possible for spirits to become the temporary associates of embodied man, to manifest before him in an assumed human shape, and to perform many acts, which, on the faith of existing evidence, are of the kind which we term supernatural. The same want of unanimity on one point which we have noticed in the writings of the mystics abounds in the literature of Spiritualism. Mediumship, on the one hand, is declared to be the gift of a few alone; by others it is considered possible to all. True philosophic prudence would have withheld both statements. While it is difficult to suppose that one section of humanity is in the enjoyment of qualities which are foreign altogether to the constitution of the rest, while it therefore seems reasonable to assume that the qualities in question are latent in all mankind, it is rash to affirm that they can be developed in all. Analogy and experience alike contradict the statement. It seems, at the same time, in all respects probable that the power, whatever it may be, is not only inherent, but would admit of development in a large number of persons who, by their circumstances, are precluded from any attempt at its exercise, and even from all knowledge on the point. The faculty is commonly connected by its students with a passive or negative temperament. Like magic power, it may be induced, it is said, by narcotics, by stimulants, or by long fasts and vigils, by prostration of body, and by an advanced degree of mental excitement; but its natural and reliable development is by sitting with investigators in spiritual circles, more especially in the presence of an already developed medium.

The rules for the formation of a circle, and the conduct of research, have been given by a number of authorities; they have little substantial difference; the most simple, complete, and practical is perhaps that which has been widely circulated, under the initials M.A. (Oxon.), by Mr. Stainton Moses, who is well known as a leader of psychic research in England, and as a medium for manifestations of a very advanced kind. The directions are, of course, written from the standpoint of one whose experience has abundantly verified the genuineness of all classes of spiritual phenomena, and they are designed for the instruction of those who intend to conduct an inquiry by means of private sittings on the part of a few earnest persons who can thoroughly rely on one another. It is thus, we are told, that the bulk of spiritualists have arrived at their convictions.

The circle of investigators should consist of from four to eight persons, and they should be divided as equally as may be into positive and negative temperaments, of which the latter are more commonly to be found among the female sex. It is to be understood that the specific object in the minds of all members of the circle is to enter into communication with the intelligences of the unseen world. The possibility of such a communication involves three things in addition to the actual and conscious existence of unseen intelligence. There is first the proximity of an invisible world of thinking beings, mentally conditioned in much the same way as ourselves, but the nature of this proximity should not be too closely connected with conceptions of space and locality. Secondly, there is the willingness on the part of unseen intelligence to respond to attempts at communication on the part of embodied humanity. Thirdly, the possibility which we are considering supposes the existence of a power which if inherent can be exercised, and if extrinsic can be adapted to establish the communication desired. If we suppose these conditions to exist, the next thing to be determined is a mode of communication, and where one side at least is invisible to the other, it must obviously take the form of signals. Now the code of signals which is commonly made use of requires no other materials than an ordinary table, preferably circular in shape; round this the investigators take their seats, positive and negative temperaments alternately, in comfortable and unconstrained positions, the palms of the hands being placed flat upon the uncovered upper surface of the table. The rest of the directions may be given most fittingly in the words of Mr Stainton Moses.

"Do not concentrate attention too fixedly on the expected manifestation. Engage in cheerful, but not frivolous, conversation. Avoid dispute or argument. Scepticism has no deterrent effect, but a bitter spirit of opposition in a person of determined will may totally stop or decidedly impede manifestations. If conversation flag, music is a great help, if it be agreeable to all, and not of a kind to irritate the sensitive ear. Patience is essential, and it may be necessary to meet ten or twelve times at short intervals, before anything occurs. If after such a trial you still fail, form a fresh circle. Guess at the reason of your failure, eliminate the inharmonious elements, and introduce others. An hour should be the limit of an unsuccessful séance.

"The first indications of success usually are a cold breeze passing over the hands, with involuntary twitchings of the hands and arms of some of the sitters, and a sensation of throbbing in the table. These indications, at first so slight as to cause doubt of their reality, will usually develop with more or less rapidity.

"If the table moves, let your pressure be so gentle on its surface that you are sure you are not aiding its motions. After some time you will probably find that the movement will continue if your hands are held *over*, but not in contact with it. Do not, however, try this until the movement is assured, and be in no hurry to get messages.

"When you think that the time has come, let some one take command of the circle and act as spokesman. Explain to the unseen Intelligence that an agreed code of signals is desirable, and ask that a tilt may be given as the alphabet is slowly repeated at the several letters which form the word that the Intelligence wishes to spell. It is convenient to use a single tilt for No, three for Yes, and two to express doubt or uncertainty.

"When a satisfactory communication has been established, ask if you are rightly placed, and if not, what order you should take. After this, ask who the Intelligence purports to be, which of the company is the medium, and such relevant questions. If confusion occurs, ascribe it to the difficulty that exists in directing the movements at first with exactitude. Patience will remedy this, if there be a real desire on the part of the Intelligence to speak with you. If you only satisfy yourself at first that it is possible to speak with an

Intelligence separate from that of any person present, you will have gained much.

" The signals may take the form of raps. If so, use the same code of signals, and ask as the raps become clear that they may be made on the table, or in a part of the room where they are demonstrably not produced by any natural means, but avoid any vexatious imposition of restrictions on free communication. Let the Intelligence use its own means; if the attempt to communicate deserves your attention, it probably has something to say to you, and will resent being hampered by useless interference. It rests greatly with the sitters to make the manifestations elevating or frivolous, and even tricky."

However absolute and however well-grounded may be the confidence of a circle in all its members individually, the certainty derived from manifestations which do not obviously transcend the capabilities of the sitters, supposing bad faith in any of them, is at its best of a moral kind, and it is still founded in faith, that is, faith in the honesty of the circle. Now such a certainty is not scientific in character, and the energies of investigation should be directed to establish experiments upon the most satisfactory possible basis. When it has been once fairly demonstrated that unmistakable raps are being produced in a fair light, and at a reasonable distance from the sitters, we shall have entered the region of positive knowledge as to the genuineness of the phenomena called spiritual; we shall have proved to ourselves the existence of a force which is still unknown to physical science, and possesses the qualities of intelligence. It will give pertinent answers to questions, and occasionally tests which will identify it with the mind of some person whom we know to have once lived in a human body upon this earth, and who is now dead to us. In other cases, it will impart information which, though not a test of identity, is of a kind that is unknown to those present, and is verified by subsequent research. In this way, by successive steps, the circle is led to the recognition of an independent understanding in another form of subsistence, and through this one rent in the veil, the possibilities of the spiritual universe begin to unfold before their eyes. In the majority of cases, the progress of the private circle is, we believe, arrested here. But should it prove that one of the company is possessed of the qualities of mediumship in an advanced degree, perseverance will be ultimately rewarded by more astounding phenomena. The course of their development will vary in every case, and the enumeration which follows must not be construed as the actual method of evolution, but merely as tabulating the chief classes of manifestation, of which instances have been hitherto recorded.

I. Intensification in the force of the raps, which become occasionally so powerful as to destroy the objects upon which they are directed.

II. The motion of inert objects, confined in the initial stages to articles of small size and weight, but subsequently extended to the transportation of things which no human being could raise by his individual efforts.

III. The levitation of human beings, in most cases of the person who is used as medium.

IV. The conveyance of small articles from a distance and through closed doors.

V. In rare instances, the transportation of the medium from a distance and through closed doors.

VI. Other developments in the experiments of the passage of matter through matter, such as the introduction of a coin into a sealed box, placing a metal ring upon the wrist of the medium when his hands are tightly locked in the grasp of other sitters, or when he is otherwise secured.

VII. The transportation of fruit, flowers, fish, and small animals from a distance, the choice of species resting with the circle, and the astonishing nature of the performance being sometimes increased by the selection of things which are out of season or peculiar to distant countries.

VIII. Performances on musical instruments, usually of a small size, such as the Oxford chimes, and occasionally on the piano.

IX. The apparition of lights, generally phosphorescent

in appearance, and sometimes in smell. In the elementary stages they are merely luminous points, but as the power and the correspondence develop large stars, emblematic characters, and radiant spheres, veined with blood-red, have been known to manifest. These, indeed, may be reckoned among the most frequent and attractive of phenomenal exhibitions at a séance, and, as may be supposed, they increase with the diminution of light.

X. The appearance of living human hands, other than those of the circle; they are seen to move objects, they grasp the hands of the sitters, pick at their garments, and in many ways give evidence of being controlled by an intelligence like our own.

XI. The entrancement of the medium, which is apparently a magnetic state induced by volition from the unseen. Usually it is a condition of the more advanced phenomena. One of its most common conseqences is a temporary possession of the human organism by a foreign intelligence, the intelligence of the medium for the time being absent or in abeyance. High moral teaching is occasionally given in this state, but it is one of the phenomena of Spiritualism which is most easily simulated by impostors, and its evidential value is therefore small. So far as it can be considered genuine, it seems one of the states of mediumship which can be most easily induced, and those who have once given themselves up to it appear to be able to command it at any time, and under the most varied and the least favourable circumstances.

XII. The spirit voice speaking through the medium is called Trance Speaking. Kindred to this, and, under proper conditions, far more valuable as evidence, is the Direct Voice, which is heard in all parts of the room, and under circumstances which preclude the supposition of ventriloquism. During such manifestations the medium is generally in a state resembling coma, and it is supposed that his organs are to some extent utilised in the production of the direct voice.

XIII. A frequent phenomenon of the spiritual trance is unconscious impersonation by the medium, acting under the influence of the unseen. In this state the subject is made to pose as a Form Manifestation of the spirits, and is even draped in materials which are said to be transported for the purpose by the controlling Intelligence. As these phenomena are peculiarly adapted to cloak the impostures of professional mediums, and as at best they are a deceptive device on the part of the spirits themselves, they should not be encouraged by any intelligent circle of inquiry.

XIV. The *magnum opus* of the spiritual séance is the appearance of human figures which are demonstrably not those of any person present in the room, and which cannot have been introduced into the room for the furtherance of any imposition. Commonly this occurs when the medium is profoundly entranced, and total darkness seems to be the best condition. For the latter reason, what is called the séance for materialisation is unsatisfactory from an evidential standpoint. But we are assured by a number of investigators whose good faith upon any other subject would pass without challenging, that it is possible to obtain the materialisation of spiritual forms in the face of open day, even in the garden, in the woods and forests, and certainly in a subdued light which shall be sufficient for all purposes of investigation. When the séance is held with shut and bolted doors, in a room where there can have been no previous preparation, where there are no secret entrances, if the few persons gathered together have more than themselves in the midst of them, they have reached the furthest point to which phenomenal Spiritualism can claim at present to carry them, and have demonstrated the actuality of what has been the dream and wonder of all the ages. The figures manifested under favourable circumstances appear in rapid succession differing in height and size, in vesture and appearance, occasionally exceeding the normal stature of humanity, while others are small children. The manifestation is sometimes so slight as to be almost of the tenuity of vapour, sometimes it is so solid and perfect that it can remain for a considerable period visible and tangible to all, speaking, walking, embracing those about it. On rare occasions more than one of these mysterious beings appears at the same time, one forming out of the side of the medium, while another is developed out of the apparition thus obtained. The first detected presence of materialisation is usually a little cloud or column of luminous vapour from which a figure is gradually built up. Those who desire a practical acquaintance with this most important form of mediumship will do well to consult the literature which exists on the subject before attempting experiment.

XV. Automatic Writing is one of the most common phenomena of a séance, and it may be distinguished broadly into two classes. First, there is involuntary writing obtained in the normal state either by holding a pen lightly and waiting for the hand to be controlled, or by the use of the little instrument called a Planchette, which is so universally known as to require no description. Automatic communications of the same kind are also obtained when the medium is in an entranced state. In either case, simulation is so easy, and the motives which actuate imposture are so numerous and so untraceable that no value can be considered as attaching to either class unless *information* is afforded by the controlling agent, which is obviously beyond the knowledge of the automatic writer, or in a language which is demonstrably unknown to him.

XVI. Spirit-writing is not confined to the automatic type, and a medium for Direct Writing is justly considered the most valuable of all his genus, as he is also the most uncommon. The phenomena in connection with this group of manifestations are familiar to the majority of persons by report if not by experience. In the test cases which are cited on the subject, a fragment of chalk or pencil is placed within a folding slate, which is locked, corded, and sealed. Intelligent observers take care to obtain one for themselves, and see that it does not pass out of their possession. It is placed on a table in front of the medium, and the most that he is permitted to do is to place one of his hands upon it while it is still being held by its owner. Investigators inform us that, despite these and still more elaborate precautions, they have obtained writing within the locked slate; that the chalk which they provided has been sensibly worn down by the process; that the communication has been a pertinent answer to a question asked mentally or written previously at their own homes upon one of the inner surfaces of the slate; that it embodies information which could not have been known to the medium, which was perhaps unknown to themselves at the time, but which they have successfully verified afterwards. It should be added that Direct Writing is not confined to the methods of the locked slate. Instances are recorded of a pencil being placed in a full light upon a sheet of paper, which pencil, under the eyes of the observers, has been raised by invisible agency, has assumed the perpendicular position which it would in an ordinary hand, and has written intelligible messages.

XVII. The last and most rarely successful of all the experiments we have been enumerating is Spirit Photography, which should not be confused with the extremely simple process of photographing the materialised form of a spirit. The experiment consists in obtaining upon the exposed plate of a camera the impression of a form which, by reason of its extreme tenuity, is invisible to the ordinary eye. The result, when successful, is usually the apparition of a ghostly human figure. The presence of a medium is indispensable, and the best method of procedure is to photograph such a person by the ordinary means, and trust to the circumstances favouring the development of a spirit from within the sphere of his magnetic atmosphere. The introduction of the dry-plate process has greatly favoured imposture in these experiments, and the facilities for fraud, combined with the complete uncertainty of every genuine method, make this feature of the spiritual séance the most laborious and unsatisfactory of all. It is well, however, to bear in mind that when a special figure is obtained *in front of* the sitter who is photographed, that this result is entirely beyond the skill of the known processes of photographic art. When a plate has been previously tampered with, the shadowy figure which is intended to represent the ghost will appear behind or to one side, and will be generally out of all relationship with the person whose portrait is subsequently taken upon the same plate. The literature of Spirit Photography is exceedingly scanty, but portraits of persons whose hands are held or who are embraced by the spectral arms of some ghostly visitant are fairly numerous, and they seem to defy explanation upon any fraudulent hypothesis.

Such are the most important branches of the phenomena termed spiritual. We do not undertake to explain them, nor to enter into a philosophical defence of their possibility. They are concerned with matters which are altogether outside the legitimate sphere of belief, and the evidence which exists in their favour should only be considered as a warrant for personal inquiry. We have placed in the hands of the student an intelligible synopsis of the alleged facts, and a sketch of the methods of experiment. If the investigations of a private circle are arrested at an early stage for want of the necessary power, recourse must be had to a professional medium, when other resources have failed. A professional medium is a person who claims to possess the required qualities in an advanced degree, and who turns them to his pecuniary profit. As the exercise of such gifts is usually very depleting, and as those who devote themselves to it have, like others, their bread to earn, it is theoretically in all respects right and reasonable that they should receive adequate compensation; but the practice·has encouraged imposture of every kind. The anxiety to give every investigator his money's value, lest he should depart unsatisfied and the trade should cease to be lucrative, has prompted the genuine medium to supplement a power, which is not at his command, by the artifices of the conjuror; moreover, the general interest in the subject has attracted impostors into the profession who have never possessed the gifts. Every precaution should therefore be taken by investigators to secure themselves against fraud when it becomes necessary to engage the services of a public medium. They should especially beware of those who decline to sit under reasonable test conditions.

It is vain to attempt, in the space at our disposal, a student's guide to the vast literature of Spiritualism. For convincing testimony on the part of men of science, reference may be made to Alfred Russell Wallace's "Miracles and Modern Spiritualism;" to Crooke's celebrated "Researches into the Phenomena called Spiritual;" and to Zöllner's "Transcendental Physics." For the experiences and testimony of an advanced medium, who is also an advanced thinker, and a man of high culture, the reader should have recourse to the numerous published works of the Rev. Stainton-Moses (M.A. Oxon.). For the history of the movement, there is "Modern American Spiritualism," and "Nineteenth Century Miracles," both by Mrs. Emma Hardinge-Britten. In inspirational writing there are the works of Andrew Jackson Davis, who is the Jacob Böhme of Spiritualism.

Spiritualism is the only branch of the occult sciences which has obtained the popularity implied by the issue of weekly newspapers. The best of these is undoubtedly *Light*, and the perusal of this journal will keep the intending student *au courant* with the progress of the movement throughout the world.

THEOSOPHY.

HOWEVER apparently at variance, magicians and alchemists were agreed on one point, that they received their knowledge by tradition. What, then, was this tradition, and whence was it derived? Nominally, in the case of magicians, it was referred to Solomon and the Kabbalah. But it is clear that the mysticism of the West had its complement in Oriental mysticism; that both had strong mutual affinities; and that Sufis, Brahmans, and Buddhists owed nothing to the Jews or their wisdom. Mysticism antedated the Kabbalah, and there was magic before Solomon. The appeal to the most wise of mankind was very evidently a device; the Kabbalah was a bigger puzzle than the transcendentalism which was supposed to be derived from it. What, again, was the tradition, and whence derived? The problem was grappled with by many writers. Some, like the author of "A Suggestive Inquiry into the Hermetic Mystery," believed that they had attained a solution, and were alarmed at their magnificent discovery. Few, however, reached any settled light or permanent satisfaction. But what may be called a partial revelation on this subject claims to have appeared within a comparatively very recent period. It reduces the pretensions of the Western mystics within measurable dimensions; while it affirms the solidity of their psychic knowledge, it defines its limitations, and it claims to be in possession of the two keys—philosophical and practical—which give entrance into the secluded sanctuary of universal mysticism. The keys have been obtained from the East, to which in things psychic, as in things physical, we are told that we must turn for light. *Ex oriente Lux.* There it bids us gaze upward and see, for another morning has broken. The

herald of which we have been speaking is called
Theosophy.

To all who are acquainted with the literature of Western
mysticism, the term Theosophy is familiar in various
ways.   We find it in magical rituals and in the writings
of Jacob Böhme.   It was used in the seventeenth
century to distinguish the divine wisdom of magus and
kabbalist from the theology of the schools,—a distinction
which was intentionally invidious, contrasting the actualities of experimental research into the hidden mysteries
of God, man, and the universe, with the wordy speculations of scholastic thought.   Concerned with facts and
not words, the Theosophy of the mystics was deemed
to be another and higher thing than any current theology
of the time.   Now, that elaborate system of transcendental life and doctrine, that master-key to the mysteries
of arcane science and philosophy, which, under the old
name of Theosophy, has become so extensively diffused,
has been so much talked of, and in a certain sense has
been in vogue at this day, attaches fundamentally much
the same significance to the same word.   Modern Theosophy is the latest and most extreme development of
supernaturalism, and alike in the character of its pretensions and in the intellectual qualifications of its pro-
moters, as well as in the work which it has accomplished, it deserves very serious investigation at the
hands of the mystic student ; nor is it possible to ignore
it in any appreciation of current psychological opinion.
It is the legitimate daughter of universal mysticism, and,
in a certain manner, it may be regarded as a mystic
synthesis.   It absorbs the transcendentalism of the West,
while it is the mouthpiece of Eastern magic.   In it the
Oriental arcane wisdom of the far past may be said to
have renewed its youth.   In principles, in comprehen-
siveness, in tolerance, it claims the mark of catholicity,
and its present diffusion is possibly to be regarded as
only a foreshadowing and promise of a geographical
universality which is yet to come.

Could Spiritualism be viewed as, in its origin and
development, historically a parallel to Christianity,
Theosophy would be the gnosticism of the new Evangel,

and the words which are made use of by Gibbon in respect of that singular mysticism may be equally applied to this. "It comprised the most polite, the most learned, and the most wealthy of the name." But though persons of respectable intelligence have believed in the identity of primitive Christianity and modern Spiritualism, the affinity—historical and otherwise— between Theosophy and the faith of the gnosis is very much closer than any that can be legitimately traced upon the other side.

It is beyond the limits of our present purpose to undertake an apology for any special system of doctrinal mysticism, new or old. Here we are simply concerned with a non-critical statement of the character and objects of Theosophy, and, with this fact in view, no expression of personal adhesion or difference should on any pretence be admitted in a short elucidatory paper. It is a subject which is still *en évidence*, it has not yet received an impartial and thorough analysis, and its promulgators are still living. For these reasons an abridged epitome of an unfinished case should not be followed by an attempt to forestall a verdict. Yet, as in other matters we have ventured to direct the student, so in this it seems legitimate to say that he will find in Theosophy an exalted form of transcendental mysticism which will not only repay investigation, but which, as one of the psychological facts of the day, he will find himself forced to investigate very early in his philosophical inquiry. For the rest, we shall, in the main, have recourse to the unadapted opinions of its best exponents ; we shall make no reference to existing controversies, or existing divisions, nor indeed to any matters of a merely historical or personal character. There will be, morover, little need to distinguish between Theosophy as it actually is and as it appears under the gloss of misrepresentation, or through the medium of public ignorance. Its unadorned presentation will be a sufficient answer to the caricatures of the moment. It will be well, nevertheless, to lay down at the outset that Theosophy is not to be regarded as a refined form of Spiritualism, though Spiritualism has undoubtedly alone made it possible to promulgate Theosophy, and though Theosophy, as would naturally follow, admits broadly the facts of the Spiritist. If we are to regard it from the standpoint of its promulgators, we should do ill to consider that it is associated integrally with the science of the circle as with an originating cause of its existence, for Theosophy, from that standpoint, is anterior to the historical religions. Nor does it differ from modern Spiritualism simply by the proffering of an alternative hypothesis to account for the existence of those psychic facts which are equally acknowledged by both. Absolutely speaking, it claims to be a complete spiritual gnosis, elaborated, like all sciences, very slowly, very gradually, with much pain, with much suffering, with much superhuman perseverance, from a remote period of antiquity, and now offered. for the spiritual illumination of the Western world which is ripe for participation in the arcane knowledge of the East. On this view the psychic facts of the period are simply the indications of that stage of spiritual development in this hemisphere which it was indispensable that our race should reach before its initiation into the mysteries of an absolute divine knowledge. Further, Theosophy is not to be regarded as a modernized form of Buddhism, adapted to the intelligence of the nineteenth century, nor, on the other hand, is it actually a reversion to the primeval fountain of Buddhist doctrine, though it has been very much identified by its promulgators with that dominant religion of the East; though it numbers innumerable Buddhists among its foremost disciples; and though, finally, and on all hands, its distinctive name has become almost interchangeable with that of Esoteric Buddhism. With the underlying principles of Buddhist faith and teaching it is undoubtedly and actually to be identified, but Theosophy recognises a common foundation for all religions, and thus Esoteric Buddhism is not to be distinguished from Esoteric Christianity, nor from the spirit of the Zoroastrian religion. The hidden principles, the arcane sense, the scientific basis of each do in fact constitute the divine wisdom of Theosophy.

From what has been already said it is equally clear

that Theosophy is not a new religion, though the term has been frequently applied to it. The common foundation of all theological systems can be a novelty only in the sense of being generally or hitherto unknown. But should its claim to this distinction be denied, it should not even then be regarded as a new departure in doctrinal belief; it is rather a new system of religious interpretation. It teaches nothing that is actually fresh to the student of comparative mythology, but it regards much that has been previously taught in a new light, and from a new standpoint. Taking the much-perverted term religion in its real sense, Theosophy is certainly a religion, for it professes to provide its followers with a scientific instrument for the union of their individual being with the universal life of God. The instrument, however, is not new; it is that of all the mystics, though it claims to be more perfect than theirs.

Theosophy at the same time must not be regarded as a harmonious combination of many mystic systems. We have said that it is a mystic synthesis, but it contains something which is over and above all of these, and that again is the essential principle which is behind them all, and which for want of a more distinctive name has been termed by Theosophists the Ancient Wisdom Religion, a term which the discriminating student will do well to interpret somewhat broadly, for, as the Wisdom Religion is the radix of all religions, it is therefore Theosophy itself from the standpoint of those who profess it. The principles of this religion may, to some extent, be recovered from the discriminating study of existing faiths and creeds, and thus Theosophy is, in one of its phases, an analysis of religious belief. To such analysis a considerable proportion of independent Theosophical literature is devoted at the present day.

"The system of thought which has been described as 'Esoteric Buddhism,'" says Mr A. P. Sinnett, "deals with a highly practical matter—the leading conclusions of a living science closely associated with the welfare of the human race at the present day—in Europe as well as in Asia. The science to which I refer is Theosophy, . . . and that science is closely associated in one of its aspects with the study of the essential principles of religious belief. Theosophists have no preconceived attachment to one presentation or form of religious belief rather than to another. They are in pursuit of truth pure and simple, convinced that there must be a real state of the facts in regard to such problems as the origin and destiny of the soul, as well as in reference to the chemical affinities of the elements or the relations of heat and electricity. And they find that the comparison of various religious beliefs will often enable them to eliminate the superficial corruptions of each, so that the residual doctrines, reduced to their lowest terms, their most abstract expression, will then be found practically identical, even when the first glance at their esoteric aspects seemed to reveal great discrepancies. In this way the study of any great religion in its esoteric aspect is a theosophical undertaking."

A theosophical inquiry into the laws of comparative mythology differs from an ordinary historical investigation in the vitality of purpose which the student brings with him into the field. He is not a mere observer; he does not merely collect, sift, and marshal the facts of universal religious belief, and when he has made out to his satisfaction the governing principles of their being, when he has, in other words, contrived some theory which accounts for their existence to his personal satisfaction, he does not consider his task ended. He believes in the existence of an undying spirit in man, and his search is prompted by a lively desire to throw light upon the mysteries of the spirit; it is therefore not dead but living, and the principles which he endeavours to discover are intimately associated with his own interior evolution.

But though the proper study of comparative mythology may result in much light to the student, it is not pretended that it will do more than provide him with a very partial theosophical illumination. It will put him in possession of the cardinal and ultimate principles of all religious belief. If he would test the truth of those principles, he must abandon the plane of history and enter that of psychology. The science of comparative religion is indeed historical psychology, but it bears the same relation to experimental psychic science that the collation of alchemical symbols bears to the practical search after the Stone of the Philosophers, and experimental psychology is a research into the activities and scope of the interior man which must be prosecuted by every man in his own interior. It is therefore the main object of Theosophy "to push our knowledge of Nature's laws on in advance of the finest discoveries of modern civilisation, keeping hand in hand with these, but ever pressing onward into the region of consciousness and super-material existence, guided by the light already in the world;—which has been in the world from the first beginnings of that union between divinity and matter which constitutes the sentient universe." To distinguish the researches of Theosophy from those of unaided mysticism in the West, it is necessary to point out that the light already in the world, to which allusion is made in this citation from Mr Sinnett, is something over and above what can be obtained from accessible supernatural history. While Theosophy by no means underrates the value of recorded psychic facts, it claims to be in possession of a superior source of knowledge—that knowledge out of which were begotten the radical principles of the mysterious Wisdom Religion, which has been perpetuated through all the ages, which has been extended in the course of preservation, which has at this day its living custodians, who have consented to its partial revelation, and from whom it will depend on ourselves whether we shall learn more.

Before we attempt the presentation of such knowledge as, it is affirmed, has been thus imparted, we must speak briefly concerning its custodians, and give some explanation of the medium by which they have come into communication with the Western world.

The existence of a secret and psychological body of knowledge which was of an absolute and momentous kind has been affirmed by all mystics, and Éliphas Lévi, as we have seen, defines magic to be the traditional science of the secrets of Nature which has come down to us from the wise men of old. So far, however, as we are aware, the name of Wisdom Religion was first applied to this science in the celebrated volumes of "Isis Unveiled," published in America in 1877, and written in English by a Russian lady, Madame Blavatsky. The existence of high intelligences, wearing a mortal form, and actual guardians of the arcane knowledge at this hour, was more recently made known in two equally celebrated books, by Mr A. P. Sinnett, "The Occult World" and "Esoteric Buddhism." While humanity in the West has devoted itself almost exclusively to physical science, and has made the progress therein with which we are all familiar, the East has been occupied with the study of the soul, and it has made even greater progress. The pursuit in the one case has been open and free to all; in the other it has been secret, more slowly accumulated, and shared and known by few. But "checked and examined at every point, verified in all directions, and constantly under examina tion," it has "come to be looked on by its custodians as constituting the absolute truth concerning spiritual things. . . . The secret knowledge is regarded not only by all its adherents, but by vast numbers who have never expected to know more of it than that such a doctrine exists, as a mine of entirely trustworthy knowledge." In America, in Europe, and scattered all over the East, there are said to be individuals and associations who have entered upon the path of attainment, who are in possession of more or less knowledge of spiritual mysteries, and who, by the fact of their attainment, would seem to be more or less in correspondence with the mundane centre of illumination, but that centre is in the far East, and the indicated abode of the grand initiates is affirmed, at the present moment, to be somewhere in the highlands of Thibet. They are not Orientals exclusively; all distinctions of race and creed are abandoned among them; they are unseen, but not inactive; they are a kind of guardian spirits, "masters of philosophy and metaphysics," says Colonel Olcott, "who benefit mankind without their hand being even so much as suspected." They constitute the "rare efflorescence" of many generations of researchers into

the great mysteries of the universe. They have
transcended the regions of the phenomenal; they have
got behind nature; they can control physical as well as
spiritual forces; they command the elements; and if
they cannot renew youth, they can at least preserve the
life of their own bodies beyond the normal period, and,
in some cases, that life is said to have been extended
over several centuries. Their science, however, is not
limited to the adaptation or conservation of energies;
it acquaints them with the past of the world's history,
with the origin of the universe and of man, with the
revolutions and the destinies of both, and it informs
them in all its depths and heights with the mystery of
the interior man, and with the infinite hierarchies of
extra-human intelligence. In the East the existence of
such beings is a matter of popular faith, and they are
known almost indifferently as Rahats, Mahatmas, and
Rishis. They are identified in the popular mind with
the regnant religions, and, whatever their position in
regard to them, we are assured that they reverence the
Lord Buddha "as the greatest among adepts of the
occult science." His religion is apparently considered to
be most in accordance with the arcane wisdom, and the
perpetuity of his incarnations also seems to be regarded
as a literal fact.

Practically speaking, all our knowledge, directly and
indirectly, concerning this mysterious brotherhood of
adepts, has been derived to us through the Russian
lady of whom we have already made mention. She was
their "accredited medium of communication with the
outer world." She was a woman of noble birth, the
widow of the late governor of Erivan; she was intimately
acquainted with the East, and for the greater part of her
life she had been a passionate student of the occult
sciences. In the year 1874, Madame Blavatsky, then
wholly unknown to fame, had extended her wanderings
to America, where she was witnessing the phenomena of
Spiritualism. It was then and there, in the village of
Chittenden, Vermont, that she and her future partner
in the propaganda of the theosophical evangel were for
the first time brought into communication with each

other. "In the year 1874," says Colonel Henry S. Olcott, "Madame Blavatsky and I met. I had been a student of practical psychology for nearly a quarter of a century. From boyhood no problem had interested me so much as the mystery of man, and I had been seeking for light upon it wherever it could be found. To understand the physical man I had read something of anatomy, physiology, and chemistry. To get an insight into the nature of mind and thought, I had read the various authorities of orthodox science, and practically investigated the heterodox branches of phrenology, physiognomy, mesmerism, and psychometry. . . . In the year above mentioned, I was investigating a most startling case of mediumship, that of William Eddy, an uneducated farmer, in whose house were nightly appearing, and often talking, the *alleged* spirits of dead persons. . . . With my own eyes I saw, within the space of about three months, some five hundred of these apparitions, under circumstances which, to my mind, excluded the possibility of trickery or fraud. . . . Madame Blavatsky and I met at this farm-house, and the similarity of our tastes for mystical research led to an intimate acquaintance. She soon proved to me that, in comparison with the *chela* of an Indian *Mahatma*, the authorities I had been accustomed to look up to, knew absolutely nothing. Little by little she opened out to me as much of the truth as my experiences had fitted me to grasp. Step by step I was forced to relinquish illusory beliefs, cherished for twenty years. And as the light gradually dawned on my mind, my reverence for the unseen teachers who had instructed her grew apace. At the same time, a deep and insatiable yearning possessed me to seek their society, or, at least, to take up my residence in a land which their presence glorified, and incorporate myself with a people whom their greatness ennobled. The time came when I was blessed with a visit from one of these *Mahatmas* in my own room at New York—a visit from him, not in the physical body, but in the ' double,' or *Mayavi-rupa*. . . . His conversation sent my heart at one leap around the globe; across oceans and continents, over sea and land, to India, and from that moment I had a motive to live for, an end to strive after. That motive was to gain the Aryan wisdom; that end to work for its dissemination." The outcome of this enthusiasm was the foundation of a Theosophical Society, for the formation of a Universal Brotherhood of Humanity—the promotion of the study of Aryan and other Eastern literature, religions, and sciences—and the investigation of the hidden mysteries of nature and the psychical powers of man.

How this society grew and flourished, in spite of the Utopian character of its first object; how its lodges exist at the present day in all parts of the world; how they are the centres of a systematic propaganda, are questions for the historical student. How also the zealous American soldier fulfilled his ambition of going to India, how he was joined there by Madame Blavatsky; how Mr A. P. Sinnett became convinced of the extraordinary psychological phenomena which took place in the presence of Madame Blavatsky; how he also, like Colonel Olcott, beheld the *simulacra* of the adepts, are matters that may be mentioned in passing, but must be lightly passed over. We have stated as briefly as possible the gist of what is at present known concerning the source of the theosophical revelation, and all that need be said concerning their accredited representatives in the outer world. The nature of this latest and ultimate message from "those who know" to those who would qualify to learn is the final stage of our appreciation.

Starting from the broad and general claim that Theosophy, or Esoteric Buddhism, as it may be indifferently called, "offers us the wisdom acquired by thought and experience on a higher plane," we shall find that its chief teachings may be classified under three heads—the Nature and Constitution of Man—the Destiny of Man—and the Way to Attain. In the first of these classes, seven composing elements, each capable of still further subdivision, are recognised as substantially existing in man as he is, though some of the highest of the series are in a still undeveloped state. First comes the Physical Body, and to that is united the Animal Vitality which changes gross earth into living flesh. The third principle is called the Astral Body, which is the duplicate of the physical envelope, and is energized by the principles above it. The fourth is the Animal Soul, which is the highest developed substance of the brute creation; it is one of the superior elements, and can be developed still further by a union with the fifth principle, which is the Human Soul, "the seat of reason and memory." The sixth principle is called the Spiritual Soul, and the seventh is the Pure Spirit.

Distinctions like this will appear to many students as mere idle refinements, but they serve their purpose in an exceedingly complicated body of transcendental doctrine, which includes not only the history and evolution of the cosmic world, or the sequence observed in the development of the phenomenal universe, but the experiment of positive knowledge, or perception into the truth and reality, and between both the theory and practice of every species of the multiform art of magic.

From the second body of theosophic instruction we learn that at death there is a final separation of the three lower principles from those which are above them, and an ascent of the superior constituents into what is called the Astral Plane, where the complicated fifth principle is disintegrated, all that is highest in its nature seeking union with the sixth, the rest becoming identified with the astral body and remaining in the world of forms. On the differentiation of the Astral Body from the real man all the apparitions of the dead are philosophically based by Esoteric Buddhism. Meanwhile, the sublimated remnant of the fifth principle departs with the Spiritual Soul, and the Divine Spirit into a Spiritual condition, an interior state of absorption, where all the superior possibilities of "sensuous emotion" are developed by the ministry of laws which are proper to this withdrawn form of visionary subsistence. There the individual remains till the arcane process of retribution begins to work and he is reborn into objective existence, the reincarnation continuing indefinitely from body to body and from planet to planet. It is, in fact, a most complex presentation of the

doctrine acquired by Pythagoras which Theosophy
offers to the student as an integral part of the arcane
wisdom, and, like Glanvil of old, as a key to the grand
mysteries of sin and evil.

Beyond all incarnations, beyond all trances of an
intermediate state, there is an abstract condition of
pure being which transcends the phenomenal world of
illusions and pain. It is possible to attain that state ;
it is possible to transcend the normal status of one's
evolution in the refining process of the ages, to reach
into the sphere of a higher law, to enter into a forcing-
house of the interior man, to walk in the path of the
adept, to tread the way of attainment. And that is
the path along which Theosophy claims to lead you,
after the manner of all the mystics, by detachment,
abstinence, asceticism of the most rigid nature,
contemplation, solitude, and instruction. It lays stress
upon the necessity of instruction, and declares that it
will certainly come, for those who earnestly seek it, if
not in the life when the effort is first made, then assuredly in the next incarnation. It affords the promise
of continued companionship through the ages—both
in the spiritual realms of Nature, and again on the
earth plane in periods of reincarnation—for those who
are truly united by the ties of a loving sympathy.
There is no material hell in the theosophical economy
of the universe, because the earth life itself, for the
normally wicked, when they reincarnate, becomes their
appropriate sphere of punishment; but there is a
condition of spiritual wretchedness—the converse of
the highest spiritual bliss, which is Nirvana—and this
supremely evil state is denominated Avitchi. Between
the terrible destiny of Avitchi, only possible for the
spiritually wicked, and the supreme state of blessedness, there lies a condition which is all but annihilation
for those who grovel hopelessly on the material plane all
through the procession of the ages, during which the
material life should be the school of spiritual aspiration.
But the complete exposition of the doctrine would be impossible here. With Nirvana, the higher consciousness—
the knowledge which is above self-knowledge, the being

which is beyond existence, the student will compare the absorption of the mystic marriage which was known to the Christian adepts. But whatever may be the final verdict of the unbiassed mind concerning the evidences which support the revelation, concerning the philosophical system which it expounds, and concerning the compensation which it can ensure to a "passionate, bright endeavour," the investigator cannot fail to learn much by its study. Whether it can take him or not into the whole truth, it is full of the beauty of wisdom and the suggestiveness of profundity and the brightness of mystic dream. If it has not transformed the world it has permeated all forms of thought. It has attracted some of the most accomplished, the most thoughtful, the most refined intellects. It is certainly worthy of study, and they are wise who suspend their judgment till the time for judgment arrives.

The literature of Theosophy is already extensive. Its foundation is "Isis Unveiled." Its culminating point is in "The Secret Doctrine," by the same writer. The investigations of Mr A. P. Sinnett are recorded in the "Occult World;" the elements of the arcane philosophy in which he was mysteriously instructed will be found in "Esoteric Buddhism."

A volume of lectures by Colonel H. S. Olcott on "Theosophy, Religion, and Occult Science," has commanded a wide circle in the reading world, and the latest developments of the subject will be seen in the "Key to Theosophy," which Madame Blavatsky had issued before her decease in the form of a catechism for the benefit of her less instructed disciples. There are also two official periodicals, of high excellence and great interest—*Lucifer*, a monthly magazine which is published in London, and *The Theosophist*, which antedates it by several years, and is the organ of the head-quarters at Bombay.

LIST OF AUTHORITIES.

ANONYMOUS—A Suggestive Enquiry into the Hermetic Mystery and Alchemy, being an attempt to recover the Ancient Experiment of Nature. 1850. 8vo.
—————— Lives of the Alchemysticall Philosophers ; with a Critical Catalogue of Books in Occult Chemistry, and a Selection of the most celebrated Treatises on the Theory and Practice of the Hermetic Art.. 1815. 8vo.
—————— Theosophia Pneumatica. *Rare Manuscript Translation,* by J. M. Rieder.
—————— The Cabalistic Science, or the Art to know the Good Genie. *Rare Treatise,* in Manuscript.
—————— Pneumatologia ; or, a Discourse of Angels, their Nature and Office or Ministry. 1701. 4to.
—————— Secret Symbols of the Rosicrucians of the Sixteenth and Seventeenth Centuries. Altona, 1785-88. Fol.
—————— Universal History of Apparitions. London, 1770. 12mo.
—————— History of Witchcraft. True Account of the Trials of Wizards and Witches. 12mo. N.D.
Arbatel—De Magia Veterum, &c. Basiliæ, 1575. 16mo.
Aristarus, of Proconnesus—Lèttre d'un Philosophe sur le secret du Grand Œuvre. Paris, 1688. 12mo.
Bacon, Roger—Mirror of Alchemy. London, 1597. 4to.
Barrett, Francis—The Magus ; or, Celestial Intelligencer. London, 1801. 4to.
Basil, Valentine—Select Works, containing Last Will, Twelve Keys, and other Treatises. Translated into English. London, 1671. 8vo.
Baxter, Richard—Certainty of the World of Spirits fully evinced. 1691. 8vo.
Berbignier, Alexis V. C.—Les Farfadets, on Tous les Démons ne sont pas de l'autre monde. 3 vols. Paris, 1821. 8vo.
Binet, A., and Féré, C.—Animal Magnetism. International Scientific Series. 1887. 8vo.
Blavatsky, H. P.—Isis Unveiled. A Master Key to the Mysteries of Ancient and Modern Science and Theology. 2 vols. 1877. 8vo.
—————— The Secret Doctrine. 2 vols. 1888. 4to.
—————— Key to Theosophy. 1889. 8vo.
Bodin, Jean—Démonomanie des Sorciers. Paris, 1581. 4to.
Böhme, Jacob, Life and Doctrines of the God-taught Philosopher.

An Introduction to the Study of his Works. By Franz Hartmann, M.D. 1891. 8vo.

Bonaventura—Itinerarius Mentis in Deum. 1864. 12mo.

Britten, Emma Hardinge—Modern American Spiritualism. A Twenty Years' Record of the Communion of the Earth with the World of Spirits. 1870. 8vo.

—— Nineteenth Century Miracles. . . . A complete Historical Compendium of . . . Modern Spiritualism. 1883. 8vo.

Burton, Robert—The Anatomy of Melancholy. Oxford, 1621. 4to.

Christian, P.—Histoire de la Magie, du Monde Surnaturel et de la Fatalité à travers les Temps et les Peuples. Paris, 1871. 8vo.

Christophorus, *Parisiensis*—Eleucidarius, seu Artis transmutatoriæ summa major. "Theatrum Chemicum," vol. vi. 1613. 8vo.

Collin de Plancy—Dictionnaire Infernale. 2 vols. Paris, 1818. 8vo.

Cross, Jeremy L.—The True Masonic Chart, or Hieroglyphic Monitor. Newhaven, 1819. 12mo.

Crookes, W. (F.R.S.)—Researches in the Phenomena of Spiritualism. 1874. 8vo.

Delancre, Pierre—L'Incrédulité et Mécréance des Sortilèges pleinement convaincu. Paris, 1612. 4to.

Deleuze—Traité du Magnétisme Animal. Paris. 8vo.

Delrio, Martin-Antoine—Disquisitionum Magicarum libri sex. Louvain, 1599. 4to.

Dionysius, Areopagiticus. *See* Migne's "Encyclopédie Theologique."

Dragon Rouge, Le, ou l'Art de commander les Esprits Célestes, aériens, terrestres, infernaux, avec le vrai secret de faire Parler les Morts, &c. 1521. 18mo.

Dupotet, J. (Baron)—La Magie Dévoilée. Paris, 1852. 4to.

Duprel, Baron Carl—Philosophy of Mysticism. Translated by C. C. Massey. 2 vols. 1889. 8vo.

Eliphas Lévi—Dogme et Rituel de la Haute Magie. Deuxième édition. 2 vols. Paris, 1856. 8vo.

—— Histoire de la Magie, avec un Exposition clair et précis de ses Procédés, ses Rites, et ses Mystères. 1860.

Elliotson, John—Numerous Cases of Surgical Operations without pain in the Mesmeric State. 1820. 8vo.

Ennemoser, Joseph—History of Magic. Translated by William Howitt. Bohn's Philosophical Library. 2 vols. 8vo.

Esdaile, James—Mesmerism in India, and its practical application in Surgery and Medicine. 1846. 8vo.

Figuier. Louis—L'Alchimie et les Alchimistes. Troisième édition. Paris, 1860. 8vo.

Fludd, Robert—Apologia Compendiaria Fraternitatem de Rosea Cruce, &c. Leyden, 1616. 8vo.

Gebelin, Court de. Le Monde Primitif. 9 vols. Paris, 1773-82. 4to.

Geber—Works, comprising Sum of Perfection, Investigation of

Perfection, Investigation of Verity, and Furnaces.   Gedani, 1682. 8vo.

Ginsburg, C. D.—The Kabbalah, its Doctrines, Development, and Literature. 1865. 8vo.

Girtanner, Christopher. Annales de Chimie. No. 100, Memoir on "Azote."

Glanvil, Joseph—Sadducismus Triumphatus. 1681. 8vo.

——— Of the Vanity of Dogmatizing. 1661. 8vo.

Grand Grimoire (Le) avec la Grande Clavicule de Salomon. 18mo. No place or date.

Gregory, W. (M.D.)—Animal Magnetism ; or, Mesmerism and its Phenomena. Second edition. 1877. 8vo.

Grimorium Verum, vel probatissima Salomonis claviculæ rabbini Hebraici, &c., à Memphis, chez Alibeek l'Egyptien. 1517. 16mo.

Hartmann, Franz (M.D.)—Magic : White and Black ; or, The Science of Finite and Infinite Life. Third edition. 1887. 8vo.

Hermes Mercurius Trismegistus—Theological and Philosophical Works. Translated by J. D. Chambers. 8vo.

——— The Virgin of the World. Now first rendered into English. By Dr Anna Kingsford and Edward Maitland. 4to. 1885.

Heywood, Thomas—Hierarchy of the Blessed Angels.

Hitchcock—Remarks on Alchemy and the Alchemists. 1865. 8vo.

Honorius—Grémoire du Pape Honorius, avec un recueil des plus rares secrets. Rome, 1670. 16mo.

Junctin de Florence—Speculum Astrologiæ, universam Mathematicam Scientiam, in certas classes digestam, complectens. 2 vols. Lugduni, 1581. Fol.

Khunrath, H. C.—Amphitheatrum Sapientiæ Æternæ. Mag., 1608. Fol.

Lane, E. W.—Modern Egyptians. 2 vols. 1836. 8vo.

Lee, F. G. (D.D.)—Glimpses of the Supernatural. 2 vols. 1875. 8vo.

Lenormant, Francis—Chaldean Magic. Its Origin and Development. Translated from the French. 1878. 8vo.

Longueville-Harcourt, M. de—Histoire des Personnes qui ont vécu plus d'un siècle. Paris, 1716. 12mo.

Lord, Frances—Christian Science Healing, its Principles and Practice. 1889. 8vo.

Maimonides, ——.—Guide of the Perplexed. Le Guide des Egarés. Paris, 1856. 8vo.

Maternus, Julius Firmicus, Matheseos Libri viii. Basileæ, 1551. Fol.

Mathers, S. L. MacGregor—The Kabbalah Unveiled. Containing Three Books of the Zohar. Translated from the Latin version of Knorr von Rosenroth. 1887. 8vo.

Migne, Abbé—Dictionnaire des Sciences Occultes. 2 vols. Paris, 1861. 8vo.

Oliver, Rev. George—History of Initiation. 1841. 8vo.

Olcott, H. S.—Theosophy, Religion, and Occult Science. 1885. 8vo.

Paracelsus—The Substance of his Teachings. . . . Extracted and Translated by Franz Hartmann, M.D. 1886. 8vo.

Paton, C. J.—Freemasonry and its Jurisprudence. 1872. 8vo.

Pererius, Benedictus—Disquisitio de Helia Artista. 1608. 8vo.

Peucer, Gasper—Les Devins, ou Commentaire des Principales Sortes de Devinations. Anvers, 1584. 8vo.

Sincerus Renatus (Sigmund Richter)—Perfect and True Preparation of the Philosophical Stone, according to the Secret Brotherhood of the Golden and Rosy Cross. Breslau, 1710. 8vo.

Reuchlin, Johann—De Arte Cabalistica. 1550. Fol.

Rich, Elihu (and others)—The Occult Sciences. Encyclopædia Metropolitana. 1855. 8vo.

Rosenroth, Baron de—Kabbalah Denudata. 4 vols. 1556. 4to.

Ross, Percy (pseud.)—A Professor of Alchemy. Denis Zachaire. 1887. 8vo.

Saint-Martin, Louis Claude de—Tableau Naturel des Rapports . . . entre Dieu, l'Homme, et l'Univers. 2 vols. 8vo.

Salmon, W.—Polygraphia. Containing chapters on Alchemy and the Grand Elixir of the Philosophers. 8vo. 1701.

Sandby, George—Mesmerism and its Opponents. 1844. 8vo.

Scott, Sir Walter—Letters on Demonology and Witchcraft.

Sendivogius. A New Light of Alchemy. Translated from the Latin. London, 1640. 4to.

Sibly, Ebenezer—An Illustration of the Occult Sciences. In four parts. 4to. N.D.

Sinnett, A. P.—The Occult World. 1881. 8vo.

——— Esoteric Buddhism. 1883. 8vo.

Stewart, Balfour, and Tait, P. G.—The Unseen Universe; or, Physical Speculations on a Future State. Sixth edition. 1876. 8vo.

Taylor, Thomas—Theoretic Arithmetic. London, 1816. 8vo.

Thyræus, Peter—De Apparitionibus omnis generis Spirituum. 1600.

Tiedemann, D. T.—Disputatio de quæstione qui fuerit artium magicarum origo. Marburgi, 1787. 4to.

Torquemada, Antoine de—Hexameron . . . Mises en Français par Gabriel Chappuys. Lyon, 1582. 8vo.

Torre-Blanca, François de la—Epitome Delictorum, sive de Magia. Lugduni, 1678. 4to.

Trévisan, Bernard.—A Treatise of Bernhard, Earl of Trévisan, of the Philosopher's Stone. Collectanea Chymica. 1604. 8vo.

Tschoudi, Baron—L'Etoile Flamboyante. 2 vols. Francfort, 1766. 12mo.

Vacherot, E.—Histoire Critique de l'Ecole D'Alexandrie. 2 vols. Paris, 1846. 8vo.

Van Helmont, J. B.—Works. Translated from the Latin. London, 1664. Fol.

Vaughan, Thomas (Eugenius Philalethes)—Magical Writings. A

Verbatim Reprint . . . with the Latin passages translated into English. Edited by A. E. Waite. 1888. 4to.

Villars, Abbé de, Comte de Gabalis, on Entretiens sur les Sciences Occultes.

Waite, A. E.—The Real History of the Rosicrucians, founded on their own Manifestoes. 1887. 8vo.

Wallace, A. R.—Miracles and Modern Spiritualism. 1878. 8vo.

Welton, Thomas—Jacob's Rod, or the Art of finding Springs, Mines, and Minerals by means of the Hazel Rod. 8vo. N.D.

Wierus, Jean—Des Prestiges des Démons : Cinq livres de l'imposture et tromperie des diables, des enchantements et Sorcellerie. . . . Faits français par Jacques Grévin de Clermont. Paris, 1569. 8vo.

Wright, Thomas (F.S.A.)—Narratives of Sorcery and Magic from the most Authentic Sources.

Zöllner, J. C. F.—Transcendental Physics. An Account of Experimental Investigations. Translated by C. C. Massey. 1880. 8vo.

INDEX.

T

TURNBULL AND SPEARS, PRINTERS, EDINBURGH.

In crown 8vo, 454 pages, with illustrations, 7s. 6d.

The
Real History of the Rosicrucians.

FOUNDED ON THEIR OWN MANIFESTOES, AND ON FACTS
AND DOCUMENTS COLLECTED FROM THE WRITINGS
OF INITIATED BRETHREN.

By ARTHUR EDWARD WAITE.

Opinions of the Press.

" We desire to speak of Mr Waite's work with the greatest respect on the points of honesty, impartiality, and sound scholarship. Mr Waite has given, for the first time, the documents with which Rosicrucianism has been connected *in extenso*." —*Literary World.*

"There is something mysterious and fascinating about the history of the Virgin Fraternity of the Rose."—*Saturday Review.*

"A curious and interesting story of the doings of a mysterious association in times when people were more ready to believe in supernatural phenomena than the highly-educated, matter-of-fact people of to-day."—*Morning Post.*

" The work not only of a refined scholar, but of a man who knows what he is writing about, and that is a great deal more than can be said for other books on the same topic. . . . Much which he has to tell us has the double merit of being not only true, but new."—*John Bull.*

"Mr Waite's book on 'Rosicrucianism' is a perfect contrast to the one we noticed a month or two back. The latter is a farrago of ill-digested learning and groundless fancies, while the former is, at all events, an honest attempt to dis- cover the truth about the Society of the Rosy Cross. . . . The study of ' Occultism ' is so popular just now that all books bearing on such topics are eagerly read; and it is a comfort to find one writer who is not ashamed to confess his ignorance after telling us all he can discover."—*Westminster Review.*

"Mr Waite is a great authority on esoteric science and its literature. Those who have read his extremely interesting work upon the writings of Eliphas Lévi, the modern magician, will expect in his ' History of the Rosicrucians ' a treatise of more than ephemeral importance, and they will not be disappointed. . . ."— *Morning Post.*

ESSAYS IN THE LITERATURE OF ALCHEMY.

Small 4to, white cloth, 10s. 6d.

The Magical Writings of Thomas Vaughan

(*EUGENIUS PHILALETHES*).

A VERBATIM REPRINT OF HIS FIRST FOUR TREATISES— ANTHROPOSOPHIA THEOMAGICA, ANIMA MAGICA ABSCONDITA, MAGIA ADAMICA, THE TRUE CŒLUM TERRÆ.

WITH THE LATIN PASSAGES TRANSLATED INTO ENGLISH, AND WITH A BIBLIOGRAPHICAL PREFACE AND ESSAY ON THE ESOTERIC LITERATURE OF WESTERN CHRISTENDOM.

BY ARTHUR EDWARD WAITE.

Opinion of the Press.

Demy 8vo, pp. xliii. *and* 349, *with illustrations, cloth extra,* 10s. 6d.

The Mysteries of Magic ;

A DIGEST OF THE WRITINGS OF ELIPHAS LÉVI,

WITH BIOGRAPHICAL AND CRITICAL ESSAY.

BY ARTHUR EDWARD WAITE.

Opinions of the Press.

" Of the many remarkable men who have gained notoriety by their proficiency, real or imaginary, in the Black Arts, probably none presents a more strange and irreconcilable character than the French magician, Alphonse Louis Constant. . . . Better known under the Jewish pseudonym of Eliphas Lévi Zahed, this enthusiastic student of forbidden art made some stir in France and even in London. . . . His works on magic are those of an undoubted genius, and divulge a philosophy beautiful in conception, if totally opposed to common-sense principles. . . . There is so great a fund of learning and of attractive reasoning in these writings, that Mr Arthur Edward Waite has published a digest of them for the benefit of English readers. This gentleman has not attempted a literal translation in every case, but has arranged a volume which, while reproducing with sufficient accuracy a great portion of the more interesting works, affords an excellent idea of the scope of the entire literary remains of an enthusiast of whom he entertains a profound admiration. . . . The reader may with profit peruse carefully the learned dissertations penned by M. Constant upon the Hermetic art treated as a religion, a philosophy, and a natural science. . . . In view of the remarkable exhibitions of mesmeric influence and thought-reading which have recently been given, it is not improbable that the thoughtful reader may find a clue in the writings of this cultured and amiable magician to the secret of many of the manifestations of witchcraft which formerly struck wonder and terror into the hearts of simple folks. . . ." —*The Morning Post.*

" The present single volume is a digest of half-a-dozen books enumerated by the present author in a ' Biographical and Critical Essay ' with which he prefaces his undertaking. These are the ' Dogme et Ritual de la Haute Magie,' the ' Histoire de la Magie,' the ' Clef des Grand Mystères,' the ' Sorcier de Meudon,' the ' Philosophie Occulte,' and the ' Science des Esprites.' To attack the whole series— which, indeed, it might be difficult to obtain now in a complete form—would be a bold undertaking, but Mr Waite has endeavoured to give his readers the essence of the whole six books in a relatively compact compass. . . . The book before us is encyclopædic in its range, and it would be difficult to find a single volume which is better calculated to supply modern inquirers with a general conception of the scope and purpose of the occult sciences at large. It freely handles, amongst others, the ghastly topics of witchcraft and black magic. but certainly it would be difficult to imagine any reader tempted to enter those pathways of experiment by the picture of their character and purpose that Eliphas Lévi supplies. In this way the intrepid old Kabbalist, though never troubling his readers with sublime exhortations in the interest of virtue, writes under the inspiration of an uncompromising devotion to the loftiest ideals, and all his philosophy makes for righteousness."—Mr A. P. SINNET, in *Light.*

" We are grateful to Mr Waite for translating the account of how Lévi, in a lone chamber in London, called up the spirit of Apollonius of Tyana. This very creepy composition is written in quite the finest manner of the late Lord Lytton when he was discoursing upon the occult."—*The Saturday Review.*

Demy 8vo, pp. 315, cloth, 10s. 6d.

Lives of Alchemystical Philosophers,

BASED ON MATERIALS COLLECTED IN 1815, AND SUPPLEMENTED
BY RECENT RESEARCHES.

WITH A PHILOSOPHICAL DEMONSTRATION OF THE TRUE PRINCIPLES
OF THE MAGNUM OPUS OR GREAT WORK OF ACHEMICAL
RECONSTRUCTION, AND SOME ACCOUNT OF THE
SPIRITUAL CHEMISTRY

By ARTHUR EDWARD WAITE.

TO WHICH IS ADDED

A BIBLIOGRAPHY OF ALCHEMY AND HERMETIC PHILOSOPHY.

Opinions of the Press.

"The chapter about Flamel is one of the most interesting in the book, but the longest and most enthralling is that containing a full account of the career of the infamous Cagliostro, whom Carlyle has immolated. This is really a romance of the highest interest. . . . There is abundance of interest in Mr Waite's pages for those who have any inclination for occult studies, and although he founds his work upon a book which was published in 1815 by an anonymous writer, yet he adds so much fresh matter that this is practically a new work. A valuable feature for students is the alphabetical catalogue which Mr Waite has prepared of all known works on hermetic philosophy and alchemy."—*Glasgow Herald.*

"Mr Waite has undoubtedly bestowed a vast amount of patient and laborious research upon the present work, inspired by the double conviction that the original alchemists had in fact anticipated and transcended the highest results of chemistry in the metallic kingdom, and had discovered in the twilight of the Middle Ages the future development of universal evolution. The biographical sketches of the alchemists, both true and false, are curious reading, and the alphabetical catalogue of works on Hermetic Philosophy is surprisingly suggestive of ages when leisure was less scarce, and literature scarcer, than in modern days." —*Daily News.*

"The alchemists more popularly known, such as Albertus Magnus, Roger Bacon, Raymond Lully, Flamel, Paracelsus, and Basil Valentine are dealt with fairly and fully, and the travels and adventures of Joseph Balsamo, *alias* Cagliostro, with his somewhat peculiar developments of Egyptian Freemasonry, are excellent and interesting reading. . . . Such an intelligent study of the subject must bring into relief the infinite possibilities which are contained in a combination of psychical insight with physical knowledge."—*Light.*

"The lives of the philosophers themselves are interesting and curious reading; the stories of Lully, Flamel, Valentine, Trevisan, and Zachaire are full of glimpses of mediæval times. To us the most instructive and valuable of the lives is that of the prince of impostors, Jaseph Balsamo, or Comte de Cagliostro, who died at the end of the last century."—*Spectator.*

"The old alchemists . . . may, however, with justice be regarded as the first experimentalists in analytical chemistry, and on this account are entitled to the gratitude of subsequent generations. The lives of the principal alchemists are briefly recorded and their works mentioned. Amongst them are such familiar names as Thomas Aquinas, Roger Bacon, Parscelsus, Helvetius, and Delisle. The volume also contains an alphabetical catalogue of works on hermetic philosophy and alchemy."—*Morning Post.*

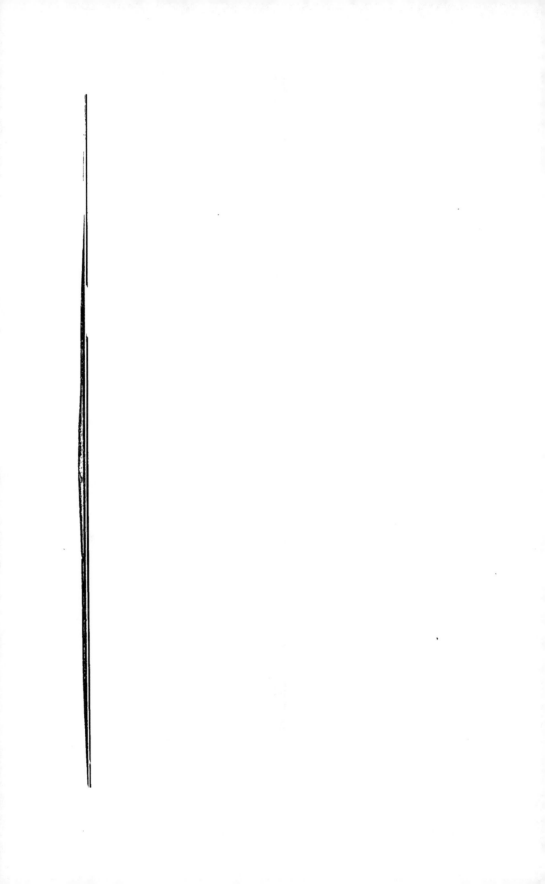